LETTERS FROM THE OPEN ROAD

(VOL. 1)

SIDHARTH SHAROTRI

ISBN 979-8-88869-036-9

For Ma.

Thank you for Rasam and Rice at 3:00am.
And everything else.

Contents

Acknowledgements

I'm sure that if I think back hard enough, I'll be able to come up with of hundreds of people upon whose shoulders I have stood. Considering that I'm writing this part though a hangover that feels like it was handmade by Satan himself, I apologise if you can't immediately find your name here.

My father always told me to go slow and be careful. I was always careful, Pa.

Off the top of my rather sore head, there are a few people I can think of who were there for me precisely when I needed them with the right contribution, advice or just their company – Vishal Joshi, Ashish Seth, Varun Swaroop, Poorva Soman, Padma Venkataraman, Joe Devasia, Capt. D.C. Sekhar, Amrut Mahajan, Romanick Aguiar, Archana Pandey, Girish Karkera, Aina Barker, Gaurav Jayaprakash and Abhishek Belmar spring to mind immediately.

I had it pretty good with the motor manufacturers as well. Reuben George from Mercedes-Benz began our professional relationship by sending me an A Class test car from Pune to Ooty practically overnight. That's unheard of. Abhay Dange of BMW, who introduces himself to me every time we meet, saw it fit to lend my 27-year-old self an M5 super saloon (among several other cars) for several days just so I could win an argument. The good people at Audi who were a bit sensitive to criticism at times, still saw fit to let me continue testing their cars. Almost all the motor manufacturers I got to work with, honestly, were wonderful.

There are hundreds of unsung heroes in public relations agencies. These wonderful men and women get short end of the stick from journalists on one side their corporate clients on the other. I admire them so much that I actually went and got myself a job in PR for a few months.

Govind Vijaykumar from Deccan Chronicle and Asian Age took a punt on an untested, inexperienced writer who only had a little bit of knowledge, a head full of opinions and a burning desire to succeed. I would throw colossal tantrums and Govind would take them all while being calm, reasonable, and continuing to protect me from the big bad newspaper world.

Most of all though, I want to thank my Class IX English teacher, Mr Kim Noble, for failing me in English Literature. That, sir, was all the motivation I needed to write nearly every day since and produce my own.

Prologue

How it Started

The funny thing about depression is that brings one to a grinding, shuddering halt. While it's got one nice and halted, it also makes it damn-near impossible to restart. My default setting was 'lie in bed and mope' and I had this perfected. It took six months' worth of therapy to bring me back to some semblance of normal. And even then, I had a problem. I'd recently moved back home and was unemployed. While I was getting better, I wasn't really sure what I was going to do.

Enter Mr. Romanick Aguiar who, by people who know him well, is affectionately called Romzy. I lived with Romzy for a few months and during this time found that I still had the ability to write in spite of having written mostly CVs for the last eight years as a recruiter. What astounded me was that I was able to write in a way that made sense to me. And Romzy. Not only was I enjoying it and getting better, I started to develop an insatiable need to write more and more. While at Romzy's I'd spin storylines, put together short stories and mess around with long format writing.

Then came the big question – now that I can write, what should I do with it?

A few years ago, towards the end of my career as a recruiter, I came across a gentlemen called Girish Karkera. Girish was then the editor of Top Gear Magazine, India. Our interactions then were work-based, of course, but I think I might have expressly expressed my admiration for his work and that of Top Gear.

Having grown up surrounded by model cars, car encyclopaedias, car magazines and, most importantly, the Top Gear UK TV programme on BBC, I decided to take up automobile journalism at the ripe old age of 26. *I would be just like Jeremy Clarkson*, I imagined.

It's all very well having a dream and even the skills and wherewithal to realise it, but I hadn't the first clue about how to actually get something printed in a newspaper or magazine with my name on it.

Remember Girish? I phoned him and took the punt of a lifetime. "Hi Girish", I said, sheepishly. "I want to be an automobile journalist. Can I write for Top Gear?"

"Hi Sid," he said, with me sweating concrete blocks from anticipation at the other end. "From what I've read of your work (I'd sent him a writing sample), I don't think it'll work for us."

What followed were the longest and most agonising ten seconds of my life. *Me thinking I could write for Top Gear just because I could string a few sentences together was like thinking I'd be able to replace Chris Cornell at Audioslave because I could hum the odd nursery rhyme.*

I decided to abandon this whole ridiculous business of even *thinking* I could write about cars. *I mean, who the hell did I think I was for even imagining that I deserved a place in this rarefied worl…*

"Here's something you can do," said the voice of hope to a man dying of shame. "Write four sample stories of about 1000 words each. Try and vary the topics as much as you can. Send these to national newspapers with a nice cover letter and see what happens."

The oracle had spoken.

It was about 2:00pm on a Thursday so I ran downstairs, jumped in the car and drove like the wind to my neighbourhood newsstand in the hope of finding some good leads in the day's news that I could spin into stories. By 5:00pm I had written four articles that I felt were good enough to be carried in national English dailies. A further two hours later, I'd made a list of all the editors of these newspapers with their contact information.

It would later transpire that editors are notoriously difficult to get through to. Even if one does get them on the phone, it is impossible to have a conversation because, let's face it - they have national newspapers to run.

I decided to email everyone and follow up on the phone. The next day at precisely 10:00am I sent out 18 emails. In less than 15 minutes I got one back from The Hindu saying that they wouldn't want to work with me because they thought my language was too aggressive. Crushing blow.

20 minutes later, my phone rang.

"Hi, is that Sidharth?"

"Yes, it is. Who am I speaking with?"

"Sidharth, hi. This is Govind Vijaykumar from Deccan Chronicle, Hyderabad. I've seen your mail. Would you like to do a weekly column for us? I'll give you a dedicated page."

It is impossible to describe the sense of accomplishment, validation, gratitude and relief that washed over me in that moment. When I moved back home, I had nothing except a loving family. I was completely miserable with no hope, no prospects no sense of purpose and an illness that threatened to keep me that way for as long as it could.

But now I could live my dream.

The Ups and Downs

The dream, of course, came with its own downsides and heartbreaks. For starters, it didn't pay very much. I was living in Bangalore at the time and would fly to Mumbai or Delhi to test cars. I would try and test two or three back-to-back per trip to make each one financially viable. I had to do this because cars allotted for journalists' use called 'press cars', 'press fleet' or 'media fleet' were all only in Mumbai, Delhi and, to a lesser extent, Pune, because that's where the bulk of the journalists are based.

Don't tell anyone but, there are times when I'd get one car manufacturer to sponsor my travel and test products of others while I was there. Every permutation and loophole you can possibly think of, I've used about five times.

There were several times when I had to fund my own travel. Even with decent savings and a lot of help, how many flights can one afford every month? How many hotel rooms? How much fuel? It all adds up. This has, at times seemed like a fool's errand and an exercise in absolute vanity.

And it can fail at any time. For example, in June 2013, I was just about beginning to build a reputation in the industry. My weekly page in Deccan Chronicle & Asian Age called HONK was getting some attention, and I was being invited by companies to review their cars. Life looked pretty good when I was offered a large SUV by an American manufacturer for a week ex-Bangalore. Straightaway I figured that we would take a family holiday in Ooty. I would get to travel with my family and share the spoils of my new profession as well. Brilliant.

But, in a cruel twist of fate (many more would rear their heads over the years), the car that was promised to me had developed a fault, which was discovered during routine service the day before we were due to leave. All the accommodation had been booked and paid for, leaves had been taken by everyone and all other arrangements made. My girlfriend at the time had flown in from Mumbai to go on holiday with us as well.

It was at 11:30pm the night before that we finally received word that they wouldn't be able to fix the car by morning.

Bugger.

If we didn't have two cars of our own, we wouldn't be going anywhere. We did, so we went.

In Ooty, slightly dejected and embarrassed that I couldn't come through, I was walking along a lake when my phone rang. It was a man called Reuben George from Mercedes-Benz. I owe him a lot, not just for what he was about to do, but how he would continue to support my little foray into automobile journalism in any way that he could.

"I heard you're looking for a car. Is it okay if I send you an A Class in two days?"

"No, Reuben. We'll still be in Ooty then."

"That's okay. The car is in our Pune plant right now being serviced. The driver can leave tomorrow and reach you in Ooty by the day after morning. Is that alright?"

"I don't know what to say, but thank you. I appreciate it."

This is something that I learnt early on in the business – to expect the unexpected. You could have the best story idea in the world and it gets rejected. You could plan literally every last detail and the car won't turn up for whatever reason. Or, like in this case, you could lose all hope only to be rescued in such style by Mr George of Mercedes-Benz.

Taking Pictures

Until I started doing this, I wasn't really a photographer of any description. After sending her some truly awful and blurry images taken from an old Blackberry phone, I was told by my editor that proper photographs were required of the cars are bikes that I tested, or else. Seeing as to how I couldn't afford pro photographers, I did what anyone else would do – I called my friends and asked if they'd pitch in. The ones who knew how to use the camera they'd found in their dads' cupboards would shoot for me while the others would lend them to me. All this would be in exchange for a quick drive in a posh car.

This went on so much that nearly all my close friends are now photographers themselves at various levels.

Among this lot, two stand out from the pack simply because of how much I work with them. The first is Vishal Joshi. Vishal is a big boy in every sense, including the fact that he's actually a big softie inside and he possesses the phenomenal ability to empty any bar; except one at a Goan wedding.

I've known him since we were both 16 and we had a great time together in school after which he moved abroad. We stayed in touch like friends do and found ourselves working together as recruiters briefly.

Then, in mid-2014, fate decried that I was once more on the lookout for a friend whose father's cupboard contained a DSLR camera. Vishal's did. So we met, I showed him how it worked and we've been working together on and off since.

And then there's Ashish Seth. Ashish and I met through a mutual friend in January of 2014. Ashish is the kind of chap who is deeply endearing, not just because he's a mild-mannered nice guy, but mostly because he's always willing to do whatever he can to further the cause. It helps that he's a pro photographer as well.

In the interest of a full disclosure, photography is the hardest part of this business as far as I am concerned. The big magazines, TV and digital properties all have professionals in their ranks who are given proper budgets. We had to just make do. Sometimes, a car company would spring for travel for two; in which case I would travel with a photographer. This happened for maybe 10% of the stories I've done. Most times, it was a car, a camera and me. I had to learn and learn fast because all the pictures had to be more or less of the same standard or I'd get a bollocking from the editor.

When I was new to this, I didn't really know what I was doing at all. Because I worked independently, I didn't have anyone to learn from either. I remember having borrowed a camera with a broken lens and spending the entire night trying to get a picture; only to discover at about 5:30am that the camera wasn't nearly good enough for night photography.

There was a time when I tried shooting the Mercedes-Benz CLS350. It was beautiful and very photogenic. The Mercedes driver who brought the car said that we should go to the road leading up to Aamby Valley because that's where all the journalists went. Aamby Valley is about an hour and a half outside Pune. We'd decided that morning that we'd go there, take pictures and leg it back to Pune Airport for my flight that evening. At the time of discussing it over breakfast, we seemed to have four whole hours to do this shoot. We figured we easily had an hour to get the car washed properly from outside. And we did.

The route we took to our location from the carwash was wet so our white CLS got a bit mucky down the sides, which needed to be cleaned. But no matter; we still had plenty of time. *We did, didn't we?*

Two minutes before we reached our location, it started raining really hard so we got there and waited. I climbed into the back from the driver's seat and began setting up the camera. Just as I was doing that the rain stopped, the clouds parted and revealed the sun in all its glory. I felt a sudden burst of joy as I instructed the driver to clean the doors on his side while I jumped out and cleaned the other side. As we were doing this, the clouds covered the sun and the light disappeared. So we got back into the car and waited. It took about 20 minutes for the sun to peek out of the clouds again, and when it did, I screwed the correct lens on the camera and jumped out to take pictures. In three minutes, just as I was setting up the camera for light, an entire cloud passed through shot. The car was 50 feet in front of me but I couldn't see it. Then it started raining again, so we had to get back into the car. This cat-and-mouse with the weather continued all day until I absolutely had to leave for fear of missing my flight. In the four and a half hours we were there, I had managed only five decent pictures; three of which were ended up in the newspaper.

Does it Have to be this Much Fun?

There are plenty of characters that one meets on the road. Some become lifelong friends, others you never want to meet again and everything in between. But the biggest character of them all is the road itself, because no matter how good you are, no matter how good your vehicle and planning are, the road tripper is always at its mercy.

I remember travelling at a certain point in early 2014 for 28 days continuously. A further six days of travelling lay ahead. The idea was that a fellow journalist and I would take a taxi from Kabini to Bangalore where I would dump my bag at home, pick up a new one that I'd packed earlier and take the next flight out to Delhi. Our press car would be waiting for us at Delhi arrivals which we would collect, meet Ashish in Gurgaon, and then drive 800+km through the night and the next day to Jaisalmer.

We got to my place in Bangalore on time and left almost immediately. I remember a having a quick cup of tea, shower, picking up the fresh bag and getting back into the taxi for the airport all in about 15 minutes. Upon reaching the airport – already quite tired – we were informed that our flight had been delayed by two hours. We should've been upset but we actually thought ourselves lucky because that meant two more hours of sleep. Just before we passed out right next to our boarding gate, we phoned the PR co-ordinator and let her know that our flight was delayed and asked her to co-ordinate with Audi who was supposed to send the car to the airport.

By the time we landed in Delhi it was 1:00am and we were really pissed off because our flight contained two crying babies who were trying to outdo one another. More than that – I needed those three hours of sleep on the plane because I'd be driving for the next 15 hours through Rajasthan. And it was bloody freezing.

As soon as we got out of the terminal, we could feel the biting chill in the air. We got out of the arrivals gate and walked quickly to our rendezvous point to collect the car; which wasn't there. At about 1:15am, there's only so many people one can call, but I had no choice. I called the PR co-ordinator a few times, but she didn't answer. We were cold, annoyed, fatigued, frustrated and late, so I started repeatedly calling everyone I knew from Audi and their PR agency at 1:15-1:30am.

After a further half-an-hour I finally got through to someone from the PR agency who told me that the car was in Audi's yard in Faridabad. Basically, 45 minutes away at that time of night. I remember getting there and having to throw stones on the window of the security booth while shouting to wake the guard to let us in. We finally got going from Faridabad by 3:00am, picked up Ashish by 3:30 and drove through some really dangerous roads covered in fog until sunrise at 6:45am.

On the way back, we figured we'd get cash on the way for fuel and our night's stay. We had no such luck because as night fell, we had over 600km still to go, not enough fuel and 861 rupees in hand all put together. We knew this because we counted several times hoping to find a 500 or 1000 note that we might've missed. This was a time when ATMs weren't always really reliable and cards hardly worked outside cities and towns. We found this out because we must've tried six or seven ATMs, five fuel stations who either didn't accept cards or they weren't working and four hotels that just didn't accept cards.

Since Ashish had left early back to Delhi, it was just fellow journalist/ then girlfriend and I. It was becoming increasingly obvious that we were would end up sleeping in the car that night. We kept driving until we found a quiet spot near a curve where our car would draw as little attention as possible, but be safely out of the way if someone lost control, at the same time be in a position to immediately drive off in case we encountered the wrong sort.

When it's two degrees at night, the engine running to keep the seat heaters on, girl on passenger's seat snoring loudly, sleep wasn't in my destiny. Plus, I was the lookout.

We discovered in the morning that we'd kipped right outside a typical highway dhaba. As the beautiful orange sun rose in front of us, the outside temperature reading six degrees, a wonderful young man who didn't look any more than 15 years of age, served us hot tea, and went off to make us parathas. When he came back with breakfast, he hesitated a bit before asking us what on earth we were doing sleeping there. After we'd explained our predicament to him, his face was awash with concern as he informed us that the 10km stretch on either side of us was one of the most dangerous roads in Rajasthan. This was apparently where brigands block roads, ambush travellers, rob them blind and often kill them.

What People Actually Like

There's nobody in history who's woken up in the morning and promptly decided that the only sensible course of action for that day is to race the national paragliding champion on his home course in a car. Well, nobody but me, obviously. I mean this not as a boast of any kind, but as an example of how my hideously under-developed nine-year-old brain works.

But it couldn't just be me, I always thought. There must be others out there who believe that life is simply too short to waste on trivial things such as fundamentally unsatisfying jobs, commuting, boring food, pop music, almost all Bollywood films, mundane sex and – most importantly – boring cars.

About six months into this gig, I'd started to figure out that people got their car reviews from expert automobile journalists who are about as much to be around as chartered accountants. I figured out that while I had to go on doing reviews, I could try and make them fun and possibly good to read for all kinds of people. I never really cared too much about dishing out any useful buying advice; although I did make the occasional suggestion.

No. I figured that every once in a while, I could do something truly ridiculous and it would end up in the paper. To test this out, I came up with something properly daft. I decided to race a car against a train.

But how would such a thing happen? And more importantly – how would I go about telling this story in a way that would interest the average English-speaking newspaper reader?

The answers to these questions were to be found (as is the way with such things) while I was tending bar at a Sunday flea market, which I enjoyed doing a few times a year. During one of these gigs, I met an old classmate from school. It's times like these that memories rush in and people become all dewy-eyed and weak-kneed with nostalgia.

"Do you remember the time when…"

My experience of meeting someone after about thirteen years was a bit different. *She could be the other writer! We could take it in turns to write a paragraph each. Like battle rap!*

I remember talking to her about it right there, and she agreed to give it a shot.

Then, it was a small question of deciding what car and train we'd use. After much deliberation and several hundred phone calls, emails and promises of getting people's kids into Ivy league colleges, we got ourselves a BMW M5 and a Shatabdi Express. The deal was that we would leave at the same time from Bangalore Cantonment Railway Station with me driving the car and her in the train. The race would end at Chennai Central Railway Station. The last one there would never hear the end of it. Simple.

At the time, the Shatabdi Express was the fastest train in the country and the BMW was as fast as a family car could possibly be. We figured it would be anyone's race.

The result of the actual race aside, we had a blast putting it together and it read a lot better than we expected it to.

Emboldened by the success of this story – and it really was properly successful – I started thinking in these terms all the time. For instance, my parents, who were on holiday at the time phoned to say that they had just been paragliding and how the road going up to the glider launch site was narrow, broken and perilous.

Upon hearing this a normal person would've said something to the effect that it was good that they made it down safely. I asked them how long the road was and how wide, what the average speed of their car was going up and then down. I asked how long the glider took to complete the descent both solo and two up.

What's the Point of it All?

On some rather ridiculous level, I've always felt a kinship with people that are obsessed with furthering humanity. While that might seem like a pompous and borderline nonsensical thing to say, what I mean is that I am truly fascinated by such people and I want to be like them. I want to be as brave and competent and important as they are.

One of the big reasons I wanted to write about cars was that cars were no longer as desirable, relevant or even part of the same social narrative that they were when I was growing up. I don't know why this was. It could've been their environmental impact or it could've the fact that they'd simply fallen out of fashion. There were a small number of dedicated enthusiasts that still lusted after them and discussed their favourites in hushed whispers behind closed doors, but for the most part, the motorcar was fast headed towards a very uncomfortable place right between the discounted refrigerator and toasted sandwich maker in the world of white goods.

I wanted to do something about it. I wanted my grandmother to read about cars like she would about food or cinema or music. None of them have fallen out of fashion. I wanted to show regular people a good time for five minutes every Wednesday or Thursday morning when they're sitting on the throne, having a cup of tea whatever else regular people do in the morning using the motorcar as a subject. To what extent I may have succeeded or failed is debatable because… No, I've failed miserably because everyone's buying hideous crossovers and nobody cares about cars anymore.

But I digress, because just being able to do this as a job is about the most fun a human being can possibly have. Not only that, it's an absolute privilege; like being a parent. Yes, it has its ups and downs, but on the whole, try and imagine having a brand-new car, a new place to go to, new people to meet, new food to eat, new music to listen to, new cultures and new experiences. Now imagine that you get to decide what you drive and where, often with friends. Now imagine doing one of these every week. It doesn't get much better.

What follow are some of my weekly reports from this life. These are as I wrote them. What appeared in the newspapers were edited and far more socially acceptable. These unfiltered versions below are full of hyperbole, four-letter words (very few, I promise) and some truly ridiculous claims, facts and figures that are almost certainly (wink wink) not true.

Part 1

The End is (Not Necessarily) Nigh

People whose record collections are still filled with Abba, Boney M, the Bee Gees and all the other '80s hideousness that once was referred to as music, probably lament the passing of the Laser Disc and its playing apparatus.

Here, as with the audio cassette player, we were presented with a device that could store your media and play it back or record it, and then play it back. Useful. I remember owning a large collection of cassettes which, even before I could finish listening to all of them, had become obsolete. Because along came CDs and you had to buy Nirvana's Nevermind all over again. All that time, some clever fellow who had never seen daylight before because he lived in his mother's basement was working out how to make the MP3. And it changed the world.

The motor industry is just as sinister. When people bought the Ferrari F430, they did so because they thought it was the best that Ferrari could do. All the while though, Ferrari was working on the F430 Scuderia and the exquisite 458 Italia. The same goes with the Lamborghini Murcielago and the McLaren MP4-12C.

But for a real taste of the motor industry's greed, one simply has to look at electric cars, or EVs as we're supposed to call them these days. There are a number of them on sale across the world like the Peugeot iON, Nissan's Leaf and our very own Mahindra E2O. The last one in particular, is something we're told that we should be proud of. Being Indian and all that.

But it was obviously styled to be deliberately ugly. Although Mahindra claims that it's good for 100 kilometres on a full charge, in the real world, it'll only do about 70-80. As long as you don't use the air-conditioning, the stereo or anything else that you would normally use in a car. If you do, the range will drop to about 60 kilometres. At best, the E2O is a car *exclusively* for the city. Mind you, no other car sold in India has such severe usability limitations. Think about that during your six-hour-long charge.

And hybrids. My God. The amount of pure bollocks coming from manufacturers about them is ridiculous. Let me quickly tell you how they work. You have a standard petrol or diesel engine like a normal car. Along with that, you also get an electric motor that powers the wheels directly. This electric motor is powered by the engine itself through a set of batteries. So, as long as the batteries are charged, the electric motor powers the vehicle by itself. But this lasts only for a few kilometres, and works only at crawling speeds, after which internal combustion kicks in again. Capice? They claim to be a tree-hugger's best friend and can apparently circle the moon on a single drop of fuel. They can't. Fuel economy wise, they're about the same as a diesel hatchback.

Everything seems to have a battery these days and not just to power the electrics, but also to provide the go-juice. I've had six cups of coffee and I still can't work out why. Because all of these technologies, and I mean all of them, are already obsolete. They're Laser Discs and VHSs when the MP3 has already been invented.

And that brings me on to the fuel cell. Granted, fuel cells have been around for some time and the idea is pretty simple - you use a fuel burning engine of some sort to power an electric motor which drives the wheels. What you have, in essence, is an on-board generator in an electric car.

So far, they've been powered by petrol, diesel, or more recently, hydrogen. Honda demonstrated with the FCX Clarity that Hydrogen fuel cells work as a replacement for petrol and diesel fuelled engines. It even sold a few cars to different government bodies in United States.

The FCX Clarity has a Hydrogen tank, where you'd normally expect to find a petrol tank. This hydrogen, when exposed to the air, combines with oxygen to produce pure H_2O. And yes, you can drink it. The by-product of this reaction is electricity, which powers the electric motor, which then powers the front wheels. And when you run out of the old H2, you pop in to a Hydrogen station and fill it up again. Just like petrol. A tank-full of the stuff will take you about 430 kilometres and that's brilliant. And in the 5 years that it's been around, it's only down 20% on performance as compared to an equivalent fossil-fuelled car. That is not a bad place to start.

But, and this is a big 'but', the technology used on this – the most advanced fuel cell car in the world – is already obsolete, and here's why. The problem with this is how the Hydrogen is stored.

A certain Professor Nelly Rodriguez and her crack eco-boffin team from the Northwestern University in Boston have worked out a way to store 32 litres of Hydrogen in a single gram of Graphite using something appropriately complicated-sounding called Nanofibers. She even owns the patent to this technology. She and her team estimate that this is enough Hydrogen to power your family car for about 8000 kilometres. In theory, if the amount of Hydrogen contained in that one gram of Graphite can fuel your average family car for a good eight months of motoring (8000 kilometres), can you imagine what a kilo of Graphite can do? Simply put, you'd buy a car that will never need to be refuelled for as long as you own it. That means that you'll never need a drop of fossil fuel again. And because Hydrogen is the most abundant gas in the universe, human beings will probably be extinct long before it ever runs out. And emissions? Pure water. That's it. You could connect it to your windscreen washer bottle or something.

If that sounds amazing, then get sink your teeth into this. Imagine a 10-kilo fuel cell powering your house. How long would that last? Would you ever need to buy electricity from the government?

There are some problems though. And as you can imagine, they have to do with the great and the good. We find on Fortune's Global 500 list that seven out of their top ten companies are in the petroleum business. Where would this leave them? What would happen to their worldwide distribution networks and infrastructure? Where would it leave the entire Middle East? The poor sheiks will have to sell their mansions and their gold-plated Ferraris for pennies. And get real jobs like the rest of us.

And things will get worse because world over, governments would lose the revenue they get from indecently taxing our petrol and diesel.

But this isn't going to happen, is it? Because let's face it. As soon as Hydrogen fuel cells start catching on, they will legislate. To think that governments won't want a piece of all this action is to think that a fat person will not eat their friends if they got hungry enough.

To be honest, I'm not the biggest tree-hugger in the world. I like the idea of flying down an open road in something powered by petrol listening to nothing but the sweet sound of internal combustion. But even I can see that it's not the future -the Hydrogen Fuel Cell is.

Food for thought.

Charge Me for What?

Since the Union Urban Development Ministry has sent out a mandate to states asking them to work out ways to implement a congestion charge in major cities, we can all expect that soon enough we'll have to fork out some more of our hard-earned/swindled money when using major city centres. This is inevitable. And this will happen sooner or later. It is much too lucrative for the government to ignore.

While people welcome and oppose this in supposedly equal numbers, motorists often forget that they pay Road Tax, Lifetime Tax, VAT, toll whenever they enter a city, toll whenever they leave, toll for most national highways (even when they're under construction), not to mention ludicrous fuel taxes. It's fair to assume that the government makes a fairly healthy sum from motoring.

And now we're staring down the barrel of the London-style congestion charge. The idea of this is to reduce the number of vehicles on congested city roads during rush-hours so that the people who pay this can have some of the stress and time taken out of their journey while those who don't want to pay can contribute to the good government's coffers by using public transportation instead. Or use a bicycle. Or walk.

The whole business of congestion charging was first seen in London in 2003. Transport for London (TfR) immediately added 300 additional busses to its fleet to cope with the additional demand as soon as the system was launched. Milan and Singapore followed shortly afterward.

All these cities quickly dispensed with the manual coupon system and moved on to completely electronic systems that either use cameras that can scan number plates of cars or overhead sensors that scan vehicles as they pass under them and deduct the tax automatically.

While the effects of this proposed (Read: inevitable) charge in India have been debated extensively, let's look at some of those which haven't been talked about. Firstly, less traffic means that businesses in the chargeable area will inevitably be affected. This is especially true for the retail industry. Less traffic = less people = less customers. Therefore, if you find that your neighbourhood grocer has shut shop, you know who to blame. Secondly, the areas surrounding the chargeable area will bear all the congestion of the chargeable area because these points will require mammoth infrastructure in terms of multi-level parking, public transport terminals and many other facilities to cater to the hoards who have decided not to pay the charge. Not to mention the congestion that will be caused at the inevitable *toll nakas* and their surroundings, which indecently will also be in the city. And how long will it be before the government decides to widen the chargeable area?

Since the time this proposal has been floated in the press, nobody seems to have spoken to the one industry that, technically, has the most to lose – the automobile industry. Those who have owned cars for a while are less likely to give up the personal freedom that they inherently offer. But first-time buyers who want a car just to go to work? They'd probably give up on the whole business and use public transport. The A, B and C segments constitute the largest chunk of the car market in India. Almost 50% of this chunk is made up of first-time buyers. Can you see the problem yet?

We spoke to 230 daily commuters across Indian cities, and here are a few things that they want for their money.

1. To begin with, if we're paying again for roads that we've already paid for with the aforementioned taxes, we'd like them to be perfect at all times. If they're being repaired, the congestion charge for the duration must be waived.

2. Public Transport must be comfortable, air-conditioned and on time. There must be enough busses and metro trains where people can commute whilst sitting down because the thought of giving up your car for a daily commute only to find out that you have to squeeze into a coach and stand up facing someone else's armparts for upwards of half an hour is as risible as sitting between two fat people on a long-haul flight.

3. All areas covered by congestion charging must be *Singapore*-clean at all times.

4. Traffic in these areas must flow at a minimum average speed of 17kph.

5. There must be constant infrastructure development in the chargeable area.

6. The charge itself must be affordable, ie. no more than INR 60/- per day. A one-time charge not exceeding the aforementioned amount per day must be applicable to all the roads in the chargeable area. Like London, congestion charge should eventually be available at retail outlets within the chargeable area as well as online and via mobile apps and should accept all credit/debit cards along with cash.

7. The chargeable area should have its own web portal where all users can monitor the area's development at every stage.

8. Residents of the chargeable area should be charged the same as people entering the area because they will be the first to benefit from this.

9. All motor vehicles must be charged the same amount within the chargeable area (No exceptions for two wheelers).

10. There should be no charge on weekends and public holidays because there is no rush hour on such days.

11. If it is proven that the controlling body is defaulting in any respect as far as its responsibilities are concerned, the congestion charge should automatically be waived and the culprits sacked.

12. All profits from this system must go into improving infrastructure for road users.

These are our terms, Mr Politician. If you can abide by all of them, we grudgingly accept your new government-sponsored extortion scheme.

All Crossed Up

Would you like a car that looks like it can go off road but can't? Yes? Well step right this way because I think we can help. They're called Crossovers and they're a bit tricky.

Crossovers were conceived in the early naughties as alternatives for hatchbacks, MPVs and proper SUVs. In almost all cases, they're derived from an existing product like a hatchback on an MPV and then tweaked with raised suspension, plastic body cladding and possibly four-wheel drive, all of which imply some degree of off-road capability.

Now, though, it is soon becoming one of the largest segments in the automotive pie anywhere. To be brutally honest, crossovers are a cynical marketing exercise because they tend to cost a lot more than the hatchbacks or MPVs that they're based on in return for some visual beefing-up and ground clearance. But that's what India seems to want.

Let's look at some examples of what's available.

First, the Renault (Dacia) Duster. The Duster was designed and engineered on the Sandero's platform. Which is an updated version of the Logan's underpinnings. Which, in turn, is adapted from an old Renault Clio. To base a Crossover on a hatchback's platform makes sense because SUVs tend to drive quite poorly - they roll in corners and so on. But the Sandero, I'm told, is decent to drive so that explains the why the Duster is as good as it is. Also, hatchbacks are light, frugal and mostly compact. None of these things are normally associated with traditional SUVs, so that's good too.

Volvo has recently launched the V40 Cross Country in India and straightaway, it looks brilliant. For me it's one of the best-looking cars on sale in India. But my worry is this: we know that crossovers are fundamentally compromised because they're derived from another product almost as an afterthought. So would you spend 30 something lakhs on the Volvo or the MINI Countryman? Or, for this kind of money, would you rather buy a proper SUV?

Reality check done with, let me get to what is undoubtedly my favourite crossover – the Skoda Yeti. To begin with this is all the car you'll ever need. Big from the inside, small from the outside, plush, sophisticated, supremely comfortable at any speed and over virtually any surface, this is the car that all carmakers should study before launching a car for India. Okay, so it's not pretty in an obvious way. But it is attractive, and that's the point. It's not trying too hard. It is what it is, and Skoda hopes you'll appreciate that. But it is quite a thing. The 4x4 Elegance retails for about 20 Lakhs and is my pick for the best car on sale in India. Why? Apart from all the other pre-requisites, it's got the Laura's 2.0L diesel and a six-speed manual gearbox to go with it. It also comes standard with power everything, a great touch-screen audio system, leather-seats, a better ride than some SUVs over twice its price, all the practicality you'd expect and then some. It'll do over 200kph effortlessly while returning 14kpl+ (Skoda claims over 17) because the awesome 2.0 TDI that does business in VWs, Audis and other Skodas, puts out 140bhp and 320 torques. And it drives like a saloon car, not a great big jiggly SUV. At just over 1.5 tonnes, it's also much lighter than its cheaper and more expensive rivals.

See what I mean? For my money, this is better in many ways, than the more expensive BMW X1, Audi Q3 and the hopeless MINI Countryman because unlike any of those cars and several other pretenders, it can do everything they can and also work properly off road. The only area in which it lacks slightly is badge. But Skoda's not exactly down-market in India, is it?

Dear Mr. Legislator

Some time ago, another motoring columnist argued in his column that putting a few *netas* in jail would be the answer all our motoring woes on the basis that roadworks, systemic changes to road pricing, delays in paperwork and substantial reductions in taxations wouldn't be held up as ploys for re-elections. And petrolheads would have the streets to themselves and would be able to enjoy motoring the way Enzo Ferrari or Ferrucio Lamborghini intended us to.

I'm sure some of you readers actually have the power, inclination and not to mention a love for motoring so strong that you could actually have this done over your morning coffee and cigarette. So why haven't you, hmmm? What's the hold up? 1.2 billion (is it more now?) Indians want motoring utopia and it's yours to provide. But you won't and I know why. Because everyone depends on the *netas* for something or other.

It is an amazing system that they've created, isn't it? Theirs to control, modify, manipulate and ultimately profit from. A system so one-sided that I've never met a politician in my entire life who is poor. In fact, every single one I've ever been introduced to gives the impression of being middle-class, until you spot the 30-thousand-rupee phone and the mandatory gold watch. Let's see if we can figure this out. They make about as much as a lowly journalist, such as me. Over that, they have a few perks such as a house, car and a few other freebies provided by a bigger politician.

Of course, when they get busted by the Lok Ayukta, they wax lyrical about how all the illegal cash, cars, jewels, land and two crore bathroom (complete with its own fireplace and gold-plated bog) were gifts from well-wishers. That could very well be the case. But would you ever give some politico things like that unless you wanted something in return? No. So these are payments in return for favours; permissions, consents and making a few calls here and there to open some doors. Or to close them for someone else.

I'd like, at this to juncture, to point out that I'm not against anybody making money. Go ahead Mr. Branson. Buy another island. What I am dead against is corruption. I hate the fact that we have to bribe people to do their jobs. If you want a driver's licence, you need to slip a little bit under the table. If a policeman, with his effervescent IQ decides that you have committed a crime, you can't reason with him. You can't explain to him that he's wrong. You've got to fill his pockets.

Narayan Murthy argued a few years ago that some bribes should be made legal. And I'm with him on this. Some of us need some things done quickly. And right now, the only way to do that is to bribe a government official. Imagine that money legitimately going to the exchequer. And getting a receipt. Sounds pretty good to me. Of course, we already do this – it's called *Tatkaal.*

Let's try some more 'solutions'. We know of businesses that employ lakhs of people. And these organisations make profits in such large numbers that I'd run out of column space before I can get through all the zeros found on their balance sheets. They are more or less governed by systems where you don't just use technology, you report to it. All you have to do is your job and let the systems manage the business. There's no room for error, because an error can only be human; who can be replaced. I know it sounds a bit Terminator – Judgement Day, but it really works.

My next solution is a reality show. God knows people love them. Imagine a channel which showed you what your public servants were doing 24 hours a day. Granted, this might be a little expensive to implement and subsequently run, and so will my IT-based solution. My source of funds to put this in place is genius as well.

I propose a raid on every single government official. Every single one. And use all the I've-never-seen-that-before-in-my-life money to get this baby up and running. In many ways, this could be the end of corruption as we know it. And if any politician refuses to participate, they are admitting that they want to go on doing corruption behind your back. They should be jailed immediately. No trial. No appeals. In prison. For life.

Second. We need someone incorruptible to run this system. Someone who fears nobody and who will always do the right thing. This is where you'd think my plan would fall flat on its face, right? But I've got that covered as well, Mr. Gold Watch, because there are organisations capable of running these systems. Corporations such as Oracle, SAP, Intel, Microsoft and Infosys have their systems in pretty well every organization in the world. And they do a bang-up job. Throw in a media company like the BBC to broadcast and you'd be able to watch your country being run. Imagine an India with no bullshit, no 'politics' where the only thing that a government could do was better the country.

But the sleazy, money grabbing politicians will try to beat this system. They'll try to find a way to outlaw it so they can go back to buying Hummers for their 14-year-old kids. But here's the thing. 99 out of a hundred politicians have no qualifications or expertise whatsoever in the Ministry that they manage. They're elected by the masses, mostly because they can lie better than their competitors and make utterly false promises sound realistic and achievable. Then they're positioned there by another politician. So what I say is this. We employ experts from across the world. Think about it. If we needed someone to manage IT, why not employ a CEO of a global IT firm? He clearly knows what he's doing. Same with Energy, Agriculture, Transportation and everything else. And to really good Executive Search firms, these people are a breeze to find. Sure, they're going to be expensive. But at least they'll know what they're doing and they will actually work for a living. If you had to choose between an expert who took a salary of 5 million USD and actually did his job well versus a politician who makes a salary of 35,000 INR and swindles 5 million USD a year and did naff all, which would you choose?

Next. These privateers are all about profit and this is great for us as well. Because they'll actually make the best use of every last rupee of collected tax. To them, it's not about how little they can do and how much money they can steal, it's about how they have to do well or they'll lose their jobs. They're used to competing and keeping their businesses competitive.

There you are Mr. Neta. Pack up and leave. Oh, and while you're at it, try to get a real job in the real world. I bet in 3 months you'll go back to being a criminal full-time. Only this time, you won't have your *pull* to keep you out of jail.

Bite-Sized Luxury

India is possibly the most confused car market in the world. We are a market that is utterly obsessed with status and not much else. Bigger is always better here, be in terms of size or badge. And for true car lovers, that's a bit sad because truly great cars are seldom appreciated while the likes of the Scorpio and Fortuner set the sales charts on fire.

And the newest culprit - Mercedes-Benz. To catch up with Audi's Q3 and BMW's X1, they launched the B-Class 'Luxury Tourer'. That's like calling Lalu Prasad Yadav tall, dark and handsome. It's a hatchback. A simple, common or garden hatchback with Merc levels of quality.

And now we have the A-Class. While this is a genuinely astonishing product, it is, I'm afraid, still a hatchback. And it costs upwards of 20 Lakhs. India seems to really love this car because in the first ten days of its launch the little Merc got 400 bookings.

Then we come to MINI. MINI has long been *the* city car. The BMW version along with the previous Leyland/Austin/Rover versions have a truly classless feel to them. They are small cars that you buy because they're just as cool as a Ferrari or an Aston Martin because they are completely unique in a marketplace that is filled to the brim with compromise. It's the same story with the Fiat 500.

But in India, MINI has lost the plot comprehensively with one simple mistake – pricing. In Mumbai, the MINI Cooper costs 35 Lakhs on-road, while the Cooper S will set you back about 39, again, on-road. That's 39 Lakhs. For a MINI.

Let's put this into perspective. The MINI Cooper in the UK costs the equivalent of 13.5 lakh INR. The Cooper S costs the equivalent of about 16.5 lakhs. Even the range-topping John Cooper Works with the automatic transmission costs about 21.5 Lakhs in INR. For the UK market, it isn't really that expensive. But in India … for a hatchback…

Now MINI India will probably wave their arms about saying that the import duties in India are exorbitant and therefore the pricing. But the last time I checked, their parent company, BMW, has a factory in Chennai. So why can't they be assembled there?

The truth is that they probably will be when there is enough demand. But do you really think that they will pass that benefit on to their customers? Or will they continue to reap the profits that result in them not having to pay the exorbitant export duty any longer?

For once, I'd like to be called a bigoted idiot and proved wrong.

Pay to Play

November is normally my favourite month of the year but last November, I was pretty ticked off because I'd been on a drive from Bangalore to Mumbai. Given the state of most of our country's roads, the national highway I took was pretty good in comparison. Smooth, fast and not very challenging. I covered great distances in very little time, and it was all very well. My trip meter told me that I'd done 1169 kilometres and my total driving time was 10 hours – a very heathy 117kph average speed. I was in a Fiat Linea T-Jet, so that figures.

What doesn't is the fact that I had to pay close to 2500 Rupees as toll on National Highways. Throw in the fact that I had to spend close to 6000 Rupees on petrol, and my travel companion and I may as well have flown down. We'd figured out what the petrol costs would be, approximately but we sure as shoot didn't see this coming. I actually leant out of the window to tell a toll-both man that I'd already paid road tax and that I shall not be paying him anymore. At first, he looked confused, and then summoned a policeman, who had no idea what I was talking about. He said I couldn't go anywhere unless I paid. So I did. And to my companion's misery, continued to pursue a half-an-hour-long conversation with him.

Not that he knew much, but what he said in essence was this: toll-booths are built and managed by private companies to manage and maintain certain stretches of road. And they're free to collect money from the users of these roads to do so. A part of this revenue is shared with the government. Okay. That's when I began my not-so-subtle interrogation.

I asked him where my income tax, life-time tax, road tax, service tax, sales tax and all those other zillion taxes go. He started getting a little annoyed and gave me the old 'don't talk too much'.

And that got me thinking. As road users, we're suckers - all of us. We're getting screwed. We know we're getting screwed. And yet we continue to let them screw us. Why? I've got to ask – are we genuinely so afraid of authority that we elect them so they can make laws which are designed to rip us off? Are we that daft? We might be, but the non tax-paying masses certainly aren't. That's over 75% of our glorious population.

If I ever came to power, I'd make it mandatory for everyone to pay tax. Everyone. There's no more reason for me to pay more out of my hard earned than someone else from theirs. I didn't get my money from sitting around. If I can afford a car and some petrol, it's because I've worked my arse off. I'm not trying to say we rip off the poor. All I'm saying is that we treat everyone equally, regardless of their financial status. Let me put it this way. We have a population of about 1.27 billion. I'm told that 480 million people are currently employed in form or another. If we charge each employed person 5000 Rupees a year, that's 2.4 trillion Rupees right there. That's one and a half times our annual GDP.

I have no financial qualifications whatsoever, and I've figured this out in the space of one afternoon. There you go Mr. Finance Minister. I'll come round next week and pick up the keys to your office.

Road Rage and Then Some

Have you noticed how everyone's getting so aggressive on the road? It's crazy, isn't it? During the day, they're either IT people or they have some sort of job in financial services. They could even be human. But the minute they get into their cars to get to or back from work, they become power-crazed, tailgating, aggressive primates. I can be certain I've met these people when they're not driving. And I'm fairly certain that they eat, sleep, fornicate and have families just like the rest of us.

Why then, when they're behind the wheel, do they suddenly transform into irrational maniacs? Some of them, I'm sure are genuinely late. But they're easy to spot. For example, if someone's furiously flashing their lights behind you, look in your mirror before you act. If the person looks worried, let them past. Their only crime is that they're late for something. If, on the other hand, you find someone 2 inches from your rear bumper, blowing their horn maniacally with an angry expression on their face, either you are driving too slowly or they are mad. In the latter case, please feel free to frustrate them until you see an explosion in your rear-view mirror. Of their head.

There are many things that frustrate me besides. Someone with no sense of urgency in a rush hour comes to mind. Maybe you're not going to work, man. But the rest of us are, so get on with it.

But my biggest crib is with inconsiderate law-breakers. You know the kind. You're the first at a traffic light and the guy (and it is inevitably a guy) behind you is blowing his horn to try and make you jump the light. As bad as that is, it gets worse. A friend of mine who lives in suburban Mumbai tells me of a similar situation, where not only did the man blow his horn, but he also came out of his car, walked up to the car in front of him, and proceeded to give him a piece of his mind for NOT JUMPING TRAFFIC LIGHTS. If that was you, and you're reading this, I hope you catch your wife with your best friend.

Then you've got people who'll change direction violently for no fathomable reason. Who are these people? How have they not died yet? I'll tell you why. Because they're the majority. And with odds like that, you my dear Good Driver, are screwed. I hate to be the bearer of bad news, but it's true. A few good apples in a basket of rot. And that's not good because how long is it before you're so frustrated by them that you decide to seek revenge, and you join the other hundreds of 'good drivers' inadvertently seeking revenge?

The root of the problem however, is in the changing socio-economic status of people. And bloody globalization. What happens when you take a city like Mumbai and add a lakh immigrants every week? Well, I'll tell you. Take a culture that was traditionally rich and cosmopolitan, to which you add every possible kind of person. The result of this, I'm afraid, is millions of people trying to make a success out of themselves in a new city, new culture, which was very liberal. And the result of that is that they start to compete with each other – fiercely. What you get is dog-eat-dog. 21 million people trying to be the next big thing. And let's keep in mind that that all these immigrants have had very little time to adjust to their surroundings. Because they've come with their hopes and dreams and not much else. Ergo, competition starts from day one. And it's a bare-knuckle brawl for trains, ATMs and of course, the roads. If someone's been driving in complete anarchy for several years in their small town, how do you expect them to change in a city which has more of them than natives? Of course, the anarchy will continue because nobody is concerned with contributing to making it better. They're there to squeeze the gonads of everyone around them to take as much as possible.

Now don't get me wrong, I know plenty of great immigrants to Mumbai and other cities as well. I'm from Bangalore and I moved to Mumbai. And I don't mean to blow my own horn, but I like to be as civilized as possible. I do a bit of cut and thrust here and there, but overall, I'm quite happy being law abiding. Assertive? Yes, I am. I'm not about to give up my space. But will I try and bully you out of yours? No.

Some call for stricter law enforcement and sterner punishments. And I'm all for this. If I see someone driving idiotically – to slow, too fast, or just being an idiot, I'd like to see him relieved of his ability to walk. But that's the trouble, isn't it? There is no known measure for idiocy and stupidity. And that could very well be the greatest invention of all time.

Escape the Fix

I'd like to begin this column with sincere apologies to S. Sreeshanth, Ankeet Chavan and the other guy whose name I can't remember. Had I written this earlier, you lot would have probably been sitting on a beach somewhere blowing your hard-swindled fixing fees on pink champagne and private yachts.

But I didn't. So if you've been doing a bit of fixing here and there and haven't been 'named' yet, take a leaf out of nine out of ten bank robbers in the UK from 1983 to 2003 and use a Ford Transit van as your getaway car. Unfortunately, they don't sell them in India. Let's see what you can get here.

But before that, let's first consider what you might need to outrun. To the best of my knowledge the fastest car that the Indian police have for tarmac is the Hyundai Accent. And Mahindra Scorpios for the off-roady bits. We're looking at top speeds of about 160kph for both – give or take. So, you'll probably need something that can spend all day on the right side of 200kph on the road, and can monster the off-roading demands that the inevitable world's-wildest-police-chases-style … police chase will throw at you.

I think we'll agree that we're looking at fast SUVs. Let's start with the most powerful of the lot – the Cayenne Turbo S. Although designed to be as ugly as cars can be, it has a massive turbo-charged 4.8L V8 that's good for 550bhp and enough torque to spin the earth the other way round. And since Porsche doesn't subscribe to the Germanic 250kph speed limit, the Turbo S is good for 278 kph. And it has most the off-road tech that a Range Rover has, so you will be able to keep going when the police have set up a roadblock and you need to turn off the road and thrash it through a field. The Cayenne also works on the tarmac. But then it would – it's a Porsche. It will handle all the ducking and weaving brilliantly as you dodge gunfire during your great escape.

But then, this big, agile V8 blunderbus will show you its Achilles Heel. If you look closely, you'll be able to see the fuel needle dropping right before your eyes. That might make you clench a little because flat out, it'll empty its 100-litre tank in about 400km. Or less. When you do run out and get caught, you'll be arrested not only for your fixings, but also for buying an ugly car.

You may think that an Audi Q7, BMW X5 or X6 is a better idea. You might even consider a Mercedes-Benz G63. But they're either too slow, or will run out of fuel before you get far enough away.

My advice? Get a Range Rover with the 4.4L V8 Diesel. It isn't as quick as a Cayenne Turbo S. It isn't as agile either. But it's comfortable, stately and will give you a dignified last few moments in your spectacular fall from grace. Also, it'll give you plenty of hope during the 900km that it can do on a full tank. N. Srinivasan has one, by the way.

Again, my sincere apologies to the three of you. I was your one shot at freedom and I suit-cased it up with my timing. My heart really does go out to you guys. In the same way that it goes out the murderers and rapists that you'll share your jail cells with.

Car Makers – Put Your Money Where Your Marketing is

If you've been watching television recently, chances are you've seen the advert from Tata saying that the Indica Vista is great to drive; a fun machine. The advert shows two 'dudes' screaming as they set off with their third friend in tow. On a parasail.

I don't want to single Tata out, of course, because we also have the likes of Hyundai singing "I want it now!" about the Eon. They followed that up with the one where someone is getting 'EON' tattooed on their arm and so on. And the list of truly misleading and overzealous adverts goes on.

To begin with, let's get something straight about the Indica Vista. The only thing in the whole of human civilization that drives worse than an Indica Vista is the old Indica. And a fairly rusty pre-World War II wheel-barrow, perhaps. As far as the Eon is concerned, the only reason you "want it now!" is because that's the best you can afford. On the petrolhead desirability index, with the Aston Martin V12 Vantage Roadster on one extreme, this comes at the other, sharing bench-space only with the Indica Vista.

The trouble is that car-makers know this. They know that their products are just that – products - consumer durables like refrigerators, washing machines and microwave ovens. And that's how they're peddling them. Look at an advert of, let's say, the Hyundai i10 and the current line of refrigerators being hawked by Priyanka Chopra. A couple of shots of the product, a couple of shots of the actor, something clever said at the end, and that's your lot.

As a car buying market, India is really a toddler. It's been barely 2 decades since we had a grand total of 10 cars on sale here. That's why we'll pay the ridiculous import tax and is also why pay extra for a sport model of a car which only has some hideous stickers and some red trim on the interiors.

And things are only getting worse. We're now being bombarded with adverts claiming all sorts of nonsense. Manufacturers use the term 'all-new' like it was going out fashion. Why? Because if one just said 'facelift', you wouldn't care because everyone else was screaming 'all-new'.

Telling the truth is clearly out of the question for now anyway, because imagine Nissan saying that the Micra is a hopeless car whose only good qualities are reliability and fuel efficiency, or Mahindra admitting that the Xylo was indeed designed whilst under the influence and all the models used in the advert (happy legs) we're about 5 feet tall. You wouldn't make a dash to the showrooms, would you?

One clear result of this onslaught of advertising is that it has taken a lot of the romance out of motoring. Once seen as a beautiful and hedonistic thing, motoring is now pretty much confined to commuting. Kpl figures sell cars nowadays, not styling. And that makes me and probably every petrolhead in the land quite sad. Because there are truly beautiful cars on sale today, even in India. The Fiats spring to mind straightaway. Why don't they sell as well as they should? Aftersales is a small let down and so are some of the engines. But what's actually delivered the hammer-blow is the aggressiveness of marketing from their competitors. It's funny, isn't it? Here are some truly great cars, killed off by their competitors and their marketers.

The only way to get around this is for the nation to fall back into love with motoring. Because if you do, the marketers will have no affect you. And they'll be forced to stop bullshitting us and spend their money on what's more important – making better cars.

On Supercars in India

A couple of weeks ago, we heard about a man who let his nine-year-old son loose in a Ferrari F430 Scuderia. We also heard that this gentleman of exquisite taste in cars and considerable wealth filmed the event; which he then proceeded to upload to YouTube. I'm not really sure about whether to congratulate him on his excellent choice of car or to smack him across the back of his head for giving supercars a bad rap.

In the interest of full disclosure, I must confess that I've been driving pretty much all my life. The first time I drove, like most people my age, was on my grandfather's lap – I did the steering and he did the throttle and brakes and so on. And I'm not ashamed to admit that I was a pretty good driver *some considerable time* before I got my licence.

I'm sure that after this seemingly shameless admission, every 'law-abiding citizen' is shaking their fists in complete outrage saying that I should be put in a straightjacket and locked up in a cell with no toilet.

But here's the thing – I've never remotely killed anybody, nor so much as caused a scratch to myself or anyone else. By now, the self-righteous among you is screaming through popping red eyes and smoking ears that joyriding is illegal and anybody found doing it should be hit repeatedly on the head until they resemble jelly.

If I ever came to power (Don't ever vote for me. Seriously), I would do the whole driver's licensing business a little differently. My first test would be to see if someone can reach the pedals and see out of the windscreen at the same time. The second would be to check if the applicant could in-fact drive. The third would be an IQ test. If anyone failed any of these, then that's it. Finito. They shall spend their lives being a passenger. If anyone passed all three, they would be given a licence, no questions asked. Age? Gender? Species (only kidding)? No problem.

Anyway, the car. As mentioned, master nine-year-old was driving an F430 Scuderia. For those not familiar, it's a harder, more powerful, more aggressive, stripped-out version of the already bonkers F430. It must feature on the list of the top 10 most unforgiving cars in the world. We're talking 500 horsepowers here. 999 out of a thousand drivers will never experience that kind power in a lifetime of driving. Mind you, all this was in India.

That's brings me to a question. Is there a point owning a supercar in India? To answer this, we must first familiarise ourselves with the breed. A supercar is typically a car with a great big engine (usually in the middle), a wide, low body, two seats, generally breath-taking looks and ground clearance lower than a hooker's morals.

It's been debated over a million times that our roads aren't good enough to handle these cars. And that our traffic is not nearly organised enough. And that since we are a relatively new car-buying population, we simply don't have the expertise to handle them. The last argument is especially compelling.

But here's something that people who make these arguments don't know. Pretty much every supercar on the market today has a little device that, at the touch of a button, raises the nose to go over speed bumps. What? Did you think that we were the only country in the world that had speed bumps? Did you think that car makers haven't thought of that? Most of them also have different driving modes to make them more manageable in the city.

Now let's look at usability. It's true that most of these cars can't handle most Indian roads. But you'd be surprised at how much they can handle. To explain what I'm on about, let me give you an example. Sometime ago, I was driving on the Bombay-Pune Expressway in my Fiat Linea T-Jet Plus. While the road itself was wide and smooth, I knew that the speed bumps at the toll booths were pretty bad. But after crossing the second one, I was overtaken by a Bugatti Veyron. I'm sure he must have had a sphincter-clench when he went over the bump, but he made it. And this is pretty much the lowest car I've seen.

Then there are Porsche 911s which I really dislike. But even I'll be the first to admit that the ones I drove in Bangalore were as easy to drive as my Fiat Linea. They're not very long, they ride beautifully on all surfaces, have enough ground clearance to handle most city conditions and are fairly inexpensive to run.

The Audi R8 is much the same. And with both these cars, you're assured of one thing – when the mood takes you, you can have some proper, world-class fun with them. With these two, you get supercar thrills without the impractically.

And this is exactly why I wouldn't have either of them. While my respect for the Audi is boundless, I can't help but get the feeling that it's been sanitized. It could have been wilder. It could have been scarier. But they held back to make the thing more practical. And, as a petrolhead, I couldn't live with that.

One of the biggest appeals of supercars is the inherent impracticality. You know it won't fit into a normal parking space. You know you can't see out of the back window. You know it will barely take two loaves of bread in the boot. And yet…

When you see one, the nine-year-old inside you feels something you can't really describe. You're instantly transported to your childhood bedroom wall where you had posters of cars like these. You can't help thinking of how great it would be to just sit in one, let alone drive it. 'If only I won the lottery', you fondly imagine.

Me? I don't care about the fact that I'll get hounded at every set of traffic lights. I don't care if I have to go everywhere either alone or with just one favourite person of the moment. I want a Lamborghini Aventador more than I want world peace. Because by driving around in the Lambo, I would be doing as much for myself as I would for all the people that feel like nine-year-olds as I drive by. I'd be freely distributing pleasure to all and sundry.

Does anyone know where I can get lottery tickets? Do let me know.

The Best Car in the World?
That's a Big One

I recently found myself in a pub with a fellow petrolhead who'd made a massive accusation, which I took altogether too gracefully. He accused me of being a motor-whore. Now this may seem offensive to a lot of people, but no sir. Not me. Because I love cars. Not all of them, but all kinds of them, with the exception of people carriers. I've had as much fun in a Maruti 800 as I have in a Ferrari 458. So I agreed with him.

After he discovered that I didn't react as violently as he'd hoped - which apparently was me inserting his head into the bottom of the rather large man sitting beside him - who, by the looks of things, had swallowed his seat. Anyway, after that he asked me a question while squinting slightly through his seventh whiskey-soda, "If you, Sidharth, could have one car, money no object, any car in the world that you'd use for the next five years as your only car, which one would it be?" I'll be honest with you; I was seeing seven whiskies. I had no idea. But I'm glad he asked me that, because for the next week or so I had the most delicious thing to think about whenever I felt a bit empty-headed.

Imagine all the incredible possibilities! I could have a Bugatti Veyron SuperSport, or a Lamborghini Aventador or Gallardo, who cares when it's a Lambo. I could even have an Aston Martin DBS. Or a Zonda. In the past week I've spent many sleepless nights agonising over vintage Ferraris and Alfas, only to dismiss them entirely in the morning and come over all Maserati-ish.

And then it dawned on me; the meat of my friend's question. Apparently, the drunken sod had thought this one through. Ferraris and Lambos are about as practical as everyday transportation as a slightly rowdy elephant. There is no way you could use them every day - especially in India. You may argue the Audi R8 would be a much better bet. But you'd be wrong. Because you'll attract so much attention in a city like Mumbai that you'll wake up one morning, slightly earlier than usual and cover it in dog turds just so people don't come near it. Owning a supercar in the city, no matter how docile it is, is infuriating. When each body panel costs bloody lakhs, you'll have 23 heart attacks in quick succession whenever someone comes close you on the road.

The Maserati Quattraporte, then. Lots of oomph for the petrolhead, and lots of discretion because it's a saloon. And, at least to my eyes, it is Monica Bellucci in automotive form. In many ways, this car is perfect. It's fast, comfortable, luxurious, stylish without being too obvious, and it's a Maserati, so it's got more character than just about anything this side of an Alfa Romeo. But best of all, it is a driver's car.

Job done then. We've found a winner. I'll see you in five years. No. Not exactly. Because its gearbox is made in hell. I have never driven or even been in a car which tries just as hard to make you comfortable and uncomfortable at the same time. In the city, its gearbox is like a monkey trying its hand at Golf. It just can't cope with the laws of motion or inertia. It simply cannot decide what it's supposed to do. Shift up? Shift down? Hold a gear? It's flummoxed.

A lot of people are now screaming at me through the windscreens of their Porsche 911s. And while it is a brilliant car, to my mind it's got no appeal at all. Why? Take a beetle, squash it, and then tell me how much it appeals to you.

And since the Honda NSX went South, the Japanese have given us the Subaru Impreza, Mitsubishi Evo and the fearsome Nissan GT-R. This last one is so immensely capable, that only proper racing drivers with reinforced titanium body parts can get close to its awesome abilities. That would be brilliant for me, because it would make me go to the gym and make me a better driver as a result. But it would also constantly give me the feeling that it was better than me. And I think it would become frustrated with me long before I get frustrated with it.

I'm inclined at this juncture to point towards the Range Rover and the Rolls Royce Phantom. But I dismissed them because I like to be involved in the process of driving once in a while. And while these are two incredible cars, they're just not meant for the keen driver.

The only two logical options that remain are the Jaguar XJ SWB with its Supercharged 5.0 V8 and of course, the phenomenal new BMW M5 Saloon.

The Jag looks so good that you could be covered head-to-toe in genital warts and you'd still be allowed into the best parties in town, as long as you arrive in it. And its all-aluminium construction means that it's much lighter than any of its natural rivals – the Mercedes S-Class, Audi's A8 and BMW's 7-Series. It also has all the gadgets you'll ever need. And the best part is that all that techno-witchcraft is hidden away behind a thick layer of British pomp and circumstance. It's hidden so far beneath that it almost feels like you could spend years getting know it. And I really like that about a car.

But there's a problem – a big one. There's too much prestige. The badge is more powerful than all it surveys. The British PM's got one as his company car. And can you imagine waking up in the morning, putting some slippers on and going down to the shops for some bread, eggs and cigarettes in this? Or try throwing your gym bag in the back seat like you would in your regular car. Just try to imagine your kids fighting on the back seat. Didn't think so. Because this is a car that constantly demands that you respect it. It needs to be treated in a certain way all the time.

And I'm sorry, but quite apart from having the best job in the world, I'm a regular guy. I wake up, I scratch, and so on. Too posh for me, then.

And (with apologies), this brings me to the meat of this week's column. The BMW M5. Or the BMW INSTANTLY SOMEWHERE ELSE, to give it its more popular name. But it's not perfect, this new love of mine and here's why: The stereo pipes a synthesised version of the engine note into the cabin and the engine has shrunk from a V10 to a V8. But that, thankfully, is the end of the bad news.

On to the good stuff. BMW's finally sent Chris Bangle to a place where he can't make us all blind anymore with his 'flame surfacing'. This new version, like the 5 Series it's based on, is a handsome so-and-so, which means that you can have one. I don't know if it's the Jason Bourne-*esque* restrained muscular lines or the beautiful dual angel-eyed headlamps, or even the way that in profile, its proportions are absolutely perfect. Show me a saloon that's better proportioned and I'll show you a BMW badge on it.

The engine's an absolute peach as well. And please don't get me started with the downsizing because the 4.4 Twin Turbo V8 unit puts out 560bhp and 680Nm of Torque, roughly 60 more horsepowers and 180 more torques than your beloved V10. Throw in BMW's 7-Speed, Dual-clutch M transmission, M's Torque Vectoring Active Differential, rear wheel drive, and the result is 0-100 in 4.4 seconds and a Germanic Top Speed of 250kph. For a small fee though, BMW will sell you what they call an M Drivers Package, which bumps up top speed to 305kph. You can also have the optional 20-inch wheels, which are just so gorgeously minimal and some beautiful deep blue brake callipers with the M logo on them. It comes standard with really fat tyres as well - 265/40/19s in the front and 295/35/19s at the rear.

But my reasoning, agree with it or not, is simple. In black, this car is an M5 for me and a common-or-garden 5-Series for everyone else.

It's a true Q car. A wolf in sheep's clothing. I can take it to the shops because you can take a 5 Series to the shops. And the best part is that that this new M5 has two programmable M buttons to setup however I want. I can have some seriously Eco-bearded fuel saving settings on one and Please-be-an-M5-thank-you-very-much on the other. Which means I can go completely mental as well. And this car does mental. Oh yes it does. You can lose your licence in less time than you'd take to say BMW M5. And it'll go around corners in whatever way takes your fancy. Gripping like a leach? Check. Drifting like a smoke machine? No problem. And you can do all of that because its technical overlord works with you. Everything from the Traction Control, Stability Control, ABS, Differential and all the other electronic aids are there to show you a good time, to entertain you, and your 3 terror-stricken passengers. And when you're done mucking about, press the other M button that you've set on everything comfort and cruise into the sunset. Because that is this car's party piece – at the push of a button it becomes a normal 5-Series.

So, my drunken friend, it'll be the BMW M5 for me for the next 5 years. Why? Because by then the new one would probably be out and I think I'll have one of those as well, please.

This Rooster Growls

An industrial estate in the IT district of Bangalore called Whitefield houses a little known but fiercely respected automobile tuning outfit called Red Rooster Performance. From the outside, it looks like any other big industrial shed, making the noise that any factory would. What caught my attention straight away was Gaurav Gill's rally-winning Mahindra Super XUV 500. Sunny Sidhu's was right next to it. And he'd come second. Both of them were rally prepared by Red Rooster. I also spotted some of Toyota's TRD Etioses. Not surprisingly, these were race-prepared by them as well – 30 cars in total, after being commissioned by Toyota themselves for the Etios Motor Racing championship as the official constructor. There were also some single-seat racers lying about.

A few days earlier, I'd been to attend their first ever Performance Motoring seminar. Alongside me were about thirty eager petrolheads trying to get as much go-faster info as they could. Now I hate seminars. I think that seminars are where dull people go to listen to other dull people explaining dull things. And yes, it was a lot of power-point-presenting and portable microphones here as well. But the difference was that it was all relevant. As a petrolhead, I ate it all up. They had specialist engineers talk about how they went about improving a car's performance. I have no engineering degree to speak of and I understood it all. "It's our first step in educating the masses about performance motoring and tuning," explained N. Leelakrishnan, Chief Technical Director at Red Rooster.

"We want to bust myths like 'high performance means low mileage' and 'a tuned car is undrivable on a daily basis'." Things like that.

A lot of tuners I've met have made such claims. But they were all bollocks. Time to put this to the test.

Back at their factory, I took one of their tuned Swifts for a road test. The puzzling part about this car was that unlike other tuners, they hadn't bothered with body-kit at all. And when I got in, there were no gauges or dials for utterly pointless things that you'll never need either. From the inside it was completely stock. No racing seats, no MOMO steering wheel. "We don't bother with the look of the car at all. Apart from the paintjob, we only do performance tuning," explained Sudhir Y R from Red Rooster, who rode shotgun with me.

On startup, all I noticed was a deep, meaningful moan from the exhaust. No drama, no shenanigans as I slotted it into first and eased off the line. In the back of my mind, I was expecting this thing to bite and bite hard. But it didn't. At crawling speeds, it's as well behaved as my Swift, and just as easy to drive. I kept searching furiously for a downside, and all I found was a little bit of tram-lining from the 205/55/R14 front tyres. If I'm honest, I only noticed this because I was looking for it. If you aren't then you won't.

My test drive took me on to the Bangalore-Chennai highway, and straight away the point of this thing became clear. It was a masterpiece in its setup. The engine was now regularly serving up its 140 turbocharged horses with absolutely no turbo lag. The whole package was so predictable that I found myself doing 150 kph – around corners! And the suspension setup from Tein was masterful. The brakes were great as well - progressive and predictable. I managed about 165 kph in the short distance that I drove. Did it have more to give? I'd say yes. And 13kpl.

If you put too much power in a front-wheel-drive car, it tends to torque-steer or understeer, or both. But as I pushed through the corners, if felt completely neutral. There was so much pure mechanical grip that even when I was stupid and trying to get it to misbehave, it just clung on and went.

By now, I was having as much fun as I was getting irritated at the thought of not being able to find anything wrong with it. Because even after a proper thrash, it settled down to a quiet potter in the city. The ride was great - firm but well judged. The steering was well-weighted but easy. The feedback was great. I saw a lizard that I ran over (by mistake, PETA, by mistake) and I could feel it through the steering wheel, pedals and seat. Feedback doesn't get much better than that. It was exactly like my Swift, just better in every way.

But then I finally found the skeleton in this otherwise perfect car's closet. The ECU is in the glove box so your sunglasses won't fit! Okay, I know. That's not really very bad.

Actually, I don't know why I'm so surprised. Leelakrishnan is one of the most successful individuals in the history of Indian motorsports. Seven-time rally champion as a driver, many time rally champion as a constructor. Red Rooster has won pretty much everything they've competed in from rally to races to superbikes. "We pulled out of motorsports at the end of 2010 due to lack of sponsorship. Now we tune race-winning machines for our customers," said Leelakrishan.

"As far as the future is concerned, we want to continue building usable, everyday cars with genuine high-performance for our customers. And with a little bit of help from sponsors, we will be back on the starting line as well." Upon some serious questioning and cajoling, he finally relented. "Yes, we are working on a supercar. But don't expect to see it any time soon."

Small tuning outfit? Yeah, right.

Part 2

More Questions Than Answers
Fiat Linea 1.3 Multijet Emotion

Yes, the diesel. And straightaway you wonder, why not the new (not so new) T-Jet that was recently launched? Actually, that's quite simple – the T-Jet wasn't available for test.

The Linea has been on sale virtually unchanged for five years around the world and its age is starting to show visually. That said, it is still properly beautiful. Masculine in its visual bulk and feminine in its voluptuous yet soft curves, it is very pleasing to the eye, this car.

Putting a diesel engine in a car that looks like this does is like pouring some cow excrement on a Gordon Ramsay Braised Stuffed Lamb Breast. And you feel that when you turn it on. It's not very loud, and it sounds more agreeable than most diesels but you do get the feeling that it is out of place. This, of course, is the little 1.3L MultiJet that puts out 90 horsepowers and 208Nm of torque. You probably know this already but this is one of the most popular diesel engines in India.

I tested the top-end Emotion version which had a fair bit of equipment on offer like leather seats climate control, rain sensing wipers, automatic headlamps, airbags and Fiat's own Blue&Me media system. All in all, enough buttons to keep you entertained.

Okay, I'm stalling because what we have here essentially, is the problem to which the T-Jet was the solution, with some more power, equipment and 185mm of ground clearance. Customers complained that the diesel was underpowered and so Fiat took cognizance and launched the T-Jet.

I've owned the old T-Jet before and thoroughly enjoyed the experience even though sometimes, some bits of trim would fall off. That's the thing about Italian cars – they will go wrong; things will fall off. But when they work, they can transport you to a place where you feel so many different kinds of pleasures, that it makes all the troubles completely worth it.

As far as the diesel's concerned, let me tell you what you have already surmised. If you try driving this car aggressively, you'll find that it is underpowered. Significantly. And since we're nit-picking, the clutch pedal had what feels like 10 feet of travel, so driving this thing in bumper-to-bumper traffic is really not easy. And the ABS is really quite intrusive and cuts in too quickly for my liking. Also, over the two days that I had it, I could never get the seat adjusted quite right. You should also know that at 6'3", I did not fit in the back seat. I'm not joking here, I really had to crane my head to one side. And the gear lever felt clunky and rubbery.

Now the good news. The automatic headlamps and rain sensing wipers worked brilliantly in Mumbai's aggressive monsoon. The wipers especially came on and at the speed I would have liked had I operated them myself manually. I also liked the isolation from the outside world. It is really quiet, apart from that engine, of course. On 16in alloy wheels with 205/55 Goodyear NCTs, it rides beautifully.

And the news gets better because this car has an incredible sweet spot. In fifth gear, between two and three thousand revs, the engine is completely quiet and you get that nice satisfying woosh at 80-100 kph as you drive along. If your good self is fortunate enough to be on a nice twisting road at the time, you'll find that the steering is perfectly weighted and the feedback is never anything other than brilliant. You'll find that while the ride is brilliant, it's no slouch around the corners. In fact, there is so much feedback from the pedals, seat and steering wheel. How have they done that? Great ride, great handling and intangibly pleasurable to drive. Hats off to Fiat.

Now you're probably wondering if you should buy one. Here's what you can expect for about 10 odd lakhs. With the T-Jet, you'll have a true barnstormer that's miles ahead in terms of sheer talent of anything that calls itself a competitor.

With the diesel, you'll get all that talent minus the hot engine. If you still want the diesel, might I suggest you get in touch with Red Rooster Performance in Bangalore, who will kindly hook you up with a tuning box to make that engine more powerful and more fuel efficient. But if you really want to enjoy your diesel Linea, don't thrash it. Instead, cruise at about six-tenths of this car's limit and enjoy all those little droplets of feedback and sensation. That alone is worth 9 lakhs out of the ten-lakh asking price.

It's a Donkey, Until You Show it the Whip
Fiat Punto 1.2 Petrol Dynamic

At 80kph, it emits a little beep to warn you that you've exceeded the speed limit. And that's annoying. In the two days I had it, I pushed every button on the dashboard twice to make this beep go away. But it didn't.

In the same two days I developed the worst backache I've probably ever had. So much so that I refused an evening out on the town because I could neither sit, stand nor lie down owing to a driver's seat that is capable of accommodating only the smallest of children. The back seat isn't much better either.

That's not all because in the city, that engine seems like a collection of parts that were never meant to work together. The throttle has little or no interest in providing the sort of power you would either want or require immediately. Honestly, at 20kph, I buried the throttle in second and the engine took a good 10 seconds to convince itself that it was responsible for my propulsion.

The tyres on my test car were certainly not the kind you would want. For a six lakh-plus car, it doesn't have climate control, airbags or anti-lock brakes. All it has is that infernal beep.

You may also have heard that Fiat has terrible after-sales service. I have. A million people told me this when I decided to buy a Linea. But we bought it anyway, and the and the after-sales is fine. It's just like any other car company – fine for the most part with the occasional problem.

I know I haven't been waxing lyrical about this car but my rather embarrassing admission is that it quite simply my favourite Fiat.

Imagine, if you will, that Gordon Ramsay has made a burger. He probably wouldn't overcook the meat, undercook the French fries and make it Big-Mac-alike. These are all the things that we, as consumers, have grown accustomed to from a burger. So much so that we've grown to like that way.

But Fiat's gone down the Gordon Ramsey route. They've designed the Punto specifically for your driving pleasure.

And it may well have been designed in the last decade, but since it emanated from the hands of a certain Italian designer called Giorgetto Guigiaro, it is about as clean, simple and beautiful as a hatchback can be. There is virtually no detailing on the body apart from the shoulder crease. This is automotive styling at its finest. Modern cars are just so Korean nowadays with their fussy detailing and their over-the-top attempts to catch your attention and you can't help but appreciate Fiat for sticking to the simple pebble-shaped two-box body.

Despite its diminutive dimensions, it feels big on the inside with plenty of leg, shoulder and headroom for the driver and front passenger. And although the dashboard hasn't aged quite as well as the exterior, all the knobs and things fall easily to hand. The boot's huge too.

But when you just want a good drive, you start to realise the point of this thing.

The little 1.2l engine that felt woefully underpowered suddenly starts to sing. You start to rev it harder and harder and realise that it feels more like a beating heart than a petrol burning motor. And on a nice twisting road, I fell in love.

When you drive this thing at the limit, you forget all about the seats, the lack of features and everything else that annoyed you. You have officially arrived in motoring nirvana.

Those poor tyres let you enjoy all the handling that the brilliant chassis has to offer. And you red-line the engine in every gear until you get to grips with the fact that driving pleasure doesn't always mean going fast. It's about the way you feel.

This isn't a fast car by a country mile. What it is, is a ton of Italian city car with all the associated Latin histrionics.

And don't bother with the diesel, or the bigger petrol engine. If you want to drive, get this tiny little 1.2. I would even go so far as to recommend it as a second car – just for that weekend pleasure drive in the countryside.

Luxury Harchbacks? Yeah, Right. Right?
Mercedes-Benz A180

Are you Stevie Wonder? No? Because I checked with him and even he couldn't deny the fact that this - the brand spanking new Mercedes-Benz A Class - is jaw-droppingly, head-swivelingly, mouth-wateringly gorgeous.

In the day I spent with it in Bangalore, I found that it had the attracting capacity of a slightly naked Monica Bellucci. It really is that good looking. That nose. Those daytime running lamps. That beautiful sloping coupe-esque roof. Those tail lamps. That beautiful bum! I think I need a moment alone.

It's not often that you hear a road-tester gush, and rest assured that this is not the result of some significant remuneration received.

Back to the road test. Unlike most road tests that begin in the city and then end up on a mountain road, my test of the A180 was the other way round. I was in Ooty when this pretty little number rocked up so my first tryst with it was in the hills. Anyone who has driven to Ooty from Bangalore will know that that the descent from this little colonial hill station has 36 consecutive hairpins. And that's where I learnt this car.

It has the stiffest suspension that I've come across on a non-AMG Mercedes. And after hairpins number five and six, I started to see the point of it. It feels like a sportscar. It's not very light, but it carries its bulk quite well. The car itself sits really close to the ground so the centre of gravity is, by default, low. Add that to a brilliant chassis, 225/45/R17 tyres and you can well imagine that this thing has all the ingredients to show you a good time.

'But what's under the hood?' you ask. An A180 should mean an A Class with a 1.8L petrol engine. But it doesn't have a 1.8. It has a 1.6L turbocharged petrol engine and it's an absolute gem. What really isn't is the 7-speed double clutch automatic gearbox. It works brilliantly in the city, in a nice creamy, lazy sort of way. And even when you're out on the highway, it shifts seamlessly through all its 7 gears. When you put it in Sport mode, it holds gears all the way to the red line and then upshifts seamlessly. If even blips the throttle on downshifts. But the trouble is that it never does any of these things when you want it to.

Let me give you an example, I was coming around a long sweeping corner at *well* over the speed limit when I saw a speed breaker. As you can probably imagine, panic braking ensued. While the brilliant braking system brought me to a perfectly poised halt, the gearbox had only downshifted as far as fourth gear by the time I cleared the speed breaker and needed power again.

This made me wonder – the gearbox does all its jobs brilliantly, only two or three seconds after you ask it to. Could it be that the software that manages this gearbox is a bit dim? MB's technical centre is in Bangalore. You're welcome to take it up with them.

Being so low to the ground might make it handle well, but it makes you clench the first few times you go over speed breakers. Although, you soon learn to take them at a particular pace and angle so you don't lose your sump.

Inside, you get lots of toys like a great stereo, sunroof, satnav, heated front seats, fully power-adjustable driver's seat with memory for 3 profiles, paddle-shifts for the gearbox and a lot of other thoughtful little touches.

The cabin is also a really nice place to be, what with leather and brushed aluminium. The coupe-style roof line gives the impression that there isn't any space for rear passengers. But there is. I did a backseat journey to test the ride and brought along a fellow six-footer for company. The only niggle was that because of the sloping C Pillar, the view from the from the rear windows was slightly hampered. Other than that, we had enough space.

Now it's time for the verdict. At 25 odd lakhs, should you buy one? Well, it looks beautiful, drives brilliantly, has a great ride for the most part, is a complete pussycat in the city and is genuinely a fantastic product. But most of all, it feels like a Mercedes should.

This is, without doubt, my car of the year for 2013. The forthcoming BMW 1 Series and Audi A3 are going to have to be a hell of a lot better than good to even come close to what is now my new favourite Mercedes-Benz.

It Works Beautifully. Just not for Me
Audi Q3 2.0 TDI

We all have memories that we don't really remember. Like the third word that our children spoke. Or that song from that band on the radio.

I'm willing to bet that all these events had a certain significance – but only at the time.

Here's what I'm willing to bet my year's wages on – after all those burnt dinners you remember your wife's birthday. You remember your wedding anniversary. You remember your first dog's name.

And happily, this time, I haven't taken too long to get to my point – driving an Audi Q3 is an event, not an occasion.

Don't get me wrong. As far as sheer competence goes, it's right up there with Tom Cruise in Mission Impossible III. And on the face of it, it has no flaws. It's attractive to the beholder - four rings and those daytime running lamps make a pretty strong case for it visually.

And there's plenty of oomph from the 2.0 TDI and the 7-speed S-tronic (Damn! That's a good double clutch gearbox) gearbox. Shall we continue to call it the S-tronic and not DSG? Just to be safe, let's ask Audi. The engine pus out 177 horsepowers and a healthy 380Nm of torque. It never feels underpowered, because this, the lightest Q, weighs in at just under 1.6 tonnes.

With that light steering, great drivetrain and an overall length of just over 4.3 metres, it's a nippy little bugger in the city. I found myself aiming for and nailing those gaps normally used by taxis and rickshaws. And people do get out of your way when you drive this in the city. Because the most terrifying thing for a city motorist is not a bus or a rickshaw – it is an aggressively driven SUV.

The ride is really good as well. It glides with great dignity on smooth roads and I really don't think that there is a big enough bump in the civilized world that will stop this thing. The high ground clearance and Quattro mean that it should be able to handle a bit of off-roading as well.

Inside you get power-adjustable and heated front seats, a huge sunroof, a brilliant music system that takes a USB, CD, SD Card and even plays music off your phone. It's also got a Bluetooth. And you can control most of this with the buttons on the steering wheel.

That, I'm afraid, is the end of the good news. Because everything about this car, from the size to the way it drives to the equipment feels like a compromise.

It has rear parking sensors but no reversing camera. There is a button on the dash for a satnav which it doesn't have. You can see Drive Select on the MMI but you can't access it.

And that last problem means that the steering is permanently set in comfort mode. That means it's always light, which is great in the city but scary as bloody hell on the open road or even in the twisties. I drove this thing aggressively for about half a kilometre on a twisting road and decided immediately to back off.

I'm sure it would be a lot better as a car if Audi gave it all the bells and whistles and a full-length glass roof like the Q5. I'm sure that would justify the resultant increase in price. And even though it has a lot going for it, I would never have one. For the simple reason that I like cars that are made to be as good as they can be.

I'm sure that many of the yummy mummies who've bought one would disagree with me, but I'm sticking to my verdict. As competent as it may be, I don't like it because I don't like the idea of it.

Budgetville Luxury
Mercedes-Benz B180 CDI

I'm going to ask the big question first. Why would you spend more money on the B180 CDI than you would on an A180 CDI? The A Class looks immeasurably better, has loads more equipment, is cheaper by a few lakhs, and vitally, tells the world that you haven't given in to middle age yet.

As you may remember from the Q3 review, I'm not the biggest fan of equipment skimpery. I like a car to be as good as it can be. And if the B Class petrol is loaded to the gills with gadgetry, then why isn't the diesel? To answer this question and a few more, we need to understand where Mercedes has positioned the B Diesel.

First, Merc is calling it a Luxury Tourer. And when you get in, you really can't understand why. There's no satnav, no sunroof, no reverse parking camera. It's got 205/55/R16 tyres which are a size too small. Where, dear Mercedes, is the luxury?

What is this thing? Is it a cynical marketing exercise? Or does it have redeeming features so strong that buyers can overlook the lack of equipment and spend a not inconsiderable 22.6 Lakhs (ex-showroom Mumbai before Octroi) when they could have had an A Class and a summer holiday for the family in Europe for the same amount?

Here are some things you should take into account before you go charging into the dealership for an A Class instead. The B is taller, wider and a lot more spacious. The cabin is typical Mercedes and has a great big slab of wood across the centre console. It feels like it's built to outlive its owners. All the materials feel like they're of the best quality. And, crucially, although it's based on the A Class platform, it's longer as well. There's more room in the back seats (enough for three adults) and the boot is humungous for a car of this size. In short, the packaging is much better than the A Class because the designers didn't have styling as a constraint.

You'd be surprised how similar it is to the A Class to drive in the city. Although, I got the feeling that Merc has softened the suspension to go with the B's more relaxed nature. That said, even with the 2.14L diesel (which you'll also find in the A, C & E Classes in different states of tune) putting out 107bhp and 250 torques, it never feels particularly powerful, but never hopelessly powerless either. It's as adequate as you can imagine.

Where the baby B really shines is on the highway. Those A Class underpinnings are almost as brilliant in the B as it in the smaller Merc. It really is great at covering ground. What I did was put in Manual using the Sport-Economy-Manual button, put it in 7th gear and just keep going. In 7th, it goes from 60kph all the way to about 195 without a fuss. And you always have enough torque low down so you don't really need to downshift. Do this, and you'll get about 17kpl in the real world. And the brilliant brakes mean that you can choose to come to a halt from 160pkh on a one-rupee coin that you've placed at a certain distance, if you so prefer.

So, the B Class then. Think of it as the bastard love child of the R Class and the A Class with the R contributing the practicality and the A contributing to the dynamics. It seems to have a depth of engineering specifically for the job it has to do - everything. Me? I'd still have the A Class. But only because I don't need the extra practicality.

Fun For the Blind
BMW 118d Sport Plus

As opposed to every other car or bike review you've ever read, Honk proudly presents our first and probably only review beginning with the verdict – if the only thing you want from a car is driving pleasure and you've got precisely 37 lakhs (on-road) burning a hole in your medium-sized pocket, buy the BMW 118d Sport Plus. Here's why.

As with the Yeti we brought you some time ago, the looks of the 1 Series will polarize opinion. Personally, I think it looks good head on. But BMW seems to have lost the plot at the rear. The 1 Series deserves to be a saloon and you can make that out straight away – it really does seem like a saloon minus the boot. But the roof is really low, so while it may not be beautiful, it certainly looks sporty – especially in Red. The 17-inch wheels shod with low-profile 225/45 tyres look the ideal size for this car.

The sportiness continues into the inside with an all-black dashboard that has a red stripe running across. And mercifully, there's no wood. The front sport seats are out-of-this-world good in the way that they support and comfort. They're also infinitely power adjustable with memory. The steering wheel feels just perfect as well, with its size and shape. Brilliant.

Okay, I'm stalling. Because you want to know how it feels to drive. So let's get on with it. First, the downer – it's a diesel. You can hear and feel that when you turn it on. And yes, you do cringe a little bit. The throttle has a typical BMW bite to it which takes some getting used to. Measured inputs are mandatory here. And once you've worked out that, you'll find that like most BMWs, it doesn't like being over-driven, it will make you a better driver.

Even though it's a diesel, it always feels alive, this car. Like it's always raring to be let off the leash. Don't get me wrong though, it doesn't misbehave. But it never feels completely relaxed either. You'd probably like that when you're going to work. But you won't when you're driving back home after a hard day's.

If, however, you find yourself on a twisting road, put it in Sport+ and prepare to be amazed. The 50:50 weight distribution, the phenomenal steering, the bite from the tyres, the inherent balance of the chassis and the sheer dynamic progressiveness will put as big a smile on your face as the day when your wife said 'I do'.

And here's the best part – most cars have a readout that give you instant fuel consumption figures. With today's technology, they're almost perfectly accurate. In the BMW, I barely saw it fall below late teens. Even when I was giving it blue bloody murder, it was in its mid-teens. Does that make it the most fuel-efficient car in India? I'm not sure. But it's definitely up there.

Now We're Talking
Audi Q5 2.0 TFSI

It's very easy for a road tester to get carried away with his opinions if all the ingredients add up to one brilliant dish. If the sun is out and I've got a great convertible on a nice twisting mountain road, I'll probably be gushing like a schoolgirl about the whole experience. I'm still human, remember?

So, keeping that in mind, I put the Q5 through the toughest conditions that I could find, given the limited time I had with it – I drove it from Mumbai to Alibaug and back.

To the average Mumbaikar, this may seem like a rather obvious 100-kilometre-long weekend drive. But in the monsoon, with roadworks and Saturday morning traffic, it will anger, frustrate and even infuriate the most patient among us. And that's precisely why I chose it – will the Q5 make me want to abandon it in a ditch and continue on foot? Let's find out.

First - the looks. It's a handsome brute, this Audi. It looks like a rugby player (one that hasn't had his nose broken as yet) in a tuxedo. Given where ze Germans are going with their styling, the Q5 is refreshingly clean. There aren't any Korean look-at-me styling creases. It looks visually large, but it's balanced. And the proportions just sort of…work. This is my kind of styling. Simple. Elegant. And not trying too hard. Throw in just a touch of bling with Audi's signature daytime running lamps and visually, the Q5 is really hard to fault. If you don't agree, please consult your nearest optician who will give you a free eye test. Or go back to school and give your art teacher an earful for not having taught appreciation well enough.

The cabin, while pretty effing large to begin with, feels double its size when you open the ceiling curtain which reveals a full-length length glass roof. It just lifts the whole experience to another level. And then there's the sunroof which, when open, gives you a hundred billion miles of headroom. The cabin itself is very well laid out. And in typical Audi quality, it feels like it's been hewn from solid, rather than made from parts bolted together. I don't really have enough space on this page to mention all the equipment but the highlights are powered, heated front seats with memory, Satellite Navigation, Cruise Control, mirrors that fold automatically when you stop, hill assist, Audi's MMI with Drive Select, a mahooosive glass roof, almost half of which opens completely and a few thousand other things. Frankly if you want more than this, get a job on the Starship Enterprise. All this means that you get the feeling Audi's pulled out all the stops in making you feel special. How they do it at 44.96 lakhs (ex-showroom Mumbai) simply beggars belief.

I first realised when I set off what a difference a petrol engine makes in an SUV. At city speeds, the 2.0L TFSI motor is near silent. Only making the odd gentle *whoosh* when you prod the throttle. In Comfort Mode, it's no harder to drive in the city than a Suzuki Swift. I thought the width would be a problem in city traffic but it wasn't. I was able to slip though congested city streets as easily as anyone else.

Getting out of Mumbai was a little more than I'd bargained for. Because of the roadworks leading up to Panvel, the traffic was backed up for a few kilometres. And this big ol' Audi crawled along nicely. With the windows up and the sunroof closed, it was eerily quiet inside. And I barely knew what kind of surface I was on until I looked in the rear-view mirror and saw cars bouncing and crashing in my wake.

"In 300 metres, take a right" said the satnav and so I did; onto the fearsome NH17. At this time of the year, this road is really not for the faint hearted. It's got every conceivable obstacle short of a meteorite storm; all in the space of 60 odd kilometres.

And the Q5, with its brilliant suspension and Quattro, did its best to hide their existence. Honestly, there were some patches where there was no road at all - just a few hundred metres of brown water. You couldn't tell where the potholes were, let alone how deep. And SuzyQ just kept on going at a steady 40kph. No fuss. No drama. Just complete composure.

About 40km from Alibag, the road became much better. And through the hills and their twisting tarmac, there was one happy chappie with a massive grin on his face, behind the wheel of his navy-blue Audi in Sport Mode overtaking everyone.

Although I did realise very quickly that you cannot be sportscar-aggressive with the Q5. You have to adopt a more fluid, more progressive driving style. If you do, you can see the miles tick away like they would in a fast saloon. And you arrive at your destination a little disappointed that you've…erm… arrived at your destination.

There were one or two little niggles that bothered me though. Like the 8-speed tiptronic automatic gearbox had just a hint of lag. I would have much preferred the 7-speed S-tronic. And it didn't have paddle shifters.

Come to think of it, I'm nit-picking. Because you can easily live with the gearbox. It took me less 5 kilometres to get used to it and adapt my driving style accordingly. And a car like this doesn't need paddle shifters.

The Q5 2.0 TFSI has genuinely been one of the biggest surprises of my motoring life and I wonder if I've found the ideal travel companion. I think I'll ring Audi and ask to borrow the car for a few years. Just to make sure.

If they can't lend me one, I may just have to walk into a dealership and put my money where my mouth is.

Low-Calorie Signature Dish
Mercedes-Benz E250 CDI Launch Edition

Getting something right every single time can't possibly be easy. Even Steven Spielberg and Shah Rukh Khan, being the titans that they are, have had their share of cock-ups. This is all over the motoring industry as well. Do you remember the BMWs that were designed by Chris Bangle? I do. All of them could conveniently be classified between drab and hideous. At some point or other, all carmakers have been found guilty of a massive cock-up. No exceptions.

That said, just about every carmaker, including the Koreans, has a nice little sweet spot. The Japanese have their no-fuss, exceptionally reliable everyday cars, the Americans have their signature evocatively-named muscle cars, the British make just about the best front-engined two-seater sportscars on the planet and the Italians do supercars.

Germany, on the other hand, has mastered the fine art of luxury. Because let's face it, a Rolls Royce (which is owned by BMW) isn't exactly a luxury car. It's a palace on wheels. It is the equivalent of dining out on the greatest hits of Heston Blumenthal, Marco Pierre White and Gordon Ramsey three meals a day – everyday. Pure indulgence.

What the Germans do best is engineer an inherent sense of luxury into their cars. Fantastic build quality, thoughtful little features that you discover over time in a package that's almost always very easy to drive. And for a while now, THE quintessential German luxury saloon in India has been the Mercedes-Benz E-Class. And now there's a new one.

Well, not completely new, but they've given it enough Botox to make it feel new.

I really do like the look of this thing. It looks like James Bond on his day off. Those daytime running lamps, especially in twilight, give it an aura of modern sophistication and panache. They blend in well with the redesigned front bumper and the new twin-slash grill which now contains the signature three-pointed star, which now has its own LED backlight. Nice.

By no means does it look racy and dynamic because it isn't supposed to. In profile especially, the E-Class borders on nondescriptness. But, and this you can take for granted, even if you've never seen this new one before, you'll instantly be able to identify it as an E-Class. Distinctive. That's the word I was looking for.

The interior is nicely laid out as well. There's leather everywhere and everything feels nice and tasteful yet luxurious. If you step inside the E and find that it's a bit spartan, your upbringing must seriously be put to question. And I don't want you at my house for dinner. That means you Mr Wannabe Liberace.

As with most Mercs these days it's got power everything, lots of gizmos to keep you entertained and a panoramic sunroof to keep the kids entertained. And then it goes a step further with mood lighting. Although I don't quite fancy the idea of turquoise lights on the dash and yellow lights on the door. Don't let that put you off, though.

On to the drive. The driver's seat is a brilliant piece of design and let me explain why. Normal cars seats have to fit a wide range of body types in whatever comfort levels their brand offers. It's a bit different here because this has to feel like a Mercedes-Benz to all who drive it. And it does. All your other interactions with the car feel good as well, in a summer's day on the beach kind of way. It is a brilliant car to drive in the city because of how well-mannered it is. The G-Tronic gearbox shifts gently and unobtrusively between its seven ratios and all you can hear from the 2.2L 204bhp diesel engine is a nice woooosh. It's a very satisfying car, this E-Class and neither I nor my passengers were left wanting for anything. And yes, as you can imagine, the back seat is legendary.

On the open road, despite not having a V6, the engine with its 500Nm of easily available torque, suits the super-cruise nature of this car just fine. It gathers pace well and has wonderful composure at high speeds. That said, it does feel out of breath when you push it hard. So, don't.

Now for the verdict – apart from the satnav screen, which doesn't reorient itself with your direction of travel, I can't think of a more complete, more well-rounded car on sale in India. This is Mercedes-Benz's gigantic middle-fingered salute to their rivals saying, 'this, gentlemen, is how it's done.' And d'you know what? I think they're right.

Utterly Beautiful and as Exciting as Being in Bed
Mercedes-Benz CLS350

Identically opposite. Humanitarian rapist. Honest politician. Four-door coupe. These are words that are just not meant to go together for the sake of logic, better judgement, or sheer distaste.

But that's what Mercedes-Benz calls the CLS – a four-door coupe. I bet you're wondering right now 'doesn't a coupe have two doors?' And yes, it did. Until the previous gen CLS came around. What they've tried to do with the new CLS, as they did with the old one, is make a low, swoopy saloon that looks like a coupe but has four doors. And both times, they've done a stellar job.

From the outside, especially in profile, the CLS is Carla Bruni beautiful. What Mercedes-Benz has managed here is beauty without any unnecessary attraction. The only chink in the big Merc's visual armour is the wheels. At 17in, they're at least two sizes too small. Personally, I'd like to see 20in wheels on something like this. Now, the way I test cars for their looks (yes, I said 'test cars for their looks') is to drive them really slowly through the poshest part of a big city. This time, it was South Mumbai. And here are some of my findings. First, people who glanced at it and looked away, immediately turned around for another look. And after trying frantically to ascertain who was in the back seat, they looked away. Second, while I was driving it, I got quite a bit of attention from the fairer sex. Seeing as to how I have no such luck otherwise, that's probably a good thing.

Through my most scientific of methods and their results, I thing we can infer that this car makes you more attractive and it makes you into someone that people want to see. With most expensive cars, all people want to do is look at the car but with the CLS, it's the person inside that's of more importance. I really don't think that this is by design, but I don't mind it one little bit.

On the inside, things are very Mercedes and the cabin is a wonderful place to be. It's got leather, wood, brushed aluminium and great plastics. And it feels a lot more than just the sum of its parts. It feels special – like an occasion. It feels really well put together as well.

The back row is strictly for two, with the transmission tunnel going right through the middle. You might wonder how much headroom there would be with that sloping roofline. Adequate. That's how much. My long dangly frame rode in the back seat for an hour and a half with no problems. Although, the roof was only an inch away from my head. And it didn't feel cramped because what the cabin may lack in height, it makes up for in length and breadth.

Mercedes expects that most of their customers would drive their CLSs themselves so they've given it paddle shifters and quite simply, the best seats ever. If I ever come to power, I will make a law which says that these seats must be fitted to every car. If you spend about 3-4 minutes adjusting them just so, they're just about as comfortable and supportive as car seats can be.

And it's got every possible creature comfort you could possibly want. I really don't want to list them here because there are far too many and they're all important. Suffice to say that you'll be entertained for as long as you own the car.

On to the drive. It had a button on the centre console where you can choose between Economy or Sport. In Economy mode it shifts up earlier while in Sport mode, it holds a gear all the way to the redline and then upshifts. It even has a button that makes the suspension stiffer for *sporty* driving. But I left it off because it made the ride worse.

On paper it has a button to raise the nose to help it go over speed bumps without scraping its undersides. And while this system works just fine, I was completely confused by its inclusion. Let me explain. To the beholder, this car looks really low. But it somehow manages to clear the kind of bumps that you would crawl over in a Honda CRV or Chevy Captiva whilst completely clenched. I was amazed every time this happened. And it was only when I was faced a scale version of Mt. Everest that I pushed the button.

I seem to be waxing lyrical thus far because it is a very good car. But in the interest of a fair and balanced appraisal, let's look at some of the bits that aren't so good. The engine, while being smooth and creamy, doesn't suit this car's character. It's a 3.5L V6 that's good for 306bhp and 370Nm of twisting force. And the 7G-Tronic 7-speed automatic gearbox suits the engine, not the car. They're both a bit lazy. The gearbox is especially so because like in the A-Class we featured earlier, it does everything well, just a few seconds after you need it to.

What the CLS needs to complement its fabulousness is 20in wheels, a big engine and a slicker gearbox. If you ask them nicely, Mercedes will fit you up with a CLS63 AMG. It's got all of that and then some.

Soccer Mom Express Has
Something for the Keen Driver
BMW X5 3.0xDrive

Big SUVs have a very prominent place in modern society. In the U.S. and A., they're the chosen set of wheels of the Soccer Mom, because most have seven seats. In Europe, they're bought mainly because they figure amongst the safest cars on the road. Well, that and the fact they can take the entire family with luggage to a country home during holidays.

India's very different. SUVs are bought here as a statement. Apart from the few buyers that actually use all the seats on a regular basis, most just have a chauffeur and a rather posh passenger hidden away somewhere on the back seat. They've nearly become a replacement for the luxury saloon.

And that brings us neatly onto the BMW X5 – a car that has to feel like BMW while being a big SUV. Does it? That's what we're here to find out. What we have here is the facelifted version of the second-generation X5, which came out *way* back in 2006. The facelift has given it the all-important LED daytime running lamps and some other clever and useful features.

The looks wont exactly set your soul on fire, but they are quite pleasing, especially in Bronze, in twilight, with the LEDs on. And even I will admit that it is proportioned very well.

But the looks, the ride quality, equipment level, boot space and third row of seats are the addendum. The meat of any BMW is how it drives, so without further ado and all that.

In the city, the throttle feels a little abrupt. Even the slightest bit of input will result in proportional output. It does take a bit of getting used to its responsiveness. But once you do, you find yourself driving more precisely. The steering is well weighted and is festooned with many useful and interesting buttons. But it's huge – the size of an elephant's face. I have relatively large hands and even they looked small whilst holding the wheel. And while the interior is fantastically built, it doesn't feel as fancy and up-to-date as some of its rivals. On paper it's a seven-seater, but the last row is a little too cramped for anything other than the shortest of journeys. It's best to fold it down and make full use of the massive boot.

But sod the city. This is still a BMW. Let's see what it can do when the going gets twisty. My friend and fellow road tester recommended Malshej Ghat, which is a beautiful mountain road outside Mumbai in the North-Easterly direction. He said this route had everything we need to test this particular BMW. And he was right. The first 25 kilometres were on a smooth flowing highway and the X5 revealed its Range Rover associations. After all, this car was designed and engineered by BMW when they still owned Land Rover. It soaks up bumps of all shapes and sizes while maintaining perfect composure. And while you get the feeling that you are in complete control, you also appreciate the extent of its predictability - after five minutes of highway driving, I knew exactly where its limits were in terms of grip, power and braking. And since every millimetre of input has a specific output, you'll learn very soon that it does not like to be over-driven.

And then we reached a ribbon of smooth, twisting tarmac. This is BMW's home turf. And it didn't disappoint. There's very little body roll for something of this size and weight. At no point in those 27 kilometres on that twisting road did I once back off because I was in an SUV. Well done on the dynamics, BMW. My only dynamic complaint is of the brakes. They stop alright but the ABS and EBD kick in a lot sooner than you'd like. This robs you of a little bit of the feel that BMWs are known for.

On to the verdict. Does it drive as well as BMW's saloons? No. It's not even close to a 3 Series. But it's vastly better to drive than other SUV of comparable price. At 80 lakhs (ex-showroom), it's certainly not cheap. Buy it if you want the driving experience. As far as I'm concerned, and this is personal, I'd rather have the Mercedes ML350 CDI because it has more toys, a better ride, costs 23 lakhs less and most importantly, makes you feel special even before you've turned the key. Granted, it's not as good to drive, but in a big SUV the driving experience must play second fiddle to the ownership experience and a general sense of well-being. Besides, the ML can do some serious off-roading, should you ever feel the need. The X5, for the fantastic driver's car that it is, can't.

All Present and Correct
Mercedes-Benz ML350 CDI

It started out as any other road test. I took the early flight into Pune and there the M-Class was, waiting for me in all its gargantuan glory. It does look a little American this ML, what with all its visual bulk and generous helpings of chrome. But unlike most American SUVs it's not ugly – it's actually a big handsome brute.

And weirdly, this got me thinking about the whole concept of dating. Bear with me. We go through our teenage years and early adulthood looking for somebody special, and in this process, we end up meeting a lot of people along the way. And then along comes someone and sweeps us off our feet. And then we marry them. So dating is no more than a process of selection.

My job is a lot like this. I drive and review cars hoping that there will be one that grabs me by the heartstrings. And just like you choose whom you date, I choose what cars I review. And just like you, I get it wrong sometimes. With a few exceptions, I really wouldn't mind owning most of the cars I've tested because they are wonderful and exciting.

But then along came the ML and changed everything. This is not just a car that I wouldn't mind owning. This is a car that I need. How can a self-confessed petro-sexual such as m'good self be completely sold on a big diesel SUV? Read on.

For starters, it comes fitted with a 3.0L turbocharged V6 diesel which makes 258bhp and a slightly mental 619Nm of torque. That's 11 more torques than the six litre V12-engined Ferrari 599. This is coupled to the 7G-TRONIC double-clutch gearbox that does duty in most Mercs. It also has 4-MATIC, which is Merc's all-wheel-drive system. Throw in AIRMATIC air suspension with options for Comfort and Sport, a dedicated off-road mode, Downhill Speed Regulator and a suspension lift option and you'll find there is quite a bit of chassis tech to deal with the big bad world.

My test car came with the Designo interior package which had beige leather on the seats and door lining and black wood on the dash and steering wheel. I normally hate a half-timbered steering wheel because they've always had brown wood. But the black just makes it work. The front seats themselves are infinitely adjustable and have memory for three profiles each. The back seats are great for having a snooze because they're slightly reclined. And they're very, very comfortable. The boot is bigger than most Bombay apartments and can easily swallow four people's luggage for a fortnight.

When you get in, you'll find Merc's signature slab of wood, which, like I mentioned earlier, was black in my test car. The combination of that and the beige seats makes you feel warm and cocooned, yet posh and stylish at the same time. It's a very wholesome feeling that's hard to describe in 800 words or less. When you're ready to set off, it eases off the line ever so gently. You'll find that there's so much more to this V6 diesel than the numbers suggest – an inner strength, if you will.

Windows up, you can neither hear it nor feel it in the city. To be honest, windows up, you really can't hear nor feel anything in the city because the suspension and NVH management are just so bloody brilliant.

No matter. I was running late for appointment in Bombay. Time for the highway blast. With the suspension set to Sport, the ML covers ground in a way that is normally the preserve of GT cars. Pace, comfort and predictability seem inherently engineered into this MB. If you just drive at your normal pace without looking at the speedo, you'll find yourself doing well over twice the speed limit. But you can't feel it because it's just so composed. I arrived at my destination as fresh as I was when I left with time to spare for lunch. Incredible.

We've established that it's great in the city and even better on the highway. There was just one more test left. Mercedes say that this car has everything you need to do some proper off roading. So, I went back to Pune to test the bigger GL on their own off-road track (more on that in the coming weeks) and came out a believer.

But would this, the smaller, cheaper ML be as good? To find out, I went exploring and found a field that was used by big earth movers with tracks. And it was raining. And there was about two feet of slush (that's only as deep as I could see). And there was a 20-degree incline. I would have thought twice about doing this in a hardcore off-roader.

But - and this is truly astonishing - I pushed all the off-road and went for it. And it just kept going. And going where all I could see was sky. Kindly note at this point that this car had 20in AMG wheels and ROAD TYRES. It's not supposed to able to do that. But it could have done that all day.

This is the first car that I'm going to give a 10/10 to because it exceeded my rather unreasonable expectations in every aspect. And besides it's a 57-lakh car that feels like an 80+ lakh car. I wonder what they're putting in Merc's water these days. Whatever it is, I want some.

Fun, Fast and Certainly Not Loose
MINI Cooper S

Let's dispense with the MINI Cooper S's more popular criticisms first. It costs an eye-watering 39 lakhs on-road Mumbai. The ride is stiffer than anything else in its class and price bracket. The back seats are fantastic only if you adopt the lotus position because there is absolutely no legroom. The boot will take about two boxes of peppermints, as many eggs and then become completely full. Also, in terms of sheer volume, this is the least amount of car that you can buy for that money. And here's one of my own – it has the most palpably annoying, flash-in-the-pan gear shifting mechanism I've ever encountered. The idea is that you use your thumb to shift down and one of your other fingers to shift up. But the problem is that you can do this with both hands on both sides of the wheel vis-à-vis a traditional paddle shift system where you click right to go up and left to go down the gears. Jeez.

Having got all that factual bollocks out of the way, it's time for me to explain why this particular MINI, the Cooper S (barring by unintelligible fondness for the Fiat 500), is the best city car on the planet. And, quite possibly, the best city car the world has ever seen.

To begin with, every inch of it oozes quality. If you can forget for a moment that it's a hatchback aka 'a small car', you'll find the kind of materials, build quality and sheer great taste that you find on posh BMWs and Mercs. Step inside and you're greeted by a tiny little cabin that feels bigger than it is owing to a full-length glass roof, half of which slides open to reveal ten billion miles of blue sky.

It has a small instrument console behind the steering wheel which has a multi-function display and a humungous circular one on in the middle of the dash. They've also thrown in BMW's iDrive with pretty much everything except satellite navigation. Below said humongous circular display (which contains the screen) you'll find beautiful toggle switches for the power windows and other things. There are toggles on the ceiling as well which operate the ceiling curtains and the sunroof.

Push the starter button and you're greeted with a deep-throated burst of revs from the turbocharged 1.6 litre 184 horsepowered petrol engine. When you slot it in D and roll ahead, you'll find that it's not intimidating at all. It's a frightfully easy car to drive. Yes, the steering is little heavy but it's nothing that you'll give a second thought to.

On the move, its perpetually naughty intensions make themselves apparent. As easy as it is to manage, it's always excited; like one of those small dogs. It also feels different from any other car I've driven before it. It feels tight, taut and very precise. This takes a bit of getting used to in the city. But when you do, you'll wonder how you did without it your whole life. If you're late for work, though, it really comes to life. Its diminutive dimensions mean that it can squeeze through gaps that are normally reserved for rickshaws. It's got plenty of power, braking and handling to get you in and out of anything that a city can throw at it. It is an absolute joy. If I had one, I'd wake up ten minutes late every day on purpose.

On the highway, the ride is a little harsh as compared to other cars for this money. But I liked that. Because what you may interpret as harshness is actually feedback – the act of the car communicating its communications with the road to you, like Chris Tucker in Rush Hour 2 because it never stops talking.

On a twisting road, you'll smile the smile of someone who's just had some great 'something I'm not allowed to mention' because it feels superb. And it covers ground at a phenomenal pace.

It really is a magical car, this MINI Cooper S. It is also one of the few cars that had me gutted when I had to return it to BMW. And the absolute best part is that BMW's just revealed the all-new MINI which is due next year which promises to be even better.

Pigs Can't Fly
Toyota Land Cruiser VXL

This is one of the most reliable cars that money can buy. Except when the fuel needle goes haywire and refuses to inform you of the amount of fuel you may have or need to get somewhere. Or when the driver's seat goes up and down (electrically with memory) but moves diagonally when you are tall like I am and wish it to move backwards. Or when the tailgate dislocates your ankle because the damper that controls its pace has fallen off.

Still, the Toyota Land Cruiser Prado VXL is one of the most reliable cars that money can buy. And that is simply because mechanically, it will never let you down. Apart from the flat tyre that it got from sitting around. Which, by the way took a small army of four people from Toyota's service team, two jacks, a slab of stone, many tools and a lot of washing up after to change.

But, if you can deal with the not-so-fatal bout of histrionics, this is a fantastic car.

You know how I treat SUVs here at Honk. You know I've taken the Yeti up a muddy slope in the rain. You know we've driven the Mercedes ML through two-feet-deep slush. You know we've seen only sky and some ungodly climb angles with the GL.

But for the Prado, I took my (patent pending) trailblazing even further. I drove it through a cornfield to test its off-road abilities.

But first let's see what this thing packs for tech. The three litre, four-cylinder intercooled turbo diesel that puts out 170 bhp and 410Nm of muscle. Add to that a low range gearbox, rear air suspension with lift, a downhill speed regulator and, of course, intelligent four-wheel-drive.

That's what you can't see. What you can is a car so big that it will make your flat look the size of an empty box of matches. It's so big that you could park your Santro inside it. Seven fully usable seats justify that, of course, but what doesn't is the quality and attention to detail in the cabin. There is an inexcusable amount of fake wood. It's great quality fake, but still.

At some point one has to mention that it weighs three tonnes. And that means that we named it Piggy, ie, a pig on the road. That said, Piggy hit 150kph before she scared us s***less when I had to slow down again. The brakes are up to the job, but man, the weight is tiresome. It rolls like a pregnant hippopotamus through corners even when you're going at medium pace.

BUT WHEN THE TARMAC RUNS OUT...

Push all the off-road buttons and Piggy comes into her own. Cornfields, remember? She can take them and so much more. Oh-my-Jesus-Christ the Prado, ahem, Piggy is a fan-chuffing-tastic off roader.

And then I realised, this utilitarian beast of a car, is so much more than its quirks suggest. It's among the largest selling SUVs on the planet for a reason. It rides beautifully in the city. It has an elephantine calm that most new monocoqued SUVs can never manage. And it's ever so manageable. Once you acclimatise yourself with the dimensions, you'll find that's it's ever so easy to drive. Yes, there's turbo-lag but the eager five-speed automatic slush box makes the best of it.

Most luxury SUVs give you more toys than a billionaire gives his kids at Christmas. The Prado, on the other hand, gives you a warm, fuzzy sense of security. Its appeal lies not in its numbers but in its range of abilities and the intangible warm blanket it throws on its occupants. This is old-school at its best.

It costs 86.2 lakhs (ex-showroom). That's more than the Mercedes GL which we brought you a few weeks ago. The big Merc is packed with much more equipment and is equally astounding off-road. And because it's made in India, it costs about 77 lakhs (ex-showroom).

Toyota needs to quickly have a meeting to figure out how to make the Prado cost half as much as it does. Because honestly, at this price, it doesn't make any sense at all.

Czech Please
Skoda Octavia

"Oh, you shouldn't have!" That's the expression we normally use when we receive a rather nice gift. We don't mean it, of course. But we say it anyway. The only time I found myself to have actually meant it is when Skoda pulled out all the stops for yours truly and set up a drive from Parwanoo to Shimla via Chail in Himachal Pradesh. I ate the finest food, stared at important old buildings en route and rested my weary head on the softest pillow available at the Oberoi Wildflower. They gave me goodie bags full of, well, goodies. They even went to the bother of giving me all the finest local produce to take home as a gift. I don't think you could have treated someone you intended to marry better than this.

I remember speaking to Miroslav Brandejsky, the affable Product Marketing person from Skoda and telling him in as many words – with a car this good, you really shouldn't have. He smiled the smile of a proud father and asked me, "What do you think its competitors are?" And that got me thinking. Considering that prices will be announced a day or two after you read this, where does it fit?

Pardon me. Where are my manners? Because this, ladies and gentlemen, is the brand-new Skoda Octavia. And as you can see, it is as handsome as a car can be. It's clean, sophisticated and full of purpose. To me, it is visually *the* quintessential European mid-sized saloon.

Things are much the same inside as well. I speak this quietly but it has the build quality of an Audi. It's all beautifully laid out and you get the impression that the engineers who did the interiors weren't allowed to go on their Vodka break until they got everything right. The high-end Elegance gets a sunroof, de rigeuer LED daytime running lamps and many more brilliant features.

I spent some quality time with two of its four drivetrain variants – the 2.0 diesel with a 6-speed DSG and the 1.4 petrol with a 6-speed manual. There's also a 2.0 diesel with the 6-speed manual and a 1.8 petrol with a 7-speed DSG.

First, the diesel DSG. The term 'easy to drive,' I feel certain, was coined for this car. You turn it on, slot it in D and away you go. At low speeds, with the windows up, you can't tell when it's shifting gear. And as speeds build, you'll find that you don't need to stamp on the throttle to get more power – just a gentle squeeze will bring on a smooth downshift, albeit in a second or two. The chassis and suspension engineers must finally be allowed to go on their vodka break because they've done an absolute stellar job. If I could I'd shake every one of their hands because the balance between ride and handling is just sublime. This time, I'll leave the figures aside because this drivetrain is about more than its numbers would suggest. It never feels underpowered unless you're driving like a complete mental. Suffice to say that it won't leave you wanting.

On to the 1.4 petrol. This drivetrain is essentially carried over from the VW Jetta. It puts out 140bhp, 250Nm of torque and you get a slick 6-speed manual to play with. Being a small petrol means that the front end is lighter than the diesel. This also means that, by default, the steering is lighter. The only criticism I have of the diesel DSG is that the steering could have been heavier. And it's a bit worse in the petrol. Also, I stalled the petrol quite a lot. And the turbo lag means that you have to keep working away at the gearbox to keep it in the power band.

Honestly, putting that 1.4 petrol engine in this car is like putting Justin Bieber's heart in Arnold Schwarzenegger and hoping for the best with two crossed fingers. But don't worry, give me a few weeks and I'll bring you a full review of the 1.8 turbo petrol.

It's time for me to answer the question that Miroslav asked me. Chevy's Cruze? VW's Jetta? Toyota's Corolla? Honda's hopeless Accord? Not a chance. The Octavia's got what it takes to worry Audi's forthcoming A3, Merc's A Class and BMW's 1 Series provided Skoda get the pricing right.

Practical, Ferocious &
Properly Entertaining
Audi S4

Over the years, I've been privileged enough to drive many different cars. Some were good and some were bad. Some were fast and some were slow. Some left an impression and some didn't. It's this last reference that I'd like to use for today's car. Welcome everyone, to the Audi S4 – a car where you remember even the shortest of drives.

And I say shortest with reference only to time, not distance. Because I picked up the car and left Audi's office in the thick of Mumbai traffic at exactly half past noon. And by 2:00pm I saw a board that said Nashik 8km. That's roughly 170km. With a quick lunch stop. Here's what happened.

The car was set in Dynamic Mode when it was delivered to me. This sharpens the throttle response, lets you rev all the way to the redline, stiffens the suspension, firms up the steering and so on. I really wondered how I was going to nurse this thing out of the city. At every set of traffic lights, I used left-foot-braking to help me set off more gently. And the ride was pretty choppy on Mumbai's roads during peak monsoon. Finally, when I reached Powai, I pulled over and decided to figure this out. I found a little button on the dash that said CAR. A quick push later I discovered that I was in fact in Dynamic Mode. Everything changed when I set the Drive Select to Comfort. The whole car just sort of relaxed. And in the remaining 20 kilometres in the city, it felt like any other plush Audi saloon.

The seats were a great mix of leather and Alcantara, with the under-thigh bit extended for additional support. The steering wheel was mercifully circular, not those stupid flat-bottomed jobs you find on some other fast Audis. The aluminium pedals, while they make sporty driving easier, gave me no trouble in the city. The dash was nicely cantered towards me as well. All this gave the impression of inherent sportiness.

20 kilometres and I had cleared the city traffic. It was time to see what's what. A quick change to Dynamic Mode and I got two perfectly timed downshifts to go with a massive increase in revs. The suspension got stiffer, the steering weighted up and the whole car felt like it was begging to be whipped.

Let the sodomy begin. Through second, third and fourth gears, the acceleration from that bee-ee-ay-youtiful 3.0 TFSI supercharged petrol motor is relentless. It puts out 333bhp and 440Nm of torque which doesn't sound like much. But none of it goes to waste thanks to Quattro and the brilliant 245/40/18 tyres from Michelin's naughty collection. And it feels fast. Really fast. If you're not careful, you'll hit the 250kph speed limiter in fifth. And then you'll have to slow down because a bicyclist has decided to cross the road about a kilometre ahead. Don't worry though because the brakes are more than up to the job. You barely feel the ABS and EBD kicking in, even at those speeds.

One more thing that must be singled out for praise is the whole drivetrain. I think that as a package, the engine, gearbox and other drive systems are (bold claim coming up) the best you can buy for this money. The aforementioned motor and Audi's 7-speed S Tronic double-clutch gearbox are a just plain fantastic in the way they work together. For this kind of money (49.39 Lakhs Ex-showroom Mumbai), you simply cannot buy any more genuine real-world pace.

Back to the road test. In the corners, there is a slight tendency towards understeer. But if you feel heroic, try lifting off gently and you'll tighten your line through the corner. But more than anything else, the S4 is planted. Audi doesn't do histrionics very well. That's for Lamborghini to do. But the flipside is composure no matter how hard you push it. There's tonnes and tonnes of grip at the limit. And when you lift off mid-corner and the back end does eventually break loose, it's ever so easy to correct.

And now we arrive at the point where I have to give it a verdict. Buy it. In red. It really does look good in red.

Desi Badassery
Feature – Rajputana Customs

Orange County Customs, West Coast Choppers, Arlen Ness and our very own Verdenchi. Custom bike building seems to have come a long way, even in India.

Trouble is that all of these bike builders seem to have gone down one route – all the bikes are large, showy and worst of all, they're all more or less the same. All of them are half a ton of styling with very little design.

My favourite bike builder of pretty much all time has been an American called Indian Larry (God rest his soul). Unlike the others, Larry had his signature old-school look that he adapted very well throughout his not inconsiderable 20 years of bike building. His bikes were so un-anonymous that you'd spot one in a crowd of a hundred other choppers.

My old boss once mentioned the name Rajputana Customs back in 2011. And he went on to wax lyrical about how these were the coolest custom bikes he'd seen in India. Jump to 2013 and I found myself, two flights later, in Jaipur to see for myself.

In the back of an unusually large house, I found Vijay Singh – owner and chief. Shorts and t-shirt don't exactly scream biker. But closer inspection revealed a few hundred tattoos so that figures. "Shall we go to the workshop?", he asked. Lead on.

In the first fifteen minutes in the shop, I knew more about this guy than he could have told me in a lifetime. He lives and breathes bikes.

And the shop is more a shrine to motorcycledom than a place where machines are built.

"Apart from the wheels and tyres, we build pretty much everything ourselves", he explains, pointing to various machines that cut and shape metal. There were bikes scattered about the place in various stages of build. Bullets, BSAs, Harleys, they had the lot. And it struck me immediately – this wasn't a chop-shop. It felt more like a studio where motorcycles are crafted from scratch. From a front suspension design I've never seen before to etched brass levers and tank lids, the detailing was just incredible.

"We took Original Gangster (their first bike) to the Delhi Auto Expo 2010. And the response we got was very encouraging. And then John Abraham commissioned a bike (Light Foot) from us. That was the first bike we sold." If it's good enough for John Abraham…

But all this is by the by. The true test of a good bike is how it rides. I rode one which wasn't named or finished as yet that I call WIP (Work in Progress). Very low seat, 300 section rear tire, 23in front wheel and you get the drift. I was expecting it to be all over the place like some of the other Indian-made choppers I've tested. But it felt tight and very well put together. "Ride it for ten minutes. You'll be completely comfortable." I tend to take such claims with a pinch of salt but he was right. After the aforementioned ten minutes, I could have ridden all the way back to Bangalore despite the fact that I'd spent the last 10 hours in airports and flights. It really was that easy.

My next concern was that WIP was running an Enfield 500cc fuel-injected motor with that 300-section rear tire. Would it have enough power and torque to cope with a rear tire as big as some supercars'? The answer came when I got off the line gently, settled into the forward set foot pegs and gave it some stick. It is as loud as it is fast – a proper roaring belter. The whole thing felt like a muscle car.

But this was just one bike. They've built over 20 in the last three-and-a-bit years and in my humble opinion, all of them are absolutely brilliant have their own respective identities. I asked him why they don't do any marketing whatsoever. "We're not salesmen. We build bikes. They do the talking for us."

Respect.

Absolutely Perfect and Not Much Else
Audi A6 3.0 TDI Quattro

I have this image in my mind of a man in a business suit with a briefcase, walking out of his minimal home with a carbon fibre dining table and stainless-steel kitchen. A man who is in senior management doing something terribly important for a large corporation. A man who barely has time for his 'hobbies'. A man who listens to classical music and likes opera and reads only the most fashionable new eccentric novel. That sort of thing.

Apparently, Audi thought the same thing. And they made the car for the aforementioned man. Behold the new A6. And straightaway we find that it is a gorgeous car. Subtle, but beautiful. I really like the clean, simple styling. I like the proportions as well. And those LED heads seem to have been introduced to the design process on the drawing board, not as an afterthought. They look like just the right amount of jewellery on a beautiful 30-something year-old woman.

It's much the same story inside. The beige and brown cabin really feels like a tastefully designed modern minimalistic home. It's got a nice wooden slab across the dash with wood adorning the centre console as well. The MMI screen slides outwards and then flips upwards when you hit the ignition button. It's a welcome bit of drama in what is otherwise a clinical cabin.

The key is only good for locking and unlocking the car and opening the boot. Once inside, you keep it in your pocket or in one of the many cubby holes because there is no slot for it. All you do it hit the big button marked START|STOP. When you do, the needles on the console do a run up and down the dials and the screen comes out of hiding. Nice.

In Normal mode, this is one of the easiest cars to drive. You barely notice from behind the wheel that the A6 is nearly 5 metres long. It's easy to scoot around the city. Top marks to Audi for the sound deadening. With the windows up, it borders on sensory deprivation – it really is amazingly quiet.

You'll also find on the go that the ride, for the most part, is top notch. Only the sharpest bumps make their way into the cabin. In a city like Mumbai, with things sticking out of the road, that ever so slightly gets on your nerves because the ride is brilliant, brilliant, brilliant, crash; over a sharp bump.

That 3.0L V6, though, is fantastic. While it puts out a modest 245bhp, it's got 500 torques from virtually no revs. This makes it never wanting power. Like all the other good Audis, it's got the 7-speed S-Tronic double clutch gearbox. In theory, that's a double act as good as macaroni and cheese. But in the real world, it feels slow to respond. In the S4 that I tested, it was as prompt as a doctor on call, but in this it felt underwhelming.

On the open road, I tested the Dynamic mode on the Drive Select. It does a few things. It makes the air suspension stiffer, adds weight to the steering, wakes up the Quattro all-wheel-drive system and holds gears all the way to the redline. If you are planning to go quickly, do turn this on. I tried going around a corner at speed in Comfort mode and I haven't unclenched yet. It really was that scary. It also has an Individual Mode where you can adjust different things individually like the steering and suspension and so on. There is even an Auto that constantly adapts to your driving style and adjusts them for you.

Back to test. There's no other way to say this. On the open road, this thing simply flies. It covers great distances in complete silence and fantastic comfort. If anything, the ride is even better at high speed. If you need it to, it will do a limited 250kph all day while giving you 13kpl. And it will easily do well over 700km on a tank of diesel.

As a car – a device to get you from A to B – it is very difficult to fault. It does everything you could reasonably expect from a car rather brilliantly. Even though it is completely uninvolving to drive and has no sense of humour, it plays the role of a German executive saloon down to the tee.

A Little Bit of Love
Vespa 125 VX

A lot of people don't understand the Vespa. They think it's too cutesy. A little feminine, maybe. I'd like to direct their attention to Ferraris and Alfa Romeos from the 60s. They we designed in the same school of thought – to please the eye rather than assault it. To be honest, most things Italian stem from the same design ideology. Take the Fiats in India for example. The Punto is one long sweeping curve and the Linea is made up of a few. The idea is to make them pleasing to the eye, not striking.

To me, the Vespa is a two-wheeled Fiat 500. And if you look at the picture of the car, you'll see what I mean. It's the only scooter sold in India that has any real style. It beckons you to put your Moccasinos on, roll up your khaki trousers and go woo the girl/boy you fancy.

But hang on a minute. It still is a bike so let's get on with the review. First things first – it's tiny. It feels about the same size as the old TVS Scooty. For those obsessed with sheer quantity, please resume your assault on your burger and buy a lorry. But for the others, who prefer quality, let me tell you what this little number has to offer. It is, and I'm not making this up, the easiest bike to ride. And there's good reason.

The dimensions, coupled with a short wheelbase and make it really nimble in the city. But there's more. While the power and torque figures (10bhp & 10 Nm) may seem fairly miniscule, the engine feels like a beating heart. And it's more than adequate for scooting around the city.

The detailing is just brilliant though. Everything, from the headlamps, switchgear, instruments, the brown leather and the generous but tasteful use of chrome a truly classless fell. Think Mini Cooper or Fiat 500.

While the scooter market is chock full of machines that are built to a price and offer nothing more than pure utility, with false pretentions at being sporty, the Vespa VX125 is as refreshing as a morning espresso. At 72 grand ex-showroom, it must seem expensive as compared to all the other scooters on the market.

But it's a Vespa. And for those in the know, it's a bargain.

This Means War!
Mercedes-Benz ML63 AMG

557bhp and 760 torques. That's probably how much go-juice God had when he created the world. You've got to wonder what in the Holy AMG's boffins had in mind when they installed such gravity-defying oomph in the sixty-something-lakh ML-Class. I mean, ze Germans aren't known particularly known for their humour. Beer, yes. Stand-up comedy? 'fraid not.

But (and this requires hindsight) think back to every single AMG-tuned car you've ever come across. Can you remember even one that threatened to compete with anything from BMW's M division or even Porsche? Of course not. While those two went down the poise and precision route, AMG did the decent thing and made cars with massive loud thrustiness and to hell with how quickly it can go round a racing track.

No, AMGs, like Aston Martins, have always been unique. They'd worked out that driving was supposed to be pleasurable - a dramatic and euphoric occasion. The skunkworks inside AMG; those crazy crazies responsible for the Black Series cars know this as well. Not one of their limited-edition specials was designed to go around a corner fast. They were designed to make corners fun and dramatic and memorable.

I loved that about them. I still do, in fact. AMG-tuned Mercs are, on the face of it, simple beings. Like muscle cars, they make huge performance accessible to you and I. And so it goes with the ML63 AMG.

Keen readers will remember that the ML350 CDI was the first ever car on Honk to get a perfect score. It blew us away completely. Pace, panache, predictability and poise – it had the lot. The loony ML has all of that as well. It also has figures that will make many a sportscar squeal. Try 0-100kph in 4.9 seconds. Or a limited top speed of 250kph in sixth gear with another one to go. One thing's for sure; if there is a faster SUV out there, it has a roll cage and a rally driver in it.

Like the AMG-fettled GL, it has a distinctly non-AMG cabin. The only visual clue to its brutality is in the flat-bottomed steering wheel. The rest is regular classy Merc – no surprises and no complaints.

The first time you put your foot down in Sport mode, you'll smile the smile of a child who's just had too much chocolate. This car has the ability to transport you back to your childhood. It makes you giggle like you did when you got away stealing mangoes. If you're not careful, you'll find yourself on a mountain road, giggling like an idiot and going 'whee!' as you hurl it from bend to bend.

And when you drive back into the city after your mountain road thrash, you will never realise that under your right foot, you have the power to make Superman blush. There's plenty of delay on the throttle response and even the 7 speed AMG SPEEDSHIFT gearbox shifts quietly and unobtrusively in the background. And all the hundreds of traction controls keep everything nicely in check.

The primary difference between it and its competitors is this. The Porsche Cayenne is a serious car for serious people. The Range Rover Sport is like an amazing workout buddy; it makes you push harder and works with you to make you cover ground faster. The ML63 AMG is like Elvis Presley – a full-on entertainer. And that's why we love it.

I Really Wanted to Hate This Thing
Audi A4 2.0 TDI

It's days like these when my job becomes really tiresome; days when I have to work out entertaining and relevant criticisms for a good car that I don't quite fancy. So here goes nothing. The new Audi A4, with its upgraded 2.0 TDI diesel motor makes 177bhp (yawn) and 380Nm of muscle. Those numbers seem pretty meek by Honk's maniacal standards because the last A4 we brought you was an S4 with such amazing abilities, that it really did leave yours truly a little out of breath.

This one doesn't have Quattro or the S Tronic double-clutch gearbox. Both of which are intrinsic parts of any good Audi. Front wheel drive and a regular 8-Speed automatic gearbox with no paddle shifts make their way in instead. You even have to adjust the steering manually.

So far, if this new and upgraded A4 hasn't set your soul on fire then I'm with you. But before you go charging into that Merc or BMW dealership, please read the rest of this review.

Audis look great in their new signature Blue. And this A4, with its sculpted lines, beautifully chiselled nose and great proportions is no different. The daytime running lamps are beautiful as well. It even has a discreet lip spoiler like the S4. All this adds us to a rather handsome looking car.

The inside feels as well built as the presidential bomb shelter. Has Audi had any quality issues in the last 10 years? I seriously doubt it.

The centre console is typically Audi, which means that the 5.3 million buttons that are on it are backlit in red. This looks very good at night. But there are at least two buttons for each of the MMI's (Multi Media Interface) functions. I quite like that, because there's one of everything for me and one for my front passenger.

Here comes this A4's first trump card – the tyres. As a stroke of brilliance, Audi's decided against giving this A4 wide, skinny, low-profile tyres on unusually large wheels. Instead, it's got 225/55/R16s which look like they stuffed themselves at Christmas and every day since. As a result, the ride is brilliant. Not just for a car of this size and price either. Only the sharpest of bumps at medium speeds make their way into the cabin. And even this won't bother you.

Trump card number two is Drive Select. This allows you to choose between pre-selected setups for Comfort which makes the steering really light and blunts the gear changes and throttle response, Dynamic which sharpens everything up, Individual which allows you to setup the steering and the throttle response as you like and an Intelligent option which reads your driving style and does it for you.

This A4 is a great city car. The gearbox shifts seamlessly without letting you know when it's working. The many ratios make up for whatever miniscule amount of turbo lag there is. This is the kind of car which makes you forget from time to time that you're driving. And let's face it, for city commuting, that's all we really want.

Trump card number three is the fuel economy. Audi claim 17.5kpl in the city and almost 21kpl on the highway. In my line of work, one often finds that these claims are a bit bollocks. But I believe Audi completely this time. This thing consumes as much diesel as a teetotaller consumes straight whiskey. The fuel needle and the range counter hardly moved on my drive.

Most of us have our spouses and significant others but we still lust for Cameron Diaz, knowing fully well that she'd be agonising on a daily basis. And it's my job to tempt you with the Cameron Diazes of motordom. Not today. Today, I bring you what is a wonderful spouse. A great everyday car that's as easy to live with as a pet gold fish.

Expect to Be Surprised. I Was
Ford EcoSport 1.0 EcoBoost

They laughed when we said we wanted to go from Mumbai to the Rann of Kutch in a day. I laughed as well. But the Ford EcoSport did it. Easily. Here's what happened.

You probably think that all I do is drive fast cars and write about them. You probably think that all I'm doing is what I wanted to do when I was nine years old. Actually, you're right. That's me. And that's all I do.

But this week, I've decided to sober down and actually consider businessy things like sales figures and demand and supply. All this has brought me to the doorstep of Ford and a car that they call the EcoSport. Aren't the words Eco and Sport like French Fries and weight loss? Beer and IQ improvement? That name shouldn't work. But it does. Somehow.

Anyway, the car. You can't buy the 1.0 three-cylinder EcoBoost because they've closed bookings. And they've closed bookings because there's simply too much demand. We've heard of bookings being closed earlier as marketing gimmicks, as with the SUV200. Or something. But I'm assured that this time it's for real – Ford can't make enough of them.

Having never driven one before, I borrowed a press demonstrator for a week to see what all the fuss about. And instead of tootling about in the city, we took it on a gruelling 2200km thrash from Mumbai to the Rann of Kutch for the Rann Utsav and back. The idea was to get there in a day. That's over 900km. Yes, I had a little giggle as well before we set off. *How the hell will a 1-litre 3-cylinder micro-SUV/Crossover do this?*

While leaving the city, it felt decidedly like a petrol hatch on stilts. Eager little engine, semi-slick manual gearbox; it felt familiar. But there was something more. It felt more substantial than most hatchbacks. It could have been the brilliant and typically Ford build quality, or even the fact that they'd thrown in every feature they could including leather seats. It's a really nice place to be.

I took it easy for the first 200 kilometres owing to rain and spray. And something struck me about a claim that Ford make about the EcoBoost engine. They say that it makes more power and more torque than the equivalent 1.5 litre petrol. The numbers suggest that it does. More importantly, it feels like it does. In the rain I held on to 5th gear all the way from 60kph till our steady 130kph cruising speed. You can do this because it has a turbo.

Indian highways in the rain are some of the most dangerous places in the world. But the EcoSport had that covered. Wonderful tyres, great suspension and brilliant ABS meant that it always felt composed. After the rain subsided, we realised that we had about 700 kilometres to cover in heavy traffic, on roads I had never driven on before, with about eight hours of daylight remaining. Time to get the hammer down.

I have to say this of Gujarat. The people are really wonderful, the food is interesting and vegetarian and novel. But my dear Gujarati friends, when you see a car behind you flashing its lights to overtake you, please don't pull out to overtake yourself. Flashing lights in India mean LET ME GO. We had so many sphincter clenching moments as a result. Gujarat is a truly beautiful place, if you can make it to your destination alive because while the roads are brilliant, the traffic is mental.

However, once we crossed Ahmedabad and turned towards Bhuj, I found a side of the little Ford that I really started falling in love with – mile munching. I can scarcely believe the 160-180kph it was averaging when the traffic died down. And it gave me the confidence to push because the chassis is so well balanced and the steering so positive. As I picked up a water bottle to have a swig, I realised that that's how much displacement the little Ford had. This is a truly and utterly astonishing engine. 22kpl at 160kph. Can you think of anything else that can do that?

We finally got to the Rann Utsav at about half past ten at night and it looked beautiful - an oasis in the middle of absolutely nowhere with pretty much all the creature comforts of home (minus meat and alcohol. Damn).

At the Rann Utsav, we decided to give the car a break after the shoot and get ourselves a couple of Trikkes. These brilliant little electric tri-skootery things were the best way to get around and we loved them.

The drive back took all of ten hours because I'd figured out a solution to the Gujarat highway chaos – hustle them, but respectfully. When we reached our destination in Mumbai a full two hours earlier than expected, I couldn't help turning around for one more look at a car that, for once, had lived up to all the hype around it.

With the EcoBoost engine, this is the most hard-working car I've ever come across. It has more to give than you can you ask of it. It's the kind of car that'll make you wonder how you've got so much for so little money. A car that stands head and shoulders above anything that considers itself a competitor. Ford EcoSport EcoBoost, it's been an absolute pleasure.

My Dear Sasquatch
Skoda Yeti 4x4 2.0 TDI

The looks will polarise opinion. Some people even went so far as to call it ugly. But I like it because it looks like no other car on the road. Someone said it looked like a Wagon-R. But the person in question had spectacles with lenses so thick that his eyes appeared to be the size of bowling balls. That said, there can be no smoke without fire and even I will admit that its appearance is not beautiful in an obvious way. But nobody can deny the fact that it is attractive.

To dismiss this car for its looks is like dismissing Ze Fuhrer for his moustache because even if you can't stomach the looks, persevere, because what lies beneath that body is deeply impressive. What it's capable of is even more so.

In one of my previous columns, I raved about how this, the four-wheel-drive version with all the goodies was the best car for India. Considering the number of brilliant cars I've driven from then until now, I thought it appropriate to review it again.

Here's something you might not be aware of. Underneath, it shares its platform with the Audi Q3 and some Seat that doesn't really matter. It even has the same diesel engine, albeit in a different state of tune. Still, 140bhp isn't that bad. And neither is 320Nm of torque.

The interior is nice and simple as well. The steering wheel is a straight lift from Audi and it has buttons and scrolls for the audio and the display between the dials. The seats, though manually adjustable, are covered in leather and are very comfortable. In most cars I like my seat really nice and low with the steering wheel just above my lap. But in the Yeti, I found a more upright position was most comfortable. It was just sort of in tune with the rest of the car. The cabin is easily big enough for five healthy adults and their luggage. There are lots of little cubby holes all over the cabin for everything from maps to sunglasses to water bottles and your mobile phones and iPods. The touch screen multimedia unit is really easy to use as well. Just don't go expecting the screen to work as well as an iPhone's.

The gearbox is a slick 6-speed manual and it shifts really quite nicely. By itself, it's brilliant. But that's probably the only thing I don't like about the Yeti. Well, that and the fake wood on the dash. Skoda could have made it even better than it already is if they had given it a DSG double clutch automatic gearbox.

The ride is just brilliant on anything from tarmac to pot holes and even on rocks on the beach. Thanks to an intelligent four-wheel-drive system you barely ever lose traction. And even if you do for a moment, the ESP restores composure barely after you've lost control. On the centre console, there is a button marked OFF ROAD. In this mode it crawls along by itself, delays the throttle response so you don't spin the wheels and sends power to whichever of the four wheels has the most traction. I tried this system on a muddy, rocky, uphill path in the rain. And it worked just fine. Granted, it's no Jeep Wrangler, but it just sort of rolled up its sleeves and got on with the job.

On the road, it feels a lot more like a saloon than its appearance would suggest. I'm struggling to think of a similarly priced SUV or crossover which is as good on the road. I think the only one that comes close, probably, is the Dacia… ahem, Renault Duster. And my dear Sasquatch gave me just over 11kpl in the city and 14kpl out on the highway.

I haven't even got to the best part yet. (Please sit down for this one) You can have all this for around 20 lakhs. That's a whole 10 lakh cheaper than its sister car – the Audi Q3. If Skoda ever made a Yeti L&K with a DSG gearbox, satnav and a sunroof, I'd be forced to give it my first ever perfect score; even if they charged 3-4 lakhs more. I would certainly buy one. But this near perfect all-round car still gets my vote for the best car on sale for India and a resounding 9/10.

Utter Nutters
Polaris Trackday

If you own a farm, live in the countryside or near the coast, this is for you. In keeping with Honk's fastidious tradition of being silly, we'd like to present an instrument of absolute hilarity, mayhem and abject lunacy not seen outside of a mental institution – the Polaris 500 Scrambler.

Until I spent day with the Scrambler, I hated quads. Primarily because the only one I'd ever ridden until then was on a beach, on honeymoon, with the old lady on the back seat. That particular quad, called the Ginseng Hakka Noodles (or something), was a horrible, unbalanced, hopeless piece of Chinese under-engineered excrement that only went to the right. Which was bad for us because that's where the sea was.

So you'll forgive me if I was a little apprehensive to begin with. First things first, get the gear on. Armour. Elbow pads. Gloves. Helmet. Check. I started out with the 90cc kiddie-quad to learn the track. The difference was obvious straightaway, primarily because it could go straight and left as well. Still, 20 minutes on this mosquito helped me learn the track, specifically built to showcase the capabilities of Polaris's quads and buggys.

Quads, for motorbicyclists are a little counter intuitive. You lean into a corner on a bike. But on a quad, you turn the handlebar in the direction you want it to go whilst your head points to the direction of travel and your bum points in the opposite direction. Rickshaw drivers will know what I'm on about.

Still, time to start with the boys. The next one on my agenda was the 200 Phoenix. This is a racing quad with full-time four-wheel drive and an automatic gearbox. But apart from the throttle being where you'd expect to find the engine start button on your bike, it had the back brake on the left and the front brake on the right like any bike. After tearing it up on this for an hour or so, I found out that all I needed to do some mental donuts was the front brake and the throttle. What followed were more one-handed donuts than Dunkin could scoff at. And it was so easy that even our photographer had a go and pulled it off. Well done, Gaurav.

With the afternoon sun burning down, it was time for the big one; the 500 Scrambler. This is a big, man-sized super-quad. The seating position is much higher than it is on the Phoenix. And that single-cylinder 500cc petrol motor makes 32bhp and a million torques. Probably.

This one felt a little more grown up; a little more serious. All that changed when I found that it had a button which allows you to switch between rear and four-wheel drive. And that means just one thing to the petrolhead - drifting. If you can stab at the front brake at exactly the right time while you're on the throttle, you can hold a drift for days. And in the empty field next to the track, I made even bigger circles around the smaller donut circles I'd made earlier. I wonder if they looked like crop circles from above.

At this point, Gaurav set me a challenge. He wanted me to try and jump this 400kg quad on the very short straight. This was really hard because no matter how many brave pills I took and how much speed I carried through the last corner, I couldn't get this heffer off the ground. I'll try harder next time.

If Elvis was Japanese
Isuzu MU-7

The year was 1993 and I was all of eight years old. A small section in the Times of India carried an even smaller image of a car called Isuzu VehiCROSS. That's the first time I'd heard of Isuzu, who at the time made some rugged, hairy-chested pick-up trucks and commercial vehicles.

In the 20 years that followed, we didn't really hear too much of them except when they forged a joint venture with the erstwhile Swaraj Mazda (after Mazda pulled out) to form SML Isuzu with the Sumitomo Corporation. And that's enough history.

Because what we have here is a luxury 7-seater SUV called the MU-7. When I first saw this at Chennai airport, I couldn't help thinking *DAMN! This thing is huge!* Then I saw the front. Wait a minute. Did someone put an Isuzu badge on a Cadillac Escalade? The resemblance is uncanny. Still, to make a car look like a Caddy that's patronised by just about every successful hip-hopper is not a bad thing to do. Only the MU-7 appears to have more chrome.

The inside, in contrast, is very different. It's as introverted as the exterior is extroverted. The driver's seat is nice and comfortable, if a little flat. From the cockpit, when you swivel your head around, you get a real sense of how big the cabin is. And the back seats appear to have tons of legroom. When you start it up, please make sure it's already in first gear because if it's neutral, the gear stick moves about six inches from side to side as the starter motor does its job. Did I mention it's based on a pick-up truck?

No? Well, that would certainly go some way in justifying the leaf-spring suspension and a steering wheel that feels like it's set in concrete. Not to mention a gear throw so long, that slick shifts are not an option. This makes life difficult if you happen to be of medium build and strength. Thankfully I am neither so I made up for having bunked gym that day as I drove it in the city.

I was really prepared to hate this car. Because while the engine was good (no turbo lag for a turbo diesel) it was really noisy and harsh. But then it hit me. While it may have the dynamic capabilities of an obese hippo, there is a certain honesty in the way it's engineered. It feels simple. It feels analogue. Yes, it has leaf springs, but they work. The resultant ride is great. And heavy steering feels nice and stable when you get out on the highway. It doesn't even roll as much as I expected it to.

That said, it really isn't a driver's car. And Isuzu themselves make no bones about it. In fact, on a recommendation from the Deputy Managing Director himself (we were testing his own car, by the way), I took a long back seat journey. The engine noise was a LOT less. I didn't have to worry about the protein shake I'd need at every set of traffic lights. It really felt like a different car – a much better car. And the back bench (60:40 split) reclines so all you need to do is lay back and enjoy the ride. In fact, the back seat is so good that it alone makes the car worth a look.

To sum up, if you've seen too much of the Fortuner and Endeavour and want a humungous, exclusive, comfortable, extroverted SUV that is also pretty economical, Isuzu's MU-7 is a rather compelling option.

Will Somebody Please Listen!
Mercedes Benz C220 CDI Edition C

Before I start my weekly ramble about some really fancy car or bike, I'd like to ask a question – what makes a Mercedes-Benz a Mercedes-Benz? Is it the three-pointed star? Or could it be the seemingly endless list of features? The distinctive looks, perhaps? No. In my mind, it's the way it makes you feel – warm and fuzzy and cool and stylish all at the same time. There is no other car maker has managed to do that quite like Mercedes.

Now for the weekly ramble – the Mercedes C-Class Edition C. Or the C Class swan song, as it were. This little number is being talked about in the media as the last iteration of this generation of the C Class. They say an all new one is expected to be unveiled sometime next year. And frankly, I can't see why. You may argue that this generation of the C Class, with a few changes here and there, has been on sale for the last seven years. That, by default, means that that its competitors from Audi and BMW are, in the very least, half a generation newer.

But Mercedes-Benz seem to have a very simple philosophy when it comes to the C Class – If it ain't broke, just make it better. And that's precisely what they've done with the C Class Edition C. The C in Edition C stands for Celebration. And they've got quite a bit to celebrate because they've sold 10 million C Classes globally.

The car itself looks great. It's got blacked-out headlamps, beautiful 17in wheels and tiny Edition C badges on the front fenders. But the interior, by far, takes the cake. The front sports seats have Alcantara in the middle with leather on the sides. This means that you don't slide around in your seat through corners. It's a brilliant idea to fuse the luxury of leather with the functionality of Alcantara. And it works.

The cabin itself is a really nice place to be. Even if you've never been in it before, it feels like coming home. It has brilliant new touches like an updated Satnav and the gear lever, unlike most Mercs, is on the floor.

As long as you're easy on the throttle, you won't be able to distinguish being in motion from being stationary. Again, trademark Mercedes. And the pure mechanical suspension feels absolutely sublime in the way it hides road conditions from its occupants. In fact, I'm going to stick my neck out and say that it rides better than an E Class (which has air suspension).

I found myself cruising in the city, a little slower than normal, not because I was wanting for power, but because I wanted to take in as much as I could of the experience. Things change on the highway, though. On the concrete-surfaced, Mumbai-Pune Expressway, it glides over the rather poor surface with grace and very little tyre roar while doing upwards of 170kph. And yes, that sounds like a really big number, but the C is completely poised even at those speeds.

It has an inherent calm, like a yogaist (or whatever they're called), that you just can't put your finger on. It feels completely at peace with itself. The 2.14 litre diesel four puts out 170bhp and 400Nm of torque in this 220 CDI guise. And it suits the car perfectly. All the power you need, when you need it, but delivered in a creamy, progressive, Mercedesy sort of way.

As with most Mercs, my primary complaint is of the gearbox. I strongly recommend that Mercedes buy themselves an Audi to see what a proper double-clutch should be. Because the Merc's gearbox, especially when you need it to quickly kick down a few gears, takes a few seconds longer than you'd like. And the steering, even in its Sport setting, feels slightly underweighted for spirited driving.

All things considered though; the C220 CDI Edition C feels like a Mercedes should. They've managed to distil the very essence of their brand into a product that's seven years old. That's quite an achievement. And if it were up to me, I wouldn't let this C Class go out of production just yet. It's a great car that I really believe has another year's worth of happy customers left in it. If only Mercedes-Benz would agree with me.

Rennsport for the Road
Audi RS 5 Coupe

While Audis look good and are impeccably built, I always wondered what their point was. I mean, if you want a plush German car that you'd drive yourself, what's wrong with a BMW? And why wouldn't you buy a Mercedes if you'd like to be driven?

But then I took the earliest flight I've ever taken in my life from Bangalore to Mumbai and found the RS 5 waiting for me at the airport. And let me make this plain. It. Looks. Fantastic. The first look shook the sleep deprivation and grogginess clean out of me. The clean lines, the low roof line, the perfect 2+2 coupe proportions – the RS 5 is a styling masterpiece. And I'm sorry, but no picture can do justice to the way this Audi looks. You just have to see one in the flesh.

A few more things happened that day that I'll never forget. First, a boy who looked about eleven years old was crossing the street in front of me. He stopped dead in his tracks right in front of the car, examined the RS 5 barge on the front grille, kissed the bonnet, gave me two thumbs up and skipped away with the world's largest smile on his face. Second, a man in one of those anonymous modern small cars beside mine knocked on my window and proceeded to tell me how beautiful my car was. And how he'd trade his A4, his liver and his children to get one.

And third, how it left a BMW 760Li for absolute dead on the Bandra-Worli sea-link. Now this is a turbocharged, V12 BMW we're talking about. D'you know the type of person that buys a big car to compensate for what God didn't give them? This was one such. His bluetooth earpiece in a car that already has bluetooth connectivity cemented his classification. And he was being annoying – tailgating me at three inches when there was an empty lane beside me which he could've used to get past. I even went to the extent of moving over and indicating for him to go past. And then he did the dumbest thing he'd done all day – he pulled up alongside, looked right at me and gave me a burst of revs to state his intentions.

I knew there was one more corner about a hundred yards ahead after which I could floor it for the next 3 kilometres. Drive Select in Dynamic. Check. The exhaust note suddenly revealed it was spewing smoke from 4.2 litre Lamborghini-derived V8 which puts out 450bhp. The RS 5 was suddenly awake. As I put foot to floor the sound became so intoxicating, so mesmerizing that I couldn't take my foot off the throttle. The way the RS 5 accelerates borders on indecent and its definitely illegal. The BMW just about kept up with me till 200kph. Between that and the 270kph that I hit, it was but a diminishing speck in my rear view mirror.

The funny part is that at no point did I feel like I was going to lose control. Such is the brilliance of Quattro. Dynamically, there's a hint of understeer through tight corners. But you can easily correct it if you ease off the throttle.

And when you're done hooning, just turn the Drive Select into Comfort and it becomes a normal Audi. You can't even hear that massive engine at city speeds. These dual personalities are nothing short of genius in the way the RS 5 pulls them both off perfectly. And don't worry about the low ground clearance. It can easily handle Indian roads.

I've been blown away by Mercs and BMWs before. But this is the first time I've ever been knocked out by an Audi. Is it the best 2+2 coupe on sale in India? Hell yes. It's also the best Audi I've ever driven. If I ever had a dream garage, the RS 5 would certainly be in it. In Blue.

Café Classic
Royal Enfield Continental GT

Royal Enfield has been given a fair bit of stick in the last few years. And this has been specifically from people that owned old Bullets. I must admit that I may have been party to said stick giving because I owned a few. What I realised, at about the same time as the other old-school Bulletheads, is that RE was taking the game drastically forward while us lot felt left behind.

In the last ten years alone, they've introduced positively horrid (read: genius) upgrades like electric start, gears on the left, fuel injection, disc brakes, LED headlamps and various other conveniences, ahem, annoyances.

But as we said with the Thunderbird 500, all this has a point. It is to make the brand more accessible to people who just love riding and save them the infuriating histrionics. And even I am beginning to appreciate the fact that it is a step in the right direction.

And then they flew a few of us jounos and hacks to Goa to ride what they call the Continental GT. And I know what you're thinking. Why would they bother naming it after a Bentley? I wondered the same thing. Then Siddhartha Lal, Chairman and Chief Bullethead at RE explained in the press conference that in 1965, RE launched a bike called the Continental GT. This was the first factory-built Café Racer that money could buy. All the others were modified classic bikes like BSAs and Nortons.

Anyway, Café Racing. The idea is that young mechanics and apprentices who'd mostly dropped out of school would buy a really cheap classic bike and go about tuning it into something that was meant to tear up city streets. They were young blades with a penchant for blue jeans and leather jackets and they all had the mandatory affinity for the James Dean/Steve McQueen look. The act of them riding together in rather large numbers was called a Burn Up.

Jump to November 2013 and I found myself looking like them and on my first Burn Up. In Goa. On a brand new, candy Red, 2013 Royal Enfield Continental GT. This is one of those bikes, possibly the only bike in India that has the gravitational force of two scantily-clad Monica Belluccis. The low clip-on handlebars, the fantastic paint quality, the styling overall. It will make you sit up and beg. In many ways, you could compare it to back-to-the-future cars like the MINI Cooper or Fiat 500.

Full riding gear on, I swung my leg over and hit the starter button. I was alarmed by the sheer volume of the burst revs. At this point I must mention that the riding position is low, with the footrests further back than RE buyers are used to. And the version I had was a single-seater where the seat was long enough for me to scootch backwards and forwards. It reminded me of my favoured riding position on a horse.

When I set off (gently) in first, a few things became clear. 1. The riding position is brilliant. 2. The suspension is firmer than any RE that's gone before it. 3. Manoeuvring this bike is manoeuvring your fingers. It is that intuitive and that easy. Top marks to RE there. They had help, of course, from Steve Harris of Harris Performance, UK, who's been tuning GP bikes for donkeys' years.

On to the ride. Forget everything you know about Royal Enfield because this is different. The engine is a 535cc single that makes 30bhp and 44Nm of very usable torque. And it loves to rev. It begs to be given hell all the time. But that said, you can potter around at city speeds and it won't bite.

This engine also has the best vocal range seen in modern times. From a clat-a-clat-a-clat at low speeds, to a deep thrum at midrange, to a full-fat angry bellow at full throttle. In love yet? No? Try this.

When you got Goa's fantastic roads as your playground, you'll soon see the Racer in Café Racer. It feels so balanced, so sharp. The steering, braking, gearshifts and all your interactions with the bike are brilliantly tactile. Telling you that I hit 135kph is purely academic because this bike is definitely more than its numbers suggest. It feels different from anything on sale today. Anywhere. It feels incredible.

I'm sure that like some of the journalists at the launch, there are people will moan about the 'vibrations'. My honest recommendation to them is to buy an electric scooter and pursue a career in hardcore IT.

As for me, the bike costs 2.05 lakh (on-road Delhi), which is about a lakh cheaper than we all expected it to be. If anyone needs me, I'll be at the dealership waving a blank cheque in a rather disorderly fashion.

Shatabdi Express vs. BMW M5

Thinking up of the most ridiculous, yet entertaining things to do with anything on wheels is what we do best. This week, we race the Shatabdi Express from Bangalore Cantonment Railway Station to Chennai Central against the best super-saloon of all time – the BMW M5. And as a special treat for you lot, we've brought back proper petrolhead and ace driver, Aina Barker, who was endlessly moaning… ahem… reporting from the train.

Here's what happened.

Sidharth Sharotri: 4:30am is a seriously chuffing ungodly hour to get out of bed. The things we do for you. It's 5:30am when we arrive at Cantonment Railway Station. It looks like a scene out of a Satyajit Ray movie. Only with neon lights. It's still dark. Last night's rain has left a blanket of dreariness on everything.

Aina Barker: I haven't seen 5:50am since I was in high school. But damn, the early morning light was made to halo the M5. She's all Monte Carlo Blue and basking and so out of place in this bourgeois train station. Sidharth is unnaturally smug about his chances and I resist the urge to elbow him square in the jaw.

SS: We're ready to start at 6:05am. The car is full of fuel and is about to lose an Aina Barker's worth in weight. I've set the M1 button on everything in comfort until I'm in city limits and the M2 button with everything including the steering, gearbox, suspension and throttle response in maximum attack. I'll need that for when I hit the open road. Time to get cracking.

AB: 6:08am – The Shatabdi Express pulls in. this hunk of steel better not make me swallow my words today. Last minute trash talk over text with Sidharth over with, I'm on board and we're off almost immediately (at least he sprung for a prime seat).

SS: My God this BMW's fast when you need it to be. It's 6:35am and I've arrived at my first toll plaza a full five minutes ahead of schedule. That's about 25km in 20 minutes. Time to push that M2 button to 'Cry havoc! And release the dogs of war!'

AB: It's only 6:30 and we've already made an unscheduled stop and now I'm beginning to really settle into my morning sulk. Hopefully Sidharth is dealing with farm animals doing their morning business across the highway. That should put a spoke in his 19in wheels.

SS: 7:35am the M5 has chewed up and spat out another 120 kilometres. That's a 150 altogether in an hour and 20 minutes. I've just gone past Palmaner. And yes, I've taken the slower and longer NH46 along the north.

AB: Oh! Breakfast. I've got steaming hot Idlis. Sidharth? Pardon me. I didn't quite get that, you're starving? Good luck with that.

SS: Sod breakfast. It's 8:30am and this is the longest traffic jam in the history of time! Honestly! Can trucks kindly find somewhere else to roll over? I'm in a race for god's sake! In the last 20 minutes, I've only covered 4 kilometres.

AB: As the dawn fully breaks, my window's just turned into a picture frame and as I'm lulled into a semi dream state, I wonder what kind of view Sidharth has. Oh wait, he can't afford a view. He's on pothole alert. How's the handling on that baby?

SS: The handling along with the power delivery, the stellar chassis and just about everything on the M5, is just sublime. It does what you ask of it every single time. It never loses composure however hard you push it. You are witnessing the process of a man falling in love. And come on, a 4.4 litre TwinTurbo V8 putting out 560bhp and 680Nm of twist - you've had it, Barker. I've seen well over 200kph quite regularly. Loser buys dinner.

AB: 9.00am. My nap time comes to a grinding halt; as does the train at Katpadi station. I call Sidharth and he's already on the outskirts of Chennai. Dammnit. He does sound beat though. I guess he didn't get in nap time. That should slow him down.

SS: It's 9:15am and I've just crossed Sriperumbadur and hit the outskirts of Chennai. How I've got here this quickly has little to do with me and a lot to do with the sheer pace of what is undoubtedly the best super-saloon of all time. I've pushed M1 to calm this nutter down again. By 9:45, I've hit rush hour traffic in Chennai city. I've just reached Ponamalle. Traffic is really well managed here. It's a lot better than Bangalore. My satnav tells me that I have 16 kilometres to run.

AB: At 10:15, a local train ambles by. We're close. My reverie of the winner's circle is rudely interrupted by my phone beeping. Sidharth's texted. Wait, he's texting… that means he has two free hands. Uh-oh.

SS: Yes, I do. And I know I've won because the train isn't due for another 35 minutes. I've got plenty of time to practice my 'winning face'.

AB: The train pulls in at 10:50am and I try to pull my most gracious loser face on. I step out on the platform and there he is; all slow smile and snarky. Spare me the victory speech and hand me the keys, Sidharth. I'm driving back and I'm about to beat your time into the middle of last week. And yes, dinner is on me.

V8 Thunderstorm. *In a Velvet Glove*
Mercedes-Benz E63 AMG

If you've been following Honk, you'll be acutely aware that we've brought you some fairly mental V8 German performance cars lately. The Audi RS 5's party piece was its ability to be two very different cars in one sen-bleeding-sational looking 2+2 package. The BMW M5 was so perfect that it's probably the best all-round car on sale on the planet.

And now we have the Mercedes-Benz E63 AMG. And let's first cut through the nomenclature confusion. A 63 AMG should mean 6.3 litres of displacement in a V8. And it did. Now however, a 63 means a twin-turbo 5.5 litre V8 (with the exception of the C63 AMG which still has the 6.2 V8). Even more so, a 55 AMG is effectively the same engine without the turbos. We'll tell you all about that when we review the new SLK55 AMG.

Anyway, the bonkers E Class. The front end, as you can see from the picture is completely revised. It's been given the full-on AMG makeover in carbon-fibre; complete with bits of aero enhancements that help increase downforce at speed. You find a similar treatment in the form of a diffuser below the rear bumper. And those double twin tailpipes mean one thing – the engine is huge. In profile though, the only giveaways to its 1.29 Crore price tag (ex-showroom) and immense performance are the 19in wheels and 'V8 BITURBO' badges on the front fenders.

Things are almost as discreet inside. What you get is a fairly standard looking E Class interior with one or two little changes. The first thing you'll notice is the wheel which isn't entirely round. It's got some annoying flat bits at 12 'o clock and 6 'o clock. That's fine if you're Lewis Hamilton, which you're not. What you end up with is bruised fingers every time the wheel slides through your hands after a turn.

The second thing you notice is the beautiful carbon-fibre strip that runs across the dash. If I had my way, all Mercs would come with this as standard. It's beautiful. The centre console is fairly standard except for the gear selection area which comes with a gear shifter, controls for the suspension, a button to turn the ESP off, a knob that lets you choose from Comfort, Sport, Sport+ and Manual for the gearbox and my favourite – a button marked AMG. This sets the car up in whatever hell-raising fashion you've pre-selected. I went for the Full Monty with the gearbox in manual (it will not shift up unless you pull a paddle), the suspension in its stiffest setting with the ESP still on.

And then I quickly realised that I didn't need any of this. This AMG - like most AMGs - is all about the engine. So even in its softest, laziest of settings, you still have all the power and the beautiful AMG soundtrack. But you can distinctly tell that you're still in an E Class, which, let's face it, is made to be accessible to the more mature buyer. The throttle's forgiving, the ride's brilliant and it's even got heated/air-conditioned seats that massage you as you drive along. Pootling around in city traffic is a cinch.

And when the road opens up, put your foot down and enjoy the 557bhp, 720Nm of slightly hilarious torque and the beautiful, if a little subdued, AMG V8 soundtrack. While the steering is precise, don't expect it to be an M5 around corners. It's not nearly as poised.

What it is, is a fantastic refinement of a breed created by the Americans in the early '60s – it's a Muscle Car. And it's also a Mercedes E Class. Which means that it will thrill you to bits, and then be a perfectly modern, perfectly German luxury saloon to drive home in. Pretty impressive, eh?

The God of Going Places
Mercedes-Benz GL350 CDI Launch Edition

Take everything you know about what a Mercedes can do and throw it away. It's the only way you'll ever get to grips with what follows. I recommend you sit down for this story.

"Sir! Sir!", shouted the little girl running towards me, as I lined the GL350 CDI up for some good old fashioned trailblazing, "Car cannot go there! Only horse can go there!" On the face of it, she had a point. I was looking at an incline of about 40-50 degrees. There was barely a visible path to speak of. There were thick bushes on either side, often overlapping each other across the track. And the most dangerous part was that there was no end in sight. Which means that had we got stuck, there was no space to turn the MASSIVE Merc around. Right.

Before I go on, I'd like you know that my new favourite motorsport is Trailblazing. Trailblazing is essentially taking a car where no car has gone before. It's an immensely satisfying experience when you do something they said the car wasn't capable of.

Anyway, 50-degree incline? No end in sight? Let's see what's what. Step 1: Push the button on the dash to raise the suspension. Step 2: Push the other button next to it that helps you climb. Step 3: Turn on the front and 360° camera (yes, and it gives you a real-time bird's-eye view of the car). And Step 4: Say a little prayer and commit because once you do, there's no looking back.

That forward-facing camera really helped, because from where I was sitting, all I could see was sky. Just to be safe, I had a spotter with her head sticking out of the sunroof. The way this thing climbs, and the places it can fit through truly mash the mind. The horse trail was about 2 kilometres long and we only chanced upon a few villagers who stopped dead in their tracks and wondered how the hell a car - leave alone one this big - could possibly be going past them at an angle so indecent. The Mercedes driver, my spotter and I got out just before turning back and scratched our heads staring at said behemoth wondering the same thing.

The Launch Edition GL350 CDI that we tested had 21in AMG wheels with 295/40 section tyres on them. If you aren't familiar with tyre and wheel sizes, they're bloody massive. And they look really good. Although, like the ML we brought you a few weeks ago, they're road tyres. They're not really meant for this kind of thing. And yet…

The next bit of astonishment came when I drove it back to Pune on the Mumbai-Pune Expressway. On the way to Mumbai on the same road, it had been near perfect. I'd even go so far as to say that it handled quite brilliantly. But I was running out of fuel on the way back. And I don't get paid nearly enough to fill its 100-litre tank. With a quarter of a tank to go, we set off for Pune with the range reading 230km. This was going to be close.

There is a feature on the multi-function display that tells you your real-time fuel consumption. And apart from the toll booths where I had to accelerate from standstill, it told me that over that stretch between 80 and 100kph, I had consumed (and this is equally shocking) 4.5 litres per 100 kilometres. That's a scarcely believable 22.2kpl from a 3.0 V6 diesel in a car so big that it should have its own post code! The same hypermiling in the city kept me at 17-18kpl.

And now for some bad news. The ride is absolutely unbecoming of a luxury Mercedes in the city. It rolls really badly over smooth bumps and crashes on the sharper ones. One of my passengers even described the ride being as bad as an Innova's.

And there's a very simple reason – the size of the wheels and tyres. The Launch Edition comes with 21in AMG wheels with skinny low-profile tyres. But you can have the made-in-India GL for 72.58 lakh (ex-showroom) with 19in or even 18in wheels with tyres that are well fed. That simple fix will improve the ride no end and make it the car it deserves to be. And if I had a family of seven, that's the one I'd have.

The New Emperor of Stuttgart
Mercedes-Benz S500 L Launch Edition

This is a very difficult car to review. Primarily because just about anybody who knows anything about cars will acknowledge the fact that the S Class is *the best car in the world*. So how in the world does one go about the business of being objective about such a thing?

With the new S Class, Mercedes has raised the bar significantly above anything that Audi, BMW and even Jaguar can throw at it. They've now got their guns trained squarely on Bentley and Rolls Royce. Let's see what this, the best Merc of all time, is all about.

On the outside, you'll find that it's even longer than the old long wheelbase S Class. Although the headlamps and tail lamps have a lot more detail, it looks quite a bit more subtle than its predecessor. That's a good thing. But then you step inside and instantly, you realise that this feels almost British in its opulence. There are many different kinds of leather, very subtle use of chrome, brushed aluminium and only the finest wood. This is, without a doubt, the best cabin that Mercedes has ever done. And that's saying something.

We tested the S500 L Launch Edition which came with something called a Chauffer Pack. This includes the most comfortable front seats that your chauffer has had the privilege of ever parking his backside on. These can be heated and cooled. But the back seats are where the S Class takes a dump on its German competitors. Not only do they recline, but the front passenger's seat moves about a foot and a half forward and out pops a little footrest from underneath to give you the whole First-Class experience. But it doesn't end there. These seats have six (SIX!) different massage options. That's two more than my neighbourhood spa. And for the first time ever in a car, you can have a hot stone massage for either your back or your shoulders.

And it gets better. The S Class gives its rear passengers a remote control to access both rear screens as well as the centre screen. You can do pretty much anything with this remote apart from drive the car.

Had enough? Good. Because here's some more. When Mercedes says interior mood lighting, they mean exactly that. Going from violet to scarlet to neutral actually changes the feel of the cabin entirely. This car even turns into a WiFi bloody hotspot and it has tray tables in the rear centre console for your laptop and Foie Gras.

I could use my entire column space telling you that it's the most comfortable car I've ever been in and how it comprehensively cuts out the outside world but there's one more side to this particular S Class that I'd like to introduce you to – the driving experience. The old S Class, while still a brilliant car, was a bit of a barge to drive. But this new one is only being sold at the moment with a 4.6 L twin-turbo V8 petrol engine that makes about 450bhp and 700 torques. This engine has all the low low-rev high-torque characteristics we like about diesels and good old-fashioned grunt as well. But it's effortlessly smooth, silent and sophisticated. Windows up, you'll never hear more than a faint burble. Never before has an engine suited a car more than now.

And it's easy to drive, either slowly or quickly. The body roll is very well managed and not just for something this size and there's always power when you need it. Yes, the gearbox is still a bit slow but that suits the wafting nature of this car.

This is the easiest verdict I've ever had to declare because this over a 7 Series, A8 or an XJ is an absolute no brainer. I'd even go so far as to recommend it over either a Bentley Flying Spur or Mulsanne. Possibly even a Rolls Royce Ghost because we all know that the Ghost is a cut-price Phantom based on a 7 Series. And you can never drive a four-door Rolls Royce yourself. But you can drive the S Class and you can be driven in it. You'd sleep well knowing that the company that invented the car has pulled out all the stops and done their best job ever. The only reason I won't give it 10/10 is because ideally, I'd like to give it 14.

Road Tripper
BMW 320d Luxury

3.6/100km. This is a fuel consumption figure. That works out to 27.7kpl. 136kph. That was our average speed over the 100 kilometres where we got this economy. Blinding. So, the BMW 320d that you've read a lot about elsewhere over the last two years is clearly very good for long distances.

Just how good? To find out, I borrowed one to go and meet friends that I rarely get to meet in cities around Bangalore. Five days, five cities and over 2000 kilometres should be a blast.

I picked up the car in Kochi Airport and the first thing that struck me was how heavy the steering was at crawling speeds. But the trade-off is that it feels very well weighted at medium and high speeds. Still, next stop – Bangalore. 517km as per Google Maps (my test car didn't have satnav). Now, 184bhp from a 2.0 diesel doesn't sound like much get up and go. But if you throw in ZF's brilliant 8-Speed automatic gearbox, it's all you'll ever need. It seems to have a perfect gear for whatever you need. The flipside is that it shifts constantly. Unobtrusively; but constantly. The roads, thanks to endless roadworks, got worse once I crossed Palakkad and entered Tamil Nadu. But the 3 came good here as well. That suspension is brilliant at soaking up bad roads and even the sharpest bumps are barely heard, let alone felt. I'd like to pat the backs of chassis engineers for discovering the Holy Grail, which is the perfect sweet-spot between ride and handling. They're still the best in the business. Bangalore came much too soon; in about six hours.

A quick overnight break later, we set off for Hubli. Morning rush hour traffic is as vicious in Bangalore as in any other city. And that got me thinking about how the X5 and 118d were a bit tricky in stop-go conditions. The 3 has some of that initial throttle bite as well, but it's much more forgiving. The size is really good as well, which means that ducking and weaving aren't very difficult. I reckon my mother could get to work 10 minutes earlier than usual in this.

I get this inexplicable sense of relief whenever I hit the highway. The sense that I am no longer confined by the shackles of traffic and I can now put my foot down. In the 320d, that felt slightly lukewarm because there's isn't any real power and the gearbox keeps shifting away. But hold on a minute. Is that 210kph on the speedo? That seems to be this Beemer's party trick, pace without the actual sensation of pace. The high-speed ride (140-230kph) is fantastic as well. It feels like that's the natural pace of this car and what it was made for.

And I don't have enough space in this column to tell you how wonderful the steering feels at speed or how balanced the chassis is or, indeed, how progressive and fluid the 320d feels on the move. But I don't like the brakes. They have little feel and even lesser bite. And as with the X5, the ABS kicks in too early.

Belgaum, Bangalore and Chennai we dispatched with similar ease and equally astonishing pace. One more thing before I close this piece. This is a very handsome car. Yes, it may look a little bland from rear, but apart from Chris Bangle's monstrosities, all BMW saloons have always been subtle and sober. And so it goes with the 3 Series. Apart from the daytime running lamps (fine pieces of jewellery), there's no visual excess. So if you want a show-off's car, please go elsewhere.

To sum up, the BMW 320d Luxury is car for the driving connoisseur who also wants to use it every day and make the occasional long-distance trip, and for whom showing off isn't on top of their list. Or to put it simply - their only car. If you look at it that way, at its price, it has no rivals.

The Real Potato
Harley Davidson Fatboy Special

One look and you know this is the real deal. If I may be permitted to use Ferrari's latest nomenclature, this should be called the Harley Davidson LaHarleyDavidson. But HD calls this, their largest selling bike, the Fatboy Special. To the oblivious, the Fatboy is the quintessence of Harley, like the Aviator is to Ray Ban – their signature dish. It harks back to the truly fat choppers of the '60s and '70s.

And fat it is. How fat? The 1690cc V-twin puts out a spleen-shattering 132Nm of torque. And in true cruiser tradition, Harley's left out the power figure. Oh, and it weighs 332kgs; which is roughly 3.3 Honda Activas.

Not being built like the Governor of California, I was reasonably intimidated by the weight. The front end appears to be made out Mr. I'll Be Back himself. It is brutally heavy if you try to turn it like any other bike. But there's a little trick that I found. What you do is lean just a little and let the front wheel fall towards your direction of choice by itself. I figured this out after about half an hour on the bike; after having lost every ounce of fluid in my bladder and every single hair on my head.

But then I found an open stretch of Goan highway and there's no other way to say this except – *Our Father who art in heaven, hallowed be thy Fatboy*. It feels just too good to have been made anything as crude as human hands and tools. There's something divine in the way it cruises at 120kph with the engine making its signature potato-potato-potato music which only proper Harleys can.

The seat was perfect, the foot pegs weren't really foot pegs, they were the size of the dead pedal in a car which can fit your whole foot. The controls were heavy, but they felt just right. The handlebar was just below shoulder level and wide, again perfect for cruising.

Then I hit traffic and thought *oh bugger, I'm in trouble now*. 332kgs worth of big V-twin and traffic go together as well as heavy metal and old people. And that's what was going on inside my head when an even bigger surprise came than the Night Rod Special we brought you earlier. Ol' Fatty here's just as easy. Harley knows that not all its customers are Beefcake Bobbys. And this conveniently means that provided you treat it with respect, the Fatboy Special will never give you anything to worry about. The throttle response is slow and progressive so there's none of that bite you find on superbikes. And the bike seems to almost balance itself at standstill and crawling speeds.

The potato-potato-potato from the exhaust means that I ended up attracting more attention than I would've liked from fellow road users. Children stared with slightly frightened looks on their faces. And people actually got out of my way when they heard me coming, only to stop and look at what in the world was making that noise. And I got thumbs-ups from every biker that I passed. Suffice to say that everybody loved the Fatboy.

This is one of those bikes that will actually change a little bit about you. It'll teach you respect, give you the most spiritual motorcycling experience that I've ever had and give everyone around you a reason to smile. And goosebumps. If I told you that the Fatboy Special costs 30 lakhs, you'd think 'hmmm, that's a bit stiff, but still worth it for a bike this good'. But it doesn't. It only costs 15 and a bit which makes it spectacularly good value for what you get. If there is a God, he works in small motorcycle factory in Milwaukee.

Suzy Q and the Real Desert Storm
Audi Q5 – 2.0 TDI

"Camel in the road!", screamed our frightened photographer for about the thirteenth time. This was going to be really stressfu… "CAMEL!" Dear god. These rather weirdly shaped ships of the desert, along with being the most relaxed animals in the world, have about as much road sense as your average inter-city bus driver. We really thought they'd be the end of us. Either that or the random clusters of four billion sheep that cross the road together.

We didn't know any of this when we landed in Delhi well past midnight to pick up our very own super camel – the Audi Q5 2.0 TDI. This, along with the BMW 5 Series and the Maserati Quattraporte, is probably the only car that looks good in beige. Although, the earlier Q5 we tested in blue was infinitely more appealing.

With the outside temperature reading 6 degrees C, we set off on a gruelling 800km drive to Jaisalmer and straightway we ran into trouble with Gurgaon five-o. Because our car had an MH registration plate, they thought they'd help themselves to our money. Since all our documents were in order, I did my best Arvind Kejriwal impression and we were back on the road in no time.

This part of India is really dangerous during the day. So you can imagine how dangerous it can be in the dead of the night, with fog everywhere. "They won't find our bodies for months," said our photographer, Ashish, as we passed through Rewari, which also happens to be the inspiration for various rural gangster flicks. Not tonight. Drive Select in Dynamic. This firms up the suspension, sharpens up the throttle response, makes the brilliant 8-speed S-Tronic gearbox shift faster, adds weight to the steering and generally helps you get the hell out of Dodge before Johnny Villager decides to take a few pot shots at you.

The result was the same as with the petrol Q5. It simply flies over broken roads. I loved that about the previous car and this one was just as good. Except the power. The petrol Q5 had some real grunt. This one sort of doesn't. For me, a car should have enough power to overwhelm you every once in a while. But in 2.0 TDI guise, the Q5 never does. That being said, the power delivery is super-smooth and creamy and progressive thanks to the sorcery that is S-Tronic.

As dawn broke, we were already about 100 kilometres into Rajasthan, being guided faithfully by Audi's ever impressive satnav system. So impressive that, since we'd chosen the shortest route in terms of distance, it took us through each town en route, completely bypassing the bypasses. And this was good because we saw so many places that we never would've seen otherwise.

After about 12 hours on the road, we finally reached Jaisalmer. And we left immediately because our actual destination was Ragasthan, which is an annual four-day music festival in the middle of the desert. And they're right. You drive and drive through absolutely nothing for kilometres on end, all you can see on the way is desert on either side, the odd windmill and then Ragasthan just appears out of nowhere.

The festival itself was brilliant and featured some of India's finest independent musicians and bands and some truly unique sounds like Neeraj Arya's Kabir Café and Run! It's the Kid. Still, after having spent the night in a tent, freezing my whatevers off, I concluded that tenting wasn't my cup of tea, and the next day, checked into the Suryagarh hotel, which must rank somewhere between 7 Star and overwhelming. They'd been kind enough to set up cocktails for us at sunset in the sand dunes.

Time for some dune bashing, then. DriveSelect back in Individual, which I'd setup with everything in Dynamic except the steering. Quattro senses when you go off road and adapts the braking and power delivery to suit your terrain. And it worked brilliantly because we scaled massive dunes and jumped off the other side. We even drove with the car at 30-degree sideways tilt along the dunes.

On the way back to Delhi, I sat back and reflected upon all what was an extraordinary experience. But at the centre of all that was a brilliant car. Granted it wasn't even the most powerful Q5, but it did a fantastic job of transporting three people and their luggage across broken and dangerous roads in brilliant comfort and at a really good pace. And it also showed its (semi) athletic abilities when it was pressed into action on the dunes. And at about 18kpl, it costs about as much to run as your faithful Royal Enfield. Still want an A6?

The Pretender
BMW 530d M Sport

BMW has made a 5 Series with an M badge. But it's not an M5; it's a diesel. I can't remember the last time I was this outraged by nomenclature. You see, an M badge on a 5 Series means something. To me, it means the best sports saloon of all time. It means one of the three best cars I've ever driven. It means the default choice for the only car I'd like to own even if I had Bugatti Veyron money. But this one seems like someone's stuck M badges to trick onlookers.

Let's see if the M5's pretentious vegetarian cousin is any good. If you can ignore the tiny M badges near the fender, it is a beautiful car – a symphony of evil in black. BMW, in my opinion, still do the most perfectly proportioned saloons. This new facelifted fiver comes with redesigned headlamps that have BMW's new double-twin daytime running lamps. It sits on 18-inch wheels with 245/45s in the front and 275/40s at the back. Visually, the 5 Series is text-book elegant. A little black dress, if you will.

Inside, you get every conceivable gadget you can imagine. It has the new iDrive infotainment system with a 16.5cm screen which only a fourteen-year-old can work out. I'm not saying it's complicated, but it has a zillion different options and sub-menus for everything. If you do buy this car, you'll really like the new iDrive because you could own it for a year and you'll still find new things in it. The rest of the interior is typical BMW. Clean, simple and efficient with a great big slab of wood right across the dash. The stand-out feature, though, is the ergonomics for the driver. The seat (infinitely adjustable in every way you can imagine), the M steering wheel and the pedals are as perfect as I've ever experienced. Well done, BMW.

What's not great about the interior is the rear legroom. BMW's been kind enough to fit TV screens behind each headrest (with remote) and then decided to curb its generosity to the people watching them. It's not cramped, but it's not as good as the E Class or the A6.

You can imagine though that all those good looks and TV screens wouldn't count for monkeys if it wasn't any good to drive. Luckily, it is good. Very good. You get four modes to choose from. Vegetarian… ahem… Efficient Dynamics, Comfort, Sport and Sport Plus. Sport and Sport Plus are the same except that in Sport Plus, the ESP is turned off.

The torques, all 540Nms feel like they're always there. It pulls like a locomotive - it's not violent acceleration but it is relentless. The 258bhp power figure from the 3-litre twin-turbo straight six diesel may seem meagre but the 8-speed automatic gearbox from ZF means that you're never left wanting. It also means that you can use all of the power all the time. I hate to admit it but it almost justifies the M badge.

Because of the progressive steering, 50/50 weight distribution and the brilliant chassis, if pulls off a trick that only the best BMW saloons do – in the corners, the whole car feels like it's pivoting around your hips. And that alone makes it worth a look.

The ride is sublime at any speed. In spite of those M wheels, it deals with Indian roads really well.

Dynamically, I've only got two criticisms. The ABS kicks in much too early and the brakes don't feel like they have enough stopping power. But this was a press car which I'm sure had been buggered to bits by every motoring hack in the land. Second, if you're not careful, your head-up display will inform you that you're cruising at well over twice the speed limit. The car can handle it, but I doubt the police can.

The verdict then, is simple. If you want a good looking, extraordinarily well-built German saloon car that's quiet, comfortable, economical, has more equipment than Bill Gate's office, is wonderful to drive, and costs less than 60 lakhs, then you only have one option – the BMW 530d M Sport. Just please take those M badges off.

Heart Attacker
Harley Davidson Night Rod Special

You don't know fear until you've fully twisted the throttle in third gear at 120kph. Because the engine is at 4000rpm and then builds revs so violently that (and I'm not joking) the rear tyre spins for a full second after which it grips and catapults you towards the horizon with such pornographic indecency, that all you can do is hold on and hope you don't die. Welcome everyone, to the Harley Davidson Night Rod Special – the cruiser's evil and very angry twin.

This is the kind of bike that you buy if you constantly crave near-death experiences. To put it simply, superbikes are fairly easy to ride. And that's because everything about them is straightforward. You take one look and you know it's going to be as fast as Usain Bolt on steroids. Basically, you know to expect the brutal pace and you prepare yourself for it. The Night Rod is a little different because it looks like a sleek, low-slung cruiser. And at city speeds, you can potter around town all day and it won't bite you once. Yes, it weighs slightly upwards of 300kgs, but the weight is so beautifully centred and low down that crawling in the city is no problem even if you're 14 years old and a girl. The stiff suspension can be a little jarring over bumps but the trade-off is a great high-speed ride.

But; and this is a big but, it looks and goes like no other Harley because when you find an open stretch of road, shift down a few cogs and give it everything. It has the ability to surprise you with more than twice the torque that you think it has. Gun it, hold on, and Bang! You're instantly somewhere else.

As a package, the Night Rod is very hard to fault because it's easy to ride at any speed, relatively comfortable, great at mile munching and looks fantastic. For what it is, all its abilities and the Joker-rivalling smile that it can put on your face while giving you the most pleasurable heart attack you've ever had, it's a snip at 21.75 lakhs.

Your Excellency

Land Rover Range Rover 4.4 SDV8 Autobiography

When you're climbing a 65-degree incline, all you can see is the sky. You have no way of knowing what's beneath wheels. Unless of course you have five cameras that feed images from all around the car to the central screen. You can choose one or two of these and enlarge them. But all this is by the by because the temperature outside was 42 degrees and I was inside looking at my camera feeds while getting an agreeable back massage on my temperature-controlled seats and listening to Radiohead on one of the best car stereos I've ever heard.

Welcome, everyone, to the Range Rover 4.4 SDV8 Autobiography – a car so damnably desirable that you'll push your mother out of the way to get one.

Let's start with the looks. It is massive; bigger than you think. And tall. At 6'3", I couldn't see over the roof. LR's Gerry McGovern has gone down a very interesting styling route with the Range Rover. Like the new S Class we brought you earlier, it's a perfect blend of subtlety and detailing. The whole body just has one clean shoulder line flowing down the side and a beautiful floating roof. The styling is almost classical. You look at it and think 'yes, this is how a Range Rover should look'. Imagine a car that looks so right that my only criticism of the outside is that the chromed grille is too blingy. You can sort that out by simply choosing something less chintzy from the options list.

The interior is an ergonomic masterpiece. Even if you've never been in it, everything is where you'd expect it to be. But more than the wood and leather and the wonderful heated/cooled massaging seats and all the brilliant and well thought out features, it's the feel of the lifts it above anything else. There's a certain majesty to this interior that's very hard to describe. It has fewer buttons than all its rivals and I love that. It makes for a cleaner, more elegant cabin. The Germans these days pack their centre consoles and dashboards with more buttons than the space shuttle but LR has resisted doing that and the result is, quite possibly, the best interior of any car on sale today.

This new Range Rover is about half a ton lighter than the one that went before it and you can feel that in its construction. Some very clever engineering and extensive use of Aluminium have resulted in a huge car that weighs just a little more than German midsized saloons.

But a Range Rover also has to be brilliant with the cut-and-thrust of daily life. And it is. The cabin completely isolates you from the outside world. I did three peak-hour runs through Mumbai to test its runabout-ability and yes, it was intimidating the first time. But I soon realised that the visibility is great and the front corners are easily visible from the driver's seat. In short, it's easy. On the open road, it cruised with a dignity hitherto unknown to an SUV. At 200kph. So that's that, then. Job Done. Range Rover 1. Competition 0.

But the RR's surprise was yet to come. When's it's off road, I doubt if there's a single road-legal SUV that can do what this can. We climbed at 65 degrees on loose rocks. We dunked it in the ocean when the water level was splashing the windscreen. We crawled along rocks at a 35-degree sideways tilt. And here's the part that amazes me – the car didn't flinch even once. It didn't so much as spin its wheels in protest.

That's Terrain Response 2 for you – the most versatile and advanced terrain management system in the business.

The verdict on the Range Rover Autobiography 4.4 SDV8 is simple. I need to get myself one. The only question is - are you going to rob the bank or shall I?

The Six Maniac
Audi S6

Again, I'm reminded of a German in management, with a Zinc-top kitchen in a house completely enclosed in glass. But the only difference is that in this case, said executive might enjoy a spot of murdering on weekends; quite like that mental in American Psycho. Because this, the S6 has a true, sword-wielding mean streak.

On the face of it, you could be fooled into thinking that it's a regular A6. It might even be a diesel. The giveaways, if you look closely, are a reshaped front bumper, tiny V8 T badges on the front wings and of course, S6 badges on the beard and the boot. Visually, it manages to pull off a neat little trick of being subtle and eye catching at the same time. Someone's probably spent years chewing the back end of a pencil to work out those headlamps because the detailing on them is phenomenal. Some might call it overdone, but these are people who think a Lamborghini is too loud and shouty.

The subtle sportiness continues to the inside as well. In true Audi tradition, there are millions of buttons for this and that. But the whole feel of the interior takes the biscuit. It's black. With a good and healthy splashing of carbon fibre where the wood used to be. Finally, Audi seems to have worked out that most of us have enough timber in our furniture at home. To their exceptional build quality, they've finally added some real style. It is a triumph of good taste over market research. The seats are brilliant as well; comfortable, supportive, infinitely adjustable and temperature controlled.

What I didn't like about the interior is the seating position itself. The brake pedal is too far to the right of the steering wheel. That feels really weird and ergonomically incorrect.

But you soon forget about the brake pedal when you start it up. The Twin-Turbo 4.0 V8 wakes up with a heavy, meaningful burst of revs. And then you're left with five choices of driving modes – efficient, comfort, auto, dynamic and individual. In truth, you only need two of these; efficient and individual. The first one's good for tootling around in city traffic because it shifts up early and shuts the engine off when you stop, only to start it up again when you take your foot off the brake. And individual works everywhere else because you can setup the steering, suspension, throttle response and the 7 speed S-Tronic gearbox the way you like.

Another particular point of interest is the engine. It makes 420bhp which is but a little more than the BMW M5 from 1998. But it's got some clever tech like cylinder shut off, which closes four cylinders when you don't need them. And it's spooky because you can never tell when it does this. It also has 550Nm of torque and rear-biased Quattro. The result is 0-100kph in under 5 seconds and an electronically limited top speed of 250kph. Thank you, Audi, for proving that horsepower numbers are just that – numbers. It's real-world pace that really matter. And the S6 has that in abundance. You could honestly own this, live in Pune and work in Mumbai. Because the urgency with which it eats up the highway is addictive. Addictive until you reach a corner.

Because that's where it starts to go downhill. The steering, no matter what setting it's in, has no feel. Its job is to turn the front wheels and that's all it does without inspiring any confidence to push on. My next dynamic complaint is about the size of the rear tyres. At 255 (same as the front) they're too narrow. That's great if the chassis was inherently sublime like it is in the 5 Series, but it isn't. And it's nose heavy. So what you get is understeer followed by an unpredictable snap of oversteer. And since you can't feel what the wheels are doing, you have to guess how much throttle and opposite lock will correct it. And that's tedious.

If you are a German minimalist with the occasional need to murder, might I suggest the BMW M5? It's better in every way. It's more expensive, but it's so much fun that you might give up decapitation and take up driving for pleasure instead. Imagine how much you'll save on body bags.

The Perfection That I Never Asked for
Royal Enfield Classic 500

Japan, as far as I'm concerned, is singularly responsible for the death of the British boutique motoring industry. In the 50s and early 60s, Britain was chock full of boutique manufacturers that made some truly beautiful machines. Triumph, Jensen, MG, Austin-Healey and Jaguar made some of the most evocative and soulful two-seater roadsters of their time. But they all had the same Achilles' Heel – reliability. Like the Alfa Romeos of their time, they were brilliant for one day in a week, because they simply wouldn't work on the remaining six.

Along came Honda with the S500 and demonstrated to the prog-rock generation that they could have a convertible sports car which was as reliable a hammer and which was nearly as much fun as their beloved 'Made in Blighty' drop-tops. As a result, most British sports car manufacturers have now gone bust. And the handful that survive have gone specifically into the track day niche.

The Japanese are very good at engineering reliability into their cars and bikes. And this brings us neatly on to the RE Classic 500. Yes, it's been around for a few years. And yes, it's sold in enormous numbers across the world. Having owned a few Bullets, ahem, Royal Enfields over the years, I can safely say that all the ones with gears on the right were a dream to ride but a pain in the arse to own. Notice anything familiar?

The Classic is different, because for a kick-off, it works seven days a week. You actually can wake up in the morning, swing your leg over and start it up. And it will start. There are none of those butterflies you got when you looked at your watch in a puddle of your own sweat, after you'd kicked it for the 43rd time, hoping and praying that it would come to life. The Classic comes with a starter button. Even that works every time.

Don't get me wrong though, I really like reliability, especially from my washing machine and my juicer. And yes, an everyday means of transport should be reliable as well. And therein lies my problem.

With the Classic, RE has turned an occasional indulgence into an everyday tool. After two days testing the bike, I began to think of it as just that – a bike. The law of diminishing marginal utility really does apply here because I did start taking it for granted. And that's not what an Enfield should do. And that's why you see IT people riding it to work every day with their name tags and their backpacks advertising the faceless corporation they currently represent.

As a motorcycle, my criticisms are few and far between. It's easy to ride, it goes pretty well, it looks like an old Enfield which means the riding position is as good as any bike you'll ever ride, it feels like it's been hewn from stone and it easily justifies its price tag. I would recommend it readily to anyone who enjoys riding. But I'd never buy one myself because I quite enjoy the occasional bout of histrionics from my Enfields, just to be reminded every once in a while that I'm riding something special. Something almost human. Something that has its own personality which must be respected. An analogue machine in a digital age of social media and fast food. In essence, a motorcycle that is ever so perfectly flawed.

The verdict, then, on the RE Classic 500 is this - it's perfect. And that's precisely why I wouldn't have one.

The Intimidator
Mercedes-Benz GL63 AMG

Remember that scene from Godzilla when it attacks the city for the 35th time and people scarper everywhere? That happens a lot with the largest and most powerful SUV money can buy in India – the Mercedes-AMG GL63 AMG.

At 760Nm, the 5.5 litre biturbo AMG V8 makes 70 more torques than a V12-engined Lamborghini Aventador. We're talking mental muscle here. And we're convinced that the 7-speed AMG Speedshiift 2 gearbox is made out of granite and bits of Arnold Schwarzenegger.

But the weird part is that Mercedes-AMG has installed this monumental firepower under the hood of their GL-Class SUV. On paper, this should be as dangerous as giving an RPG Launcher to an enraged gorilla because high-performance and big SUVs go together as well as... umm... RPG Launchers and enraged gorillas.

You see, the GL is meant to ferry seven people about in great comfort and luggzury over just about any terrain. That's its purpose. Where the hell does a 552bhp twin-turbo AMG-built V8 fit into that? How does it contribute to this car's purpose?

For starters, you can feel its presence. Sitting that high up, in a car that big, with that engine burbling all the time is a bigger ego trip than Mrs Queen bowing for you. The holier-than-thou factor here is higher than I've ever experienced before. And here's the other weird part. As you sit in your Intimidator watching people scampering out of your way, you'll realise that this blunderbuss, this Leviathan, this tank-buster is no harder to drive than the diesel GL. The throttle has plenty of delay so even the most lead-footed driver (me) can potter around in city traffic and not worry about all that power being unleashed en route to a tree. The fact that it can shut off four out of eight cylinders when you don't need the power has a lot to do with this as well. This makes it all the more ego-trippy – being so convincingly in control of all that power.

We've already brought you a comprehensive off-roading report of the diesel GL, so we'll skip that bit in the interest of finding out what Affalterbach's largest monster is like on the road. It's fucking hilarious, is what it is.

When you step into the distinctly non-AMG cabin, you don't expect that this souped-up soccer-mom-mobile can crack 100kph in less than five seconds. But it can. It can also scare the shit clean out of your 'chute in the process. And it just keeps on piling on the power like a boxer bludgeoning his opponent to death. And don't worry about the corners. AMG's boffins have ensured that there are various traction management systems to keep you on the road. This is actually an SUV that you can punt into corners with a vague certainty that you'll come out alive on the other side. The four-wheel-drive system is setup to understeer in comfort mode which is good because most drivers don't know what to do when the tail kicks out.

The body roll has been managed very well considering it weighs as much as the country it was made in. The only time you'll feel this weight is under braking. It stops alright, but not before dislodging some of your vital organs from their mountings.

All in all, I can sort of see the point of this car. It's big (full-size SUV even by American standards), imposing, insanely powerful and very very loud. It is all of these things while being no more difficult to drive than a shopping cart. It's like Tony Soprano who can do a hundred-metre sprint as well.

I could almost conceive of having one because it is a million billion times better looking than the Porsche Cayenne. And more powerful.

The Cat's Pyjamas
Jaguar XF 2.0 Petrol Luxury

Before we get to the fantastic wonderfulness that is the Jaguar XF 2.0 Petrol, let me explain my slightly weird choice of title. 'The Cat's Pyjamas' is a very 60's expression that was used to describe music that was *way cool*. 'It's the cat's pyjamas, man! The bees knees!', they'd rabbit on in their semi coherent state with reference to a new song by Led Zeppelin. There's no modern-day equivalent of the expression.

There's no modern-day equivalent or substitute to this Jaguar either. There's nothing else that feels quite like it. But stop me here please, because this is a car review. So let's see what it's like. First things first; the XF has been on sale for seven years. That makes it older than any of its competitors. And in many ways, you can tell. Although I don't know what these ways are because after Tommy Jag's facelift in 2012, it still looks and feels as fresh as tomorrow morning's newspaper. And would you look at it. Aside from those 17in wheels, which give it a brilliant ride, it is bite-the-back-of-your-hand beautiful. Where ze Germans are all about muscular lines and sharp edges, the XF is curvy like Shakira. It just flows from end to end and across. It's got real beauty – the kind that survives the test of time and ever-changing preferences.

Not everybody knows how to use wood tastefully in their interiors (see Audi and Toyota for details). Jaguar does. The XF's interior has the correct kind and the perfect amount used in the most tasteful way. This is the kind of interior that lends its own character and feel to a car – like Jimmy Page's guitaring did to Led Zeppelin. It's got AC vents that reveal themselves when you turn the car on and a gear selector that rises from the centre console. It's a nice bit of drama that lifts the experience even higher. The steering boss is Jaguar's signature growling cat which tells me one very important thing – the XF 2.0 Petrol, like all Jaguars, is a driver's car.

What's it like to drive? Well, it isn't the M5-worrying Supercharged 5.0, so it's not fiercely powerful. But it's not as dull and dreary as an Audi A6 either. It's superbly progressive. It flows from overtake to overtake with phenomenal finesse. The engine puts out 240bhp and 340Nm of muscle. Jaguar claim 7.9 seconds to 100kph but that only tells half the story because like many luxury cars these days, it comes with ZF's 8-speed automotive gem. What this does to the tiny 2 litre four-pot is keep the acceleration smooth, progressive and relentless all the way to 200kph.

But this Jag isn't just about the power, it's about the sensation of driving. That's where the XF leaves everything behind. Not even BMW's phenomenal 5 Series feels this good. It just feels like there's less interference between you, the driver, and the car. Jaguar made the XF to drive and the result is something that will make you grin like an idiot every time you go around a corner. It feels so DAMN good, it could almost be sexual. And the ride is perfectly judged. Nothing gets through. How in the name of all that's criminally insane have they found a balance of ride, handling and feedback where they're all beyond belief? Honestly, there's no downside.

But yes, we finally come back to one point that you won't overlook – its age. What with BMW, Mercedes and Audi flogging Bradley Coopers and Ryan Reynoldses, it's hard to consider something that's as old as the Jag. But look at it this way, in automotive terms, the XF is George

Clooney – getting on a bit, but your wife still fancies him, doesn't she? If that's not enough, imagine turning to her one Saturday evening when you have a posh party to attend and saying, "Darling, shall we take the Jag?"

Pick Me Up
Isuzu D-Max

I don't have a commercial vehicle licence, which meant that I couldn't drive the D-Max pick-up truck (which can only be registered as a commercial vehicle) on public roads. Luckily, the good folks at Isuzu came up with a cunning plan. The booked the Wabco proving grounds test track for Honk. If that wasn't enough, they lined up all three variants of the D-Max for our trucking pleasure.

Having never tested a commercial vehicle before, I sat back and thought about what you might want to know about a pick-up truck. Since a standard road test was ruled out, I thought I'd load it and drive around in an erratic manner. That didn't work because I couldn't find anything to load it with. So what follows is a CV road test Honk style.

The first one is a bog-standard single cab. This has two seats, power steering and a massive flat bed at the back. Then there's Space-cab. This is just like the single cab, except the cab itself is a little larger with storage behind the seats and the loading bay is smaller. Both of these pick-ups look distinctly like commercial vehicles and neither has air conditioning.

Then the D-Max really gets cracking with the Space-cab Arched Deck. This doesn't look like a CV at all. It looks like one of those posh American pick-ups. This D-Max, minus fog lamps, shares its face with the MU-7 we brought you earlier. That in turn appears to be a straight lift from a Cadillac Escalade. On the D-Max though, it looks really good. Much better than the Tata Xenon. And this variant also has air conditioning and powered windows.

All of the D-Maxes have the same 2.5 litre four-cylinder turbo diesel with a five-speed manual gearbox. Hold on to something because this engine makes 134bhp and 294Nm of torque. The result is a bargain basement pick-up that tops out at 175kph (tested) and never feels out of breath. Come to think of it, is this the most powerful sub eight lakh *vehicle* on sale in India? Do write in and tell us.

The light steering make manoeuvring a breeze and at it feels very sure footed at high speeds. Isuzu claims and ARAI kpl figure of 13. Figure 11 in the real world. That is still a range of 836km on a 76-litre tank. Not bad at all.

As far as I can tell, there are only two drawbacks. The first is that they all have leaf-spring suspension at the back. They feel like really good leaf-springs, but still. The second is that all variants are classified as commercial vehicles. This means you can't drive one on public roads unless you have the right licence. I'm told Isuzu is in talks with the authorities to be able to sell the D-Max as a passenger car. I really hope that works out because for less than eight lakhs (the most expensive variant), what you get is a Japanese pick-up that is meticulously engineered, thoroughly well put together, honest, hard-working, powerful, efficient, decent looking, economical and brilliantly priced. The D-Max gets a resounding 9/10 and a big hand. Well done, Isuzu.

Christmas Comes Early
Mercedes-Benz B180 CDI Edition 1

We really like Mercs here at Honk. They're great luxury cars with just the right amount of tasteful snobbishness. But the one that never really floated our boat was the B Class. When we tested it last year (I remember wrapping the test up in two hours), we found that it was trying to be too many things and ended up being none of them. It felt, not surprisingly, like a large wonderfully-made hatchback that just happened to be a Mercedes-Benz.

Here we are about a year later, and Mercedes has rolled out the Edition 1 version which should be the solution my problem with the B Class – not enough luxury. Mercedes-Benz has always called it a luxury tourer, which is quite a claim for a car that is essentially a family hatchback. Let's start with the luxury bit.

As you'd expect, the quality is there. All your physical interactions with the car from the key to the buttons on the centre console feel very Mercedes-ish, ie, of great quality. The seats, as we found, along with being electrically adjustable, were also very good for many hours of continuous driving. But here comes the kicker – reversing camera, panoramic sunroof, rear seat arm rest, rear seat entertainment with two screens that will take your entertainment in pretty much any form it comes. Individually these make things a bit better. But put them all together and you have a package that feels a few notches more expensive than it actually is. It feels like a proper luxury car.

If you can ignore the slightly tacky Edition 1 decals along the sides (discreet badging would've been much better), you'll find that it has really nice gloss black rear-view mirrors that give some much-needed visual sportiness. Merc has thrown in different wheels 16 inch as well.

So that's the luxury taken care of. Let's get to the tourer part. The B Class never pretended to have sporting intensions. That was for the A Class. The B Class was supposed to be quiet, comfortable and smooth. And it does quite well on at least two out of three of those things. Merc has given it revised suspension which has been tweaked and raised slightly to better cope with Indian roads. The B Class was always quiet and the suspension tweak has made no perceptible difference to that. And it's comfortable in a firm and controlled sort of way. What it's not is particularly smooth. Bumps make their way into this nearly 30 lakh luxury car a lot more than they should.

It's an absolute doddle to drive anywhere, especially in the city. The engine hums along quietly as the gearbox goes about its business without so much as a cough. At this end of the luxury car market, Mercedes is aware that all of its customers aren't going to be Lewis Hamilton. So they've given it lazy throttle response, brakes that feel very progressive and a forgiving steering setup.

The engine is the usual 2.14 litre four-cylinder diesel that does duty in everything from the A Class to the ML Class. In 180 CDI tune it produces about 110bhp and 250Nm of torque. Don't let the figures fool you, though. The B180 CDI is fairly brisk in the real world. Get the 7-speed auto box into top gear and it will do 150kph all day while returning over 20kpl. The best part is that you wouldn't realise that unless you looked at the speedo. That makes it a good tourer.

The bottom line on the B Class is a pat on the back for Mercedes. All manufacturers make big claims in their marketing bumph, but nine out of ten of them are utterly rubbish. This isn't. The B Class B180 CDI Edition has finally become able to cash the cheques that its 'Luxury Tourer' tag are writing.

Das Audi
Audi A7 3.0 TDI

If we're honest, Honk has given quite a bit of stick to Audi. Some of their cars like the Q5 and the RS 5 are spectacular. But the A6 is about as interesting as the people that bought it, the Q3 is a Skoda Yeti in drag and the S6 damn near killed me with its diabolically dead steering. I'm only going to go out on a limb and say that Audi couldn't have been too pleased with this.

In what was probably their 'allow us to retort' moment, they sent round the A7 to show yours truly what's what. And I'm going to come straight out and say this; humble pie eaten. Lesson learned. The A7 is the best Audi there is. How have they managed to sway me so definitively you ask? Read on.

To begin with, just look at it. There is no angle from where it won't make you sit up and beg. The low roofline, the stretched back headlamps, the massive grille, the hatchback… erm… fastback tail (Audi calls it Sportback); they all come together to create the kind of visual drama that is the essence of what every Audi should be.

The drama extends to the inside as well. Like the Mercedes CLS, it has four doors and they all have pillarless windows like a coupe. Unlike the CLS, when you get in and turn on the ignition the Bang & Olufsen tweeters rise from the top of the dash, the steering wheel drops down into your lap, the mirrors fold outwards and the screen folds out and flips upwards. We've seen each of these things separately of course but together, they're S-Class cool. Make no mistake; you could impress Angelina Jolie with all this. Once the robotic Cirque de Soleil has done its thing, you'll find that the cabin is distinctly Audi – festooned with more buttons than a Blackberry phone. The thing is, all those buttons become intuitive in about 15 minutes and you never feel like you're trapped in Bill Gates' brain. The front seats are fairly comfortable until you discover that they can be heated and cooled. Then they're very comfortable. Then you discover that you can have six different kinds of massage while they cool you down on a hot day and you're in heaven.

The ride is really good for the most part, but it does tend to crash over sharp bumps. You can barely feel them, but the harshness does filter through more than you'd like. But, like most new expensive cars, the faster you go, the better the electronic air suspension gets.

Like most Audis, the A7 isn't really a proper driver's car. And that's perfectly fine because what it lacks in driving dynamics, it makes up for in just about everything else.

The engine, for example is Audi's 3.0 V6 TDI. That means 240bhp and 500Nm of double cream. I love the torque spread. It makes the delivery nice and progressive. It's also got what is probably the best gearbox on the planet – the 7-speed dual-clutch automatic that they call S-Tronic.

The result is 0-100kph in a claimed 6.3 seconds and a limited top speed of 250kph. But in reality, it means progressive, relentless power, complete stability courtesy of Quattro and biblical long-distance abilities in supreme comfort. Do you see why the below-par dynamics can be forgiven? Because it does everything else brilliantly. And unlike the A6 or the Q3, the A7 communicates the best of Audi's strengths to its customers. It costs just shy of 90 lakhs ex-showroom and for that you get a really unique car that costs as much to run as a Suzuki Swift. Is it the best car that Audi make? No. That'll be the RS 5. But it is the best Audi that Audi make.

Return of the Nutters!
Polaris Trackday – Two Years Later

Regular readers of Honk will be familiar with our penchant for off-roaders and off-roading. It's our most favourite thing in the whole word. Man and machine against the elements. Being Christopher Columbus with a V6. The satisfaction of actually having 'conquered' terrain that you previously thought was unconquerable is as big a rush as the aforementioned Mr Columbus must have felt when he… erm… landed in the wrong place.

But even something as stupendous as the Range Rover is fundamentally designed to be a car first and then an off-roader. This is possibly the best road-legal off-roader that money can buy, but something with air-conditioning and a glorified home-cinema with more screens than I have in my house is inherently compromised.

The only solution for hardcore off-roading enthusiasts is a buggy or a quad-bike of some sort. Enter Polaris with their range of off-roaders so capable, that none of them are road legal. We've told you all about their quads. But in that test, we were limited to a small track to learn them and a big open construction site for cocking-about.

For the RZR (pronounced: Razor) 800 buggy, we wanted to do something special so we went to this place called Dirt Mania just outside Bangalore. They had a track which was jolly nice. But they also had wilderness all around which meant one thing – trailblazing.

On really craggy uphill paths I found myself crawling to begin with; inching the two-seater left-hand-drive buggy like I would in a big SUV. This wasn't working.

"There's a reason it has 18 inches of suspension travel!" shouted Raj Kumar, Owner of Dirt Mania, "Go faster!"'

I started building up speed. He was right. The body stays flat and the suspension takes all the beating. This was an astonishing revelation for me because I've driven the best SUVs in the world and none of them came close to this little 800cc fourteen-lakh lunatic. It can do everything a Jeep Wrangler can at 10 times the speed.

Yes, fourteen lakhs does seem a bit excessive for what is essentially a toy. And yes, you don't even get doors or a windscreen for that. There isn't power steering either. But for someone who loves off-roading as much as we do, all these omissions mean that there's a lot less to go wrong or damage. It also means that there's a lot less weight.

As a device, it is as single-purposed as a gun. Not only is it illegal to use on public roads, it is impossible as well because you'd end up wearing out the tyres in no time. But if you lived in wilderness (I think I might soon), this would be all the vehicle you'd ever need.

I made a claim with the Range Rover that I'd like to retract because this, the Polaris RZR 800 is the best off-roader sold in India.

The Flying Man vs. The Flying Elephant
Range Rover Sport 3.0 TDV6 HSE

"It takes 35 minutes by road to the landing site. By glider, it's 20 minutes." said Paragliding National Champion Arvind Paul as he pointed to the downhill semi-road of twenty murderous kilometres. *Bugger.* The deal was the he jumped off a cliff and I raced him along the road in a Range Rover Sport to the same finish line – his landing site. Last one down buys lunch.

This was adrenaline like I had never felt before. Partly because I wanted to win, but mostly because if we fell off, we'd die of old age before we hit the ground. Plus, the road was inches wider than the car. The job was simple – go like hell, and try to bring the car back in one piece. The road from Billing to Bid (Himachal Pradesh), broken as it is, has no straights. It has millions of blind bends. I had to average 60kph just to stand a chance.

"Get Ready. Go!" said Sonu Kumar, himself a veteran paraglider pilot as soon as he jumped into the passenger's seat. He'd be my navigator.

Gearbox in manual, full throttle. *Remember to stay alive.* The brilliant four-wheel-drive system hurled the 2.1 tonne monster forwards with all four wheels spinning into the first corner. They came up at the rate of one every second or two. It was immediately apparent that five out of eight gears in this auto 'box were redundant. And then it hit me. While this was hard work, the Range Rover Sport felt like a hot hatch. The point-and-squirtability of this huge luxury off-roader is nothing short of breath-taking. You fling it hard into corners even on gravel and provided you're on either the throttle or the brakes, the electronics will keep you in check. They feel like they're there to make you faster, not slow you down. But more than the computers, it's the chassis and suspension that impress.

You see, the old Range Rover Sport wasn't a Range Rover at all. It was an LR Discovery in a Range Rover dress. This new one shares its chassis and running gear with the new Range Rover. And like its big brother, it's half a tonne lighter than its predecessor. To put that into perspective, imagine taking four Honda Activas out of the boot. The outcome is as dramatic as the love child of Stephen Fry and Usain Bolt – fierce competence, intellect and composure meet genuine athletic ability.

Being sporty isn't just the ability to go quickly around corners. Real sportiness is the sensation of speed, excitement and control. The Elephant has every other SUV in the world licked on this count.

"Take right! Take Right!"

Thank you, Sonu, for interrupting my reverie. We'd done seventeen kilometres. The hard work was done. The remaining three kilometres past a monastery and through the Bid village tested my patience. Not running the locals down had to take precedence over the final push to the finish.

We were in the valley now, and for the first time since the flag dropped, we had clear skies. "There he is!" screamed Sonu as he pointed to Arvind's glider. I stole a quick glance and he was descending fast. "Landing site on your left! Go Go Go!" I jumped the Sport over the two feet drop to the landing site because I'd lost sight of the glider. *Where the hell was he?*

As I stopped and jumped out, I could see Sonu hooting and hollering at a glider. Arvind landed a few seconds later. The car had won. But only just.

"How the hell did you come down so fast?" asked an exhausted Arvind.

"It was the car. I couldn't have done 20km in 20 minutes on a road like that in anything else," I said trying to dissipate the adrenaline. "Any other car would have killed us on that run. The Elephant brought us down in one piece."

On the drive back to Delhi I had time to reflect on the RRS as it transformed completely into a super-cruiser. It's other-worldly as piece of engineering and design, fabulous to drive, beautiful to behold, supremely comfortable and best of all, prices start at just over a crore (Ex-Maharashtra).

If you still choose to buy a Porsche Cayenne in spite of this, I never want you round my house for dinner.

Unfinished Sympathy
Ford Fiesta 1.5 TDCI

Yes, the title's a bit of a giveaway. But with this (sort of) new Fiesta, you won't believe how close Ford has come to the perfect city car. But first let's have a bit of a history lesson.

Remember the Ford Icon? That was a facelifted Mk IV Fiesta badged Ikon for India. The Figo? That's based on a Mk V Fiesta. The EcoSport? That's the current Mk VI Fiesta on stilts. And then there's the Fiesta Classic which is essentially the Mk V Fiesta still being made and sold to taxi operators.

We have four iterations of two generations of the same car currently on sale and the one that sells the least is the flagship. Funny, eh? It is when you consider that the Fiesta is selling brilliantly across other markets.

The Fiesta that's doing brilliantly elsewhere in the world is the hatchback. As a piece of design, it is completely inspired. If you take away the MINI and Fiat 500, it is probably the best-looking hatch in the world. Secondly, Ford has shut us all up with the 1.0 litre EcoBoost engine. To get that much power, economy and drivability from an engine whose block will fit on an A4 sized piece of paper is, and I'll take no argument on this, historic. If you fondly imagine that the combination of the two; super swish hatchback body and that Hail-Mary EcoBoost engine would make the ultimate city car, then I'm with you. It gets better because the Fiesta's also the best driver's car in its class. Anywhere.

The one we'll get in India, in many ways is just as good. The front-end is identical to the hatchback which means it looks stunning. And since the chassis is the same as well, the ride and handling are superb; class leading by a light year.

The interior is nice and funky (straight lift from the EcoSport), with many buttons that do many things. Ford even went to the extent of bringing Microsoft into the mix to create something called SYNC which is a Bluetooth-enabled interface for your phone. They went to great lengths to describe how the whole system is voice activated. Brilliant. Now if you'd please send someone with my challan to retrieve my licence from court since it is now illegal to use your phone even with Bluetooth on.

Now the bad news. Like every hatchback that's been turned into a saloon, the addition of the third box ruins the looks. The Fiesta is particularly hurt by this because its hatchback sibling is so achingly beautiful.

And I'd like to meet the person who decided that this particular 1.5 diesel engine must be fitted to this car, because I think he is either an impostor or he secretly works for Hyundai. It is so out of character with the rest of the car that Justin Bieber on stage with Metallica would seem a more cohesive experience.

Let me explain the problem. It is either lazy or harsh, but more importantly, you can hear it all the time. There is no point at which it is completely silent. This is the first car I've come across with this problem. Second, Ford claim that it has 90ps of power, which should be adequate. But it certainly doesn't feel like it. The just never is enough power for things you'd reasonably need. 25kph, second gear, accelerator welded to the floor and nothing, nothing, nothing, groan. Ford's argument is that it's very economical, and it bloody well better be because it's no good it being anything else.

The verdict on this Fiesta is difficult, because I adore it as much as I despise certain bits of it. All I'm going to say for now is this; if Ford does a Fiesta 1.0 EcoBoost hatchback in India, I'll be the first to buy one.

You're Not Ready
Jaguar F-Type V8 S Convertible

I can go on and on about the looks for about fourteen weeks and I still won't be able to aptly describe just what a pleasurable assault it is on the senses. I have never seen an object this beautiful with my own two eyes. And I'm including Astons, Lamborghinis and I daresay; the E-Type. In a day's driving, no other car in my hands has attracted so much attention before. And my test car was a simple white. It's not mad and shouty like most supercars. It's beautiful in the true sense of the word. It has tremendous sex appeal, but it's not in the least bit excessive or vulgar. This is a masterpiece of styling.

My tagline applies to the interior as well. In most super-sportscars, you'd expect the interior to be full of he-man space-thruster buttons. You'd expect it to be more complicated than the Starship Enterprise. You may even expect no equipment at all and on all counts, the F-Type's is none of those things. It's all black, simple, elegant and very Jaguar.

I was expecting it to intimidate me with its mental V8, but it didn't. At least not to begin with. To get this thing going is as easy as any other luxury car. You unlock, jump in, press the start button, put it in D and you're off. In about 23 seconds you'll realise that it's as docile as the family Golden Retriever. The throttle's progressive, the steering's easy and the visibility all round brilliant. This is an easy car to potter around town in. Even the largest of Mumbai speed breakers and the deepest of her potholes didn't cause any part of the F-Type's body to come in contact with them. How in heaven have they managed that I wonder. Something that's this low and swoopy should cause cheeks to be clenched permanently throughout the duration of the drive. But no. Not even slightly. Properly amazing, that.

In a small break in the rain, I dared to put the top down. Oh man. This perfectly completed the F-Type experience, I thought as the engine set about showing me its mid-rev vocal range – a deep, if slighted subdued bellow. I tried this out on the open road for half an hour and a few things popped into mind. One – the ride takes some getting used to. It's controlled, but quite firm. Two - even in excess of 150kph, there's hardly any buffeting that you normally get in cabrios. The design of the windscreen helps immensely in keeping your hairstyle in order. This makes it an excellent GT car. Three – this is motoring nirvana.

Flooring the throttle changes everything. It turns this cool cat into a raging… erm… Jaguar. The engine note changes completely. It sounds violent. Visceral. And seriously pissed off. It's not just noise either. It's real 488 cat power. The 8-speeder bangs in each gear like a blacksmith hammers out a sword. There's a real and clear intent to make the whole experience more and more euphoric the harder you push by attacking your senses (pleasurably). I've never felt that in any car before. Take your foot off the throttle and a makes angry cracking and popping noises on the overrun.

It has a tendency to hang its tail out in the corners which is hugely enjoyable if you know what you're doing. You can hold a drift in this thing till the tyres burst because it's just balanced so bloody well. Ham-fisted drivers will need to be a little careful to begin with though.

I love my job on days like these because what we have here, ladies and gentlemen, is a petrolhead's wet-dream. An Ian Callum masterpiece.

A more-than-worthy successor to the E-Type. An everyday super-sportscar that makes every drive an occasion. And finally; something to make that damn holier-than-thou Porsche 911 shut the hell up.

This is my new favourite car.

Fading Rhino
Audi Q7 4.2 TDI

Eight years is a long time. Most marriages don't last that long. World wars have been won and lost in less. In car terms, eight years is an ice age. Especially these days since preferences are so fleeting and buyers' minds so fickle.

That Audi has thought to keep the Q7 on sale for that long is a moot point for the pub. It stands to reason that no car, no matter how unique and special it was, could have survived this long.

When the Q7 launched in India, it was a massive hit. It was the obvious choice for the rich and infamous. Big, bombastic and four-ringed, it was the only proper luxury SUV on the market. It had a great run for many years until Land Rover, Mercedes-Benz and BMW joined the party. And even then, the Q7 held its own. The trouble with this scenario is diminishing exclusivity. Rich people always want to be different. Particularly with their cars. And we've arrived at a point now where the Range Rover is the best Uber SUV and the Mercedes GL and BMW X5 fill in the rest. The Q7 has become irrelevant. Or has it? Let's find out.

It's still big. No, wait. It's still bloody huge. Imagine two Adnan Samis (circa 1998) and you know what I mean. The looks, whether good or grizzly, are debatable. What isn't debatable is its presence. Or rather it is because the Q7 is just too familiar a sight on city streets. Its head-turning capabilities have left the building.

Inside, the age is beginning to show as well. There's a slot for the key leftover from the old car. This is odd because it has keyless entry and keyless go. The DriveSelect only gives you suspension options. It has separate buttons to start and stop. And the selection for Sport mode on the gearbox is below Drive, not beside it. This meant that I found myself wondering a few times if I hadn't inadvertently awakened the God of war while parking and doing 3-point turns.

On the upside, the quality is legendary Audi. Everything feels solid and extremely well put together. It has a full-length glass roof, a high-quality stereo from Bose and the MMI has many things to fiddle with in traffic jams.

It is a little difficult to drive in the city, especially if you've driven the similarly-sized Merc GL. It feels like a land-yacht. We've said time and time again that all luxury cars and even sportscars are easy to drive in cities. And the Q7 is in some ways. Except in terms of manoeuvrability. You can feel the distinct lack of enthusiasm for agility. Let me put it this way; if you see a gap, don't bother.

But it does have a sweet spot. Like our beloved Q5, it has the inherent ability to cruise exceptionally well over bad roads. And good ones for that matter. Unlike the Q5, it has a 4.2L V8 Diesel. The V8 diesel Range Rover has 700Nm of torque. An AMG Mercedes GL with a biturbo petrol V8 makes 760Nm. This has the same. The result of this is cruising as effortless as I've ever experienced. The power is relentless through all eight gears. It never peaks. It's just one long constant surge. I loved it. As engines go, this one is brilliant when you want to simply haul arse long distance. And long distance it goes because it has 100L fuel tank and a highway kpl figure of 13kpl. Theoretically, that 1300km on a tank. Practically, it's about a 1000. But 1000km is almost Mumbai to Bangalore.

In the face of its modern competition, the Q7 4.2 V8 TDI is a difficult car to consider, especially since the all-new Q7 is due next year. But I like it for its long-distance abilities on real Indian roads. If you have a family of seven - all of whom are afraid of flying – that need to be carted long distances regularly, then the Q7 is the car for you.

Are You Worthy?
Jaguar XJL Portfolio Diesel

JLR's being difficult because every single car of theirs is brilliant. I'm having the devil's own time criticizing them. This new made-in-India XJ is the toughest one to pick apart. But that won't stop me trying.

Tiny issues first. The brakes take a few minutes to warm up. They make a jarring sound at low speeds until they do. The seats aren't as plush as the S-Class's. And the steering wheel has wood on it which makes it a tad slippery.

But there's a bigger, more alarming concern with the XJ – its image. To understand this, we need to look at what it means in today's context. The Mercedes S-Class is the last word in fidelity - doubtless, the best car in the world. BMW's 7-Series is built and engineered ruthlessly and without compromise so that as you drive along, you can marvel the great job their engineers have done. Audi's A8 is engineered just as beautifully. Their buyers are mostly Ivy league and IIT types who are CEOs or MDs of some particularly hefty conglomerate. In other words, corporate fat cats.

The XJ, on the other hand, is meant for a different kind of cat. The cool ones, if I may. XJ owners are the kind of people who you'd have around to your house for dinner because they're interesting. When I say interesting, I don't mean took-a-break-from-mergers-and-acquisitions-and-went-fishing interesting, I mean the likes of Stephen Fry, George

Clooney and Amitabh Bachchan. These are the kind of owners the XJ commands. You've got to ask yourself (even if you can afford one) if you really deserve it.

It is, in my opinion, the most beautiful four-door-saloon in the world. Strange, because the C-pillar extends so far back that, theoretically, it ruins the proportions. But it creates a shape that is unusual, visually evocative and very pleasing to the eye.

The interior has as much leather and brushed aluminium as any of its German counterparts but it just feels better, somehow. There's a uniquely British sense of understatement and opulence to this cabin. Don't think it's high on image to compensate for a lack of engineering depth. It's built just as well the Germans and has all the toys and tech that they do.

But there's one crucial differentiator - the way it feels. The others (7-Series to a lesser extent) feel big and cumbersome, especially around corners. The XJ has a balance, a poise, a majesty that really is very uncharacteristic of its size. I found this in just about every environment I threw it into. You get the feeling that it considers speed bumps and potholes to be almost trivial. It treats them like you or I would a treat the average SMS joke; one glance and delete.

On the open road you can choose to drive it however you like. If you want to just cruise, turn the seat-massager on, turn up the spectacular 20 speaker Meridian stereo and waft at 120kph as it deprives you of the world's existence. Or turn the gearbox knob to S, push the Sport button on the dash and be amazed at what this Jag can do. The 3.0 turbodiesel V6 thrums as it delivers 270bhp and a monumental 600Nm of torque. It is a relentless, smooth and controlled surge through all 8 gears in the auto box. This is the most effortless and controlled way of doing 250kph all day long. And more pleasurable than in anything that calls itself a rival.

The conclusion is inescapable. The BMW and the Audi will only ever compete with each other in the S-Class's shadow. The S-Class will always own the plutocrat market because it will always be the default choice. The Jag, on the other hand, will continue to do what it does best; be the only choice for people who think that a Rolls Royce is a bit excessive and the Germans haven't quite got the hang of true luxury yet. The kind of people that the world needs more of. If only so there'll be more Jaguars in it.

Late for a Reason
Mercedes-Benz GLA200 CDI

In India, small SUVs will sell like bloody hell if they have an upmarket badge. Unlike luxury hatchbacks (MINI, A Class, 1-Series) which haven't sold as well as their makers hoped, Audi's shambolic Q3 (the slowest, least powerful version was badged 'S') and BMW's hideous X1 sold in inexplicably huge numbers. They both had a point, though. And entry point into their respective brands for those afraid of Indian roads.

What surprises me is how long Mercedes took to join this party. It stands to reason then, that they've had plenty of time to study the competition and therefore shouldn't get this wrong.

What they've cooked up for this particularly competitive potluck is called the GLA and it is striking. It's got all the small SUV bases covered on looks front. It's imposing, it got big wheels and fat tyres, some plastic body protection and most importantly, it's not cute. There's plenty of detailing in the rather intricate headlamps and the rest of the body to warrant second looks as well. I'd even go so far as to call it handsome.

There are two trim levels you can choose from for the interior. The Style trim (diesel only) has a clean, all-black interior. This is my kind of cabin because I like simplicity. The one you'll buy, however, is the Sport trim with has both petrol and diesel to choose from. This cabin has a lot more beige and gives the distinct impression of being much more luxurious. This means that, for a change, you can choose how your cabin feels – simple and sporty or lap of luxury. So far so good.

The next big concern with all SUV buyers is 4x4. If an SUV doesn't have it, then it's not an SUV, right? So, when was the last time you went off-roading? Yes, you with the Range Rover. And let's face it; even if you go up to your farmhouse or coffee estate every once in a while, the GLA's got your back. A 4x2 SUV is not a good idea for me because I do a lot of off-roading for your reading displeasure. But I doubt if you'd care.

It never feels particularly sporty to drive, does the GLA, so I'd stick with the smooth diesel which makes 134bhp and 300Nm of torque. The result of this is surprising. It feels like any other Merc in the city; silent and never flustered. But out on a twisting mountain road, it keeps strong pace with its power delivery and the smooth shifts from the 7-speed double-clutch gearbox. The 'box itself comes with 3 settings Eco, Sport and Manual. Eco works best in the city. It shifts seamlessly, if a teensy bit late. Sport works well when you want some performance. Even though it has paddles, I wouldn't bother with Manual because you can always feel the lag between the instruction and result. It's probably the only thing I don't like about what is otherwise an amazing car.

Prices (ex-Delhi) start at 32.75 for the GLA200 CDI Style diesel. The Sports come in at 36 for the GLA200 petrol and 90k more for the diesel. Whichever way you look at, that's spanking good value. If you're not convinced, you need to speak to the 600 people who booked the car in 18 days even before it was launched.

He-Man's Vegetarian Cousin
Harley Davidson Street 750

All modern Harley Davidsons are big, heavy, loud, proud, intimidating holier-than-thou machines that make you feel like The Governor of California, even if you have job in app development. They exaggerate your manhood considerably and even put some serious butch in the women that ride them.

Except the Street 750. It is and does none of those things. It appears to be the vegetarian option in a restaurant that otherwise serves only bloody, lightly-killed steak. This is not good.

It's cheap, of course. If it isn't already, at 4.10 Lakh (Ex-showroom Delhi), it will be the largest selling Harley Davidson in India. Let's not forget that we're a people desperate to move up the social ladder. We must be. There'd be no other way to explain the success of the Audi Q3.

Every teen, college-goer and young professional is probably salivating to the point of flooding the room at the idea that owning a Harley Davidson is now so much more realistic; so achievable. This means that HD sells a ton of bikes and its new customers will finally get dates. You will probably see as many of these on our roads in two years' time as you do KTM Dukes right now.

In the near future, Harley Davidson will be laughing all the way to the bank. But this bike, I personally believe, will lead to the untimely demise of what Harley Davidson means because there will come a point when the words Harley and Davidson will cease to stand for everything in the first paragraph of this story and mean the Street 750.

People on Harleys will be found commuting to work in their bad formal clothes with Cisco or HP or Dell or some such faceless corporation on their backpacks for the world to see. We've seen this epidemic affect Royal Enfield.

What makes things even worse is that the bike, as a bike, is pretty good. The riding position is great for people of average height, the controls are all standard, the 222kg kerb weight is very well centred and low down as well. The only thing I found a little discomfort with was the clutch. My left hand went pretty sore after a few hours of riding because of how heavy it was.

Let's look beyond the obvious and try to work out how HD's been able to price this so low. The tyres are from MRF. Yep. You read correctly. MRF rubber on a Harley. And they're really average. There's adequate grip in the dry on open roads, but it never really gave me the confidence to find its limits. Mind you, wringing its neck is something that takes a lot of consideration on a 750cc bike with no fuel gauge. And no range/distance to empty either. All you get is a low fuel warning light which comes on for a moment and then goes off again. It does this every few minutes. If you aren't looking at the display, it's very easy to miss during the day. There's no rev counter either, so it takes a while to work out how hard you're actually riding the thing.

It does have one or two Harley genes though - it eats up highway like a fat man eats chips. It's most comfortable cruising at 110kph in sixth gear. Its smallness and lightness also mean that it handles really well. Quick overtakes on highways and even in the city are a breeze. This has a lot to with the engine which is liquid cooled and very smooth. They call it the Revolution X and it's a scaled-down 750cc version of the one in the

Night Rod Special that you read about here. There's hardly any noise but it has endless reserves of torque at any revs.

But it still doesn't feel like a proper Harley, ie, it doesn't feel special like all other Harleys do. As we speak, the organisation is readying their electric bike. And the Street 500 is already on sale elsewhere. How long d'you think before that makes it to India? Oh dear.

What Price Exclusivity?
Triumph Speed Triple 1050

Earlier this year, Ashish and I were at India Bike Week and we couldn't help but wondering that India is full of really rich biking nuts. The regular hardcores were present on Japanese superbikes and there were endless <10 lakh Harleys. That's acceptable. But we also spotted Ducati Panigales and BMW S1000RRs and Harley CVOs. These cost anything up to 45 lakhs. Stands to reason, doesn't it? The more expensive the bike, the more exclusive it will be. Not anymore.

Have you seen the second Transformers film? Do you remember that annoying little Decepticon that Megan Fox's character carried around in a box? The Triumph Speed Triple has the same face. The rest of it though, is brilliant.

This is a tall bike. I have fairly long and dangly legs, and I took a while to climb aboard comfortably. But the trade-off is once you're on, the tall seat, upright bars and the resultant supermoto riding position make it really comfortable for whatever kind of riding you've got in mind.

Don't let its easy riding position fool you though, because the Speed Triple is a full-fat litre-class mental. And that's easily explained by the huge 1050cc inline 3-cylinder making 133bhp at 9400 revs and a whole 111Nm of torque at 7750 revs. What these numbers don't completely convey is the smooth and creamy spread of power that makes riding this Triumph ever so manageable. This is probably the only big performance bike I've ridden that feels so progressive and forgiving.

It responds to the way you're treating it at the time. If you're doing big bursts of throttle in traffic to squeeze into gaps, then that's exactly what it does. If you pin the throttle open on an empty stretch, the front wheel immediately lifts to salute the horizon. When it comes down, it pulls with a maniacal addictiveness that, so far, has been the preserve of superbikes. And when you're done making a racket and you just want to get home, it turns into a quiet city bike.

To be honest, I've been struggling to describe the way this bike rides. Until now. It feels like a thoroughbred that you've trained yourself. It feels like it knows every one of your commands and precisely how you'd like them executed and when. More than that, it feels like it knows you.

You obviously want to know things about the suspension, the chassis and the brakes. Well, they're all brilliant. Nothing to worry there. So are the super-sticky Metzeler tyres which feel sensational at the limit, especially under braking.

You get all this for about 10 lakh and 70 grand ex-Delhi, which makes it the cheapest litre-class bike in India. It's really funny because had this been a BMW, it wouldn't have been less than 20 lakhs. The people at Triumph India know this. And I'm sure they're secretly smug about their pricing. In many ways, then, this is like an Aston Martin. It's always going to be cheaper than anything from Ferrari and Lamborghini, but to the petrolhead, it's ever so slightly more desirable.

The Sweet Spot
Mercedes-Benz CLA 45 AMG

The modern-day four-door sports saloon like the M5 or E63 AMG has nearly 600bhp. F1 world championships have been won with a lot less than that. It's not like you're taught to use this power either. You just buy it, and find out for yourself what it feels like to drain your bladder and those of your passengers before you hit 100kph. In other words, absolute power may be properly exciting as it corrupts absolutely, but it is also bloody terrifying. It's not as if I don't like power or speed, but even I can admit when it's too much.

With the CLA 45 AMG, Mercedes seem to have found a balance which is as close to the edge of exploitability as I have ever known. I haven't done any checking but at 355bhp I'm fairly certain that this is the least powerful AMG car on sale today. It is worth mentioning that this much power has been screwed out of a 2 litre four-cylinder by some extraordinary engineering and a whacking great turbocharger. Since Mitsubishi makes the 400 and 440bhp EVOs only as special editions, this engine gets the dubious distinction of being the world's most powerful turbocharged four-cylinder in series production.

And it's got the 7-speed AMG SPEEDSHIFT which is good and 4Matic which is great. The result of this is 0-100kph in 4.6 seconds and that's completely irrelevant. More on that later.

First look at the thing. Styled with the four-door-coupe (still bonkers) idea to be a smaller version of the CLS, the standard CLA is quite the looker. With all the AMG visual paraphernalia, it looks even better. Hunkered down and menacing. Like the CLS, it has pillar-less doors and like the CLS it will get you lots of attention, especially in Red.

The interior is rather excellent with really comfortable sport seats, which are fully electric at the front, satnav, panoramic sunroof, AMG gear lever and plenty more besides. More than all the gadgets you get as standard, this feels like a Mercedes AMG interior; very high quality, no-compromise long feature list and genuine sporting luxury.

It's been a while since I've driven a high-performance four-cylinder so the exhaust note reminded me of the street-racing tuned cars I used to drive many many years ago. It was a nice bit of nostalgia. As with all AMGs, the CLA is genuinely benign. It's as well behaved as Prince Charles until you provoke it. It's here that it is completely different from anything else you can buy today.

With most high-powered cars, you're always wary of the huge reserves power so you tend to drive them more carefully than you would otherwise. The CLA 45 has just the right amount and you can use all of it for a lot of the time. This car's limits are at the edge of usable. On any normal Indian highway, you can put it in Sport mode, mash the accelerator pedal and you will not be scared of what happens next. It is a great deal of speed, yes. But it feels like it is the result of your bravely not a gigantic engine. Honestly, this is the most I've ever felt in control of a car on the wrong side of 250kph.

This is a very special car to me. It took me to a place in the motoring world I'd never been to before – just about enough power to be really fast but completely controllable. Not to mention the chassis, brakes, steering and electronics all have a role to play in what is the first of a new breed of performance cars. The price for the privilege is 69 lakhs (ex-showroom). If you have the money and the wherewithal but you buy a 'bigger' car, I'll be very disappointed.

Surprise Surprise
Audi A3 35 TDI

Keen followers of Honk (all three of you) will remember our love/hate relationship with Audi. We've given – with good reason – many of their cars a bit of a hard time because we thought they deserved it. Still, let's give the poor buggers a little respite because they've reinstated themselves into the top spot in luxury car stakes (without blatant discounts this time) with the all-new and all-brilliant A3.

Let's be honest, the A3 is a shoo-in for Honk's car of the year 2014. It's based on Volkswagen's MQB platform which has spawned the current Golf, the new Skoda Octavia and the new Audi TT and some cars you've never heard of. And this has to be one of the best platforms in the business.

The A3 we had on test is called the called the 35 Technology which costs 32.6 lakhs, which, in logical circles, is called 'bloody expensive'. More expensive, in fact, than some A4s and Q3s. That would be great, except that it's a size smaller than both of them.

But look beyond the price for a moment and you'll see why the A3 is Audi's masterstroke. In the flesh, in red particularly, it looks fantastic. It's nearly as good looking as the A Class and 10 billion times better than the gawping 1 Series BMW. Visually, everything about it works brilliantly. Things are much the same on the inside as well. It's all clean, simple and sexy. This is what all Audi interiors should feel like. The relatively tiny exterior does a good job of masking a rather large and roomy interior.

And in Technology (top-end) trim, Audi has packed the A3 with every conceivable feature they could. Satnav, huge sunroof, electric seats, the lot. This certainly feels like a proper luxury car.

The drivetrain is a direct carryover from the Octavia – 2.0 diesel with a 6-speed DSG auto box, conveniently badged S Tronic for Audi. If you think that 143bhp and 320Nm of torque doesn't sound like much then you ought to know that the A3 weighs about as much as your lunch. The result of this is the first Audi saloon I've ever driven that feels good to drive. And I mean really good. The gearbox feels more alive in the A3 somehow and keeps piling on the 320 torques gear after gear. The suspension is very well judged and there virtually no roll through corners even without Quattro. And corner it can because Audi's fitted great steering. It's impossibly light in the city, which is great. But then it progressively weighs up as you build speed. This is a bit much from the people who make the severely sanitized A6. They've actually made a car that is fundamentally enthusiastic and entertaining. Sure, Audis work better than anything else on the planet as just cars; devices to get you to work and take the kids to school and such. And the A3 is brilliant at this as well.

But, and this is an important one, I'm sure you've got one eye on the price. Realistically this is a 36-lakh car on-road. More if you live in Mumbai or Bangalore. But do keep in mind that prices start at 22.9 lakhs ex-showroom for the Attraction trim which has most bare necessities. The in-between Premium trim is the best option because you get all the stuff you'll actually use like electric seats and the big sunroof. This only costs about 26 lakhs ex-showroom.

Many people, myself included, saw the BMW X1 and Audi Q3 as just a status buy for people looking to make the cut into a luxury brand. But the A3 never strikes you as that car. It's a great car first that just happens to be an Audi. So buy it for whatever reasons you want. But only in red.

Your Everyday (Sports) Car
BMW Z4 35i sDrive

People who think that BMW is ever going to make a car that drives badly are probably in a meeting of the Flat Earth Society whilst hammered on copious amounts of granola bars, listening to evocative speeches about how the world would be a better place if we all adopted mice and forced our children to eat only vegetables.

Anyway. Some BMWs are a little less than perfect, but they still have that inherent BMW*iness*. Weirdly enough, even the X3 has it. It's just in their DNA somehow. If we've deduced that they make, on average, the best driving everyday cars, then you can well imagine what our expectations were of the sportiest non-M car till the i8 came along earlier this year. I am, of course, alluding to the Z4.

This is the first car I've ever heard of to be designed exclusively by a team of women. 'Pah!' I hear you say. 'Women and car design? That's like a man designing high heels'. After you've satisfactorily examined the work of Christian Louboutin and Jimmy Choo, take a good look at the Z4. Is it not a perfectly styled and perfectly proportioned sportscar? Do you still care what gender it was designed by? Didn't think so. Let's move on to the interior.

The seat is really low. I mean that in the literal sense and in relation to the height of the doors. This makes it feel even lower. Call me crazy but I sort of like that. It gave me that feeling being discreet, but in something really attractive. To call the interior typically BMW would be both true and false. True, because it is unmistakably BMW in its design and layout, and false because it feels like no other BMW. Still, there are no real disappointments in terms of lack of appointments.

During the week that I had it on test, there were times when I actually forgot that it was a convertible. I just treated like hard-top sportscar and it worked perfectly fine as one. Goes to show, I suppose, that if you have to have a cabrio, get one with a folding metal roof.

And on a beautiful day, take the top off, put your shades on and enjoy 50 million miles of blue sky, a beautiful engine note and a great driver's car. But let's face it, you know this just by looking at the ingredients. I mean, turbocharged 3-litre straight six putting out 306bhp and 400Nm of torque isn't exactly a shrinking violet. Throw in a 0-100kph time of 5.1 seconds and a limited top speed of 250kph and this is the real deal – a proper sportscar with BMW's dynamics and those looks.

I could end it here and you'd still be mighty impressed by this 70 lakh (Ex-Delhi) sportscar. But to do that would miss the point of this car. I'll make no bones about it. You can use this every single day. If you are SINK or DINK, this is all the car you'll ever need. Apart from the attention you get from people around you, it feels like a normal car in the city. It's easy to park, easy to drive, goes over bumps like a normal luxury saloon, and at about 8-9kpl if you're careful, easy to live with as well. It's not often we do buying advice here at Honk. But think long and hard if you *really* need a luxury saloon or SUV. Or would you rather something more… unique?

C Section
Mercedes-Benz C200

If an S Class was to be pulled out of Merc's womb about four weeks premature, this is what it would be; the brand new, next generation C Class.

You've seen the A4 reviewed here. It did very well. So did the BMW 3 Series. And with all due respect, they are now as relevant as last Monday's newspaper. Why? Because the new C Class has taken the game so far forward that until Jaguar turn up sometime next year with their XE, it will probably have the market all to itself.

The magic begins with the body. It looks as sporty as business suit. And that's precisely the idea. It's a luxury car and it unequivocally looks like one. While everyone else tries to add a hint of sportiness to their styling, Merc has simply played to their strengths. Sure, there are superbly detailed LEDs fore and aft, and the body looks more muscular. But all this hints at an inner strength, not sporting pretensions.

At the risk of sounding like an idiot, the inner is where its real strength lies. Wood, leather and brushed aluminium combine to create an interior that feels crafted and very tasteful. It is a beautiful place to be. If a salesman were to blindfold you, get you in the driver's seat, shut the door and say, 'this costs 70 lakhs, sir/madam', I can guarantee you that you will be convinced it's good value. But that's the thing. It doesn't cost 70. For the pleasure of one of the four best interiors (S Class included) that I've ever seen, it costs a measly 40 lakhs. It has a Burmester stereo like you get on the S Class and sounds like it's from another planet. It's got electric everything and a voice-activated system that actually works. Even the plastics feel like they were made to withstand a nuclear holocaust.

I was a little sceptical about the electric power steering, to begin with. It's a step towards making the whole thing more efficient, of course. But in reality, it feels like you can turn the wheel with just the power of suggestion. It's the lightest I've ever felt at low speeds. And spectacularly devoid of any sort of feedback. Over time, I realised that, as an everyday convenience, it's a boon. Even if you drive to work through a riot, you'll be able to politely and confidently slip through the petrol bombs.

Merc has almost managed to pull off the 'riding on a cloud' effect that the S Class is famous for. It really rides beautifully on any reasonable surface. We took it on some shocking rutted paths that tractors use and even there, the suspension held its own.

The launch car has the same 2.0L turbo petrol engine and 7-speed dual-clutch auto box as the GLA 200, you read about earlier. And that means 181bhp and 300Nm. And that also means smooth, creamy delivery and an engine that is as quiet as a graveyard. If you really want to hear it, mash your foot into the throttle and it will rev cleanly and smoothly until 6250rpm, shift up smoothly, and do that six more times until you find yourself at 230kph.

Despite the 225/50 R17 tyres, I never found it short on grip. Even while cornering at well over twice the speed limit, it felt planted, with just a hint of tyre squeal letting me know that the tail was at its limit. Fantastic high-speed manners, has the C Class. Even that deceased steering firms up and provides a decent amount of feedback. This is to be expected of course, because the new C Class weighs 1500kgs plus the weight of your lunch.

Yes, of course the boot is huge and the back seats are really comfortable and the NVH is very well engineered. But that you can take for granted from a Mercedes saloon. What you can't, is that they've done everything you've read about here for 40 lakhs.

Honk's Car of the Year 2014 is the Mercedes C Class C200. Big hand.

The Time Machine
Triumph Bonneville T100

I'd ask you to close your eyes and imagine you were in the sepia-tinted '60s where everyone was groovy, the music was outta-sight and most of the youth movements we take for granted today were busy being born. But that would make it difficult to keep reading.

Every era has its icons. And the 60s were no different. Marlon Brando, Steve McQueen, Bob Dylan and countless others all had one thing in common. They were all Rockers. And they all had Triumph Bonnevilles. It was *the* motorcycle back then.

As it turns out, it is *the* motorcycle even today. George Clooney, Tom Cruise, Ryan Reynolds, Hugh Laurie, Ewan McGregor and many other pap targets own the modern Bonneville in one form or other. Suffice to say that the Bonneville, along with being the most famous motorcycle of all time, is also one of the finest.

I'm almost certain I can't act, I'm not famous at all and I am to rock and roll what a headless chicken is to professional golf. Besides, I only don leathers to either ride or for 'special occasions'. So, the Bonnie shouldn't particularly appeal to me. But it does.

The T100 that I had my fling with (while wearing leather) has a classical simplicity to it. The styling is instantly recognisable, especially from the front and in profile. The effect is completed with the spoked wheels and the optional leather saddle bags.

As holiday romances go, this is as good as I've had. The minute you climb aboard and park it on the brilliant but flat twin seat and put your hands on the handles, the outside world feels different. It feels like it exists only for you to ride through it. It's hard to explain really, because even before you've thumbed the starter button, you begin to understand why this is the world's most loved motorcycle. And yes, it does feel like a bit of a privilege.

Still, leathers on. Time to hit the open road. Next stop – Jaipur.

Getting out of Delhi isn't that bad but Manesar is a nightmare. But none of that mattered because between my legs was a Triumph Bonneville. The 865cc engine felt subdued yet substantial. It was never designed for out-and-out speed. It was designed for feel and tractability. And that's where it really shines. On paper, the parallel twin makes 61bhp and as many Nm of torque. This is mated to 5-speed gearbox. That came as a bit of a disappointment to someone who was going touring but I quickly fell in love with its fifth gear.

I barely needed to downshift at highway speeds because the Bonnie (two up with full luggage) can do anywhere between 50kph and 165kph in fifth. It doesn't really cruise like cruiser. It feels more like a sports tourer in the way it deals with highway. We were able to keep a constant pace of 120-140kph throughout. But if I'm honest, it feels comfortable even at higher speeds.

My only crib about the epic Bonneville is that it sounds a little too happy and friendly. But that's an easy fix with Arrow exhausts that Triumph themselves will sell you.

The Rajasthan tour threw up many questions. Firstly, why doesn't everybody have one? It only costs 6.75 lakh Ex-Delhi. How can Triumph possibly make any money on this considering it has no visible evidence of cost-cutting. And finally, how do I go about starting a career in acting?

Tata Bolt. Crash Tested
Tata Bolt 1.2 Revotron

Imagine me taking your brand-new baby, accidently dropping it and breaking one of its legs. And then imagine you dealing with that rather uncomfortable situation gracefully; assuring me that all was well and that I wasn't to worry about it. This was precisely the situation that faced Tata Motors when they graciously flew me out to Udaipur to test the new Bolt. I'll make no bones about it; I crashed my test car quite badly whilst trying to avoid an absolute idiot on the highway. First time that's ever happened to me.

Since my job (most times) is to review very expensive cars and bring them back in one piece, I'm a very careful driver. Quick, but safe. But Rajasthan got me. I hope the idiot who changed lanes without looking in his mirrors gets violent, debilitating and incurable diarrhoea.

And I hope that because I like the Bolt. It's sort of the perfect recipe for a city car; small on the outside and big on the inside with a tiny petrol engine and loaded to the gills with useful features. In the past that would be an obvious cover-up for shoddy engineering. So, here's the big question – has Tata Motors made their second ever good car? In short, yes.

At the Zest launch, we were treated to billions of first-in-class this and best-in-class that during their marketing presentation. This one was different. 'Hello everyone. This is what we've made. We hope you like it' was the general inference. Much better.

It looks pretty good, the Bolt. Considering the Pratap Bose (Chief Designer) we know, he must have taken one look at the Vista and decided to start all over again. All things considered; he's done a fine job on the Bolt. I could bore you with the smiling grille and something that is trapezoidal but I'll just say that the overall styling is pleasing, yet striking.

The inside is 20,000 light years better than old Tatas. There's genuine quality here. To say that it feels as well built as the Swift's and a lot better than the Etios's (Oy! Toyota! Wake up!) is as good a compliment as I've ever given a Tata. Harman's been at work here as well, so you get a great 8-speaker stereo, many things to play with on the touchscreen system, and…wait for it… satnav! It's not the usual sort of thing. Mpmyindia gives you maps that you download on your phone and connect your phone through a cable to the system for satnav via an app. It's a lot easier to do than I'm making it sound.

The petrol version we had on test had Tata's on 1.2L turbo that puts out 90bhp and 140Nm of twist. Even though it has a slick 5-speed manual, driving the thing takes some getting used to. It has 3 modes; City, Eco and Sport. I was expecting this to be something to make fun of, but they really work. They change the engine characteristics, throttle response and many other things make it feel genuinely different. We used City mode in the city, Eco mode on the highway and Sport mode on twisting mountain roads on the way to Kumbalgarh and, weirdly, they all worked.

The steering, though electric, feels positive. Only at very low speeds do you feel the assistance. As speeds build, it firms up nicely and lets you know quite a lot about the surface you're driving on. Throw in a nicely sorted chassis that rides well over just about any surface, well-judged suspension, 9th generation ABS with EBD, Goodyear NCT tyres and you've got a dynamic package that is going to send the Hyundai i20 scurrying into the woods.

Again, if you do meet someone from Tata Motors who's been a part of the Bolt project – their glasses should be empty by now – please buy them another round.

The Pitbull Special
Mercedes-Benz GLA45 AMG

Something strange is going on in Affalterbach. It's almost as if amino acids and anger serum have been clandestinely laced in their water. In spite of having been curbed and curtailed by various emission and efficiency regulations, AMG seem to have a bit of a giggle like naughty public schoolboys and continue to unleash upon the world machines of such ferocity that Dr Frankenstein's monster, in comparison, is about as threatening as Stuart Little.

AMGs have always baffled us, here at Honk. I've driven them for years and I still can't wrap my head around the fact that they take the most sensible, obvious luxury cars (Mercs), and give them hearts and souls of great vengeance and furious anger. And they do it in a way that still retains all the Mercedesness.

And the most baffling AMG to date is (deep breath) the Mercedes-AMG GLA45 AMG. A car that, with the best intentions in the world, is mis-marketed as an SUV.

They'll have you believe that it's the raucous version of the GLA. Which is a small SUV. But it isn't an SUV at all. It isn't even a crossover. What it is, is the perfect naughty little b*s***d.

That decal round the side is a bit iffy, I'll admit. It looks like McLaren's logo. And no Mercedes, AMG or otherwise, should be sold with decals.

Just takes away the class. Visually, the rest of it is part hot-hatchback and part rally car. Aggression is something that the 45 is not short on.

The inside's a lot like the CLA45. In fact, it's damn near identical. If you were under your rock when we brought you that review, it's all black with red stitching, body-hugging seats and a steering wheel that been flattened at half past midnight. The latter might work when you're on a track, but on the road, it's very annoying. Especially when you make tight turns and let the wheel slide through your hands. Dear Mercedes, if you're going to call it a steering wheel, please make it round.

Turn the key and you get a deep sonorous moan like you'd expect from a Mitsubishi EVO X that's been to Red Rooster Performance for tuning. We've got to bear in mind that, barring their Formula 1 engine, this is the smallest engine that AMG has ever made. And even here, they've shattered the mould. At two litres, it's less than half the size of their 5.5litre biturbo and yet it's good for 355bhp. In a car the size of your left foot, that's biblical power.

The result, as you can imagine, is acceleration times that will make the Lamborgini Diablo (and the original Murcielago) run home to mama. Good job it has four-wheel drive. And in the real world, that means the ability to cover ground at massive speeds on any surface. I always liked the Audi Q5 for this reason. But the GLA45 costs not much more, so I've decided that I like this better. It's not a full-on mud-plugger, but neither is the Audi.

I'm not joking here. You could arrive at the Raid De Himalaya in this, win, and drive back home in supreme comfort. Lest you forget, it still is a Mercedes. That means it's quiet, comfortable, forgiving and very easy to live with.

Mercedes say that that they have no intention of bring the A45 to India. If it did make it here, it would cost about 65-70 lakhs. But we're not complaining. Because the GLA45 is more suited to us. In fact, it may just be the new perfect car for India (step aside Skoda Yeti). It costs 70 lakhs and is made by lunatics who clearly know exactly what they're doing.

All Crossed Up
Fiat Avventura 1.4 Petrol

Sometime in 2013, the editor of this newspaper asked me to compile a story on crossover cars. You know the kind; hatchbacks with a bit of visual beefing up. Some of them like the Duster or the Ford EcoSport had a little more done than just some cosmetic alterations. They felt like genuinely new cars.

This brings us onto the new raft of cross dressers that have flooded the Indian market. The Etios Cross, Polo Cross (or Cross Polo. I can never remember which) and the meat of this morning's missive; the Fiat Avventura.

These three are classic cases in crossing over. That said, the Avventura is just a little more than that. Firstly, Avventura is Italian for adventure. That gives it an aura of being competent when the tarmac runs out. This aura is further enhanced with the aforementioned visual beef in terms of black body protectors, roof rails and the all-important spare wheel that hangs off the boot lid.

I'm not sure what trim level my car had but it's the only car I've ever known to have both leather and fabric on the same seats. Seriously. There's leather on the sides where it can be seen and fabric for the bit you sit in. Eh? The confusion is compounded by the fact that above the aircon controls, there are three dials that look like they've been borrowed from a cheap children's toy. One's a compass that shows you your 'general' direction of travel, and the other two – apparently – are inclinometers of some sort. To be honest, this smacks of a little desperation from Fiat because it's a classic automotive afterthought.

What also definitely was never on the drawing board was the spare wheel mechanism. The idea is that you press a button either on the dash or the key which releases the arm that holds the spare wheel. You then swing that arm to the right which reveals all the grizzly inner workings that no customer should ever have to see in a car. Then you flip the boot lid up like you would on a normal car which reveals a rather cavernous boot. To close, you simply flip the boot lid down, press a button on the spare wheel mount, and swing it around until it shuts. This is generally followed by delirious and uncontrollable urge to pull your eyes out from anger and frustration.

That, thankfully, is the end of the bad news because at least it looks more like an SUV than the Toyota or the VW. In fact, it looks pretty good in the flesh.

And come on. It's a Fiat. Of course it drives well. Even the completely pointless 1.4L petrol with no turbo that I had loved to be revved all the way to 6750rpm in every gear. It only makes about 90bhp. And they're not particularly easy to access because there's only 115Nm of torque so you end up driving the nuts and bolts off of it. And when you do, it comes over all Italian.

'But wait, what's the point of the beefing up?' I hear you ask. Not too much, really. Except that the Avventura comes with 16" wheels with 205/45 tyres. That's the same as the Linea. What that means is a great ride and the ability to handle really bad roads rather well. It also means proper Fiat handling in the corners because the Goodyear Eagles feel really planted.

All in all, this is a rather curious car. But it does have a point. The body cladding may be as useful as a bicycle is to me, but it does lend a bit of character to the Avventura. Besides, when it rides this well, and drives as well as it does, there's a lot you'd forgive it. Just buy the diesel.

Red is the New Black
Mercedes-Benz CLA200

While you were brushing your teeth and doing your taxes in 2014, Mercedes had their biggest ever year India and sold a whopping 10,201 cars. As far as we're concerned, they were our manufacturer of the year for 2014. Why? Ten new launches. All of them great cars. Before you can catch your breath, they've got fifteen (fifteen!!!) new launches lined up for this year. And what we've got here, is probably their most important new car – the CLA Class.

In theory, this is marriage made in heaven because it's a small, sensible, presumably well-priced saloon that has the driving dynamics of the A Class with the svelte four-door-coupe styling cues from the CLS. But has it worked? To find out, I went to Goa to eat lots of seafood, drink lots of cheap booze and soak up…erm, sorry… to drive the CLA and see what's what.

This first thing you've got to know is that it looks stunning. Literally. People stopped and stared as I drove by in a red one. It has a low roofline with a wide stance, much like the A Class. This is one of the few times that fussy detailing has contributed to a fine-looking car. In front, the A Class's silver diamond grille has given way to black. The front and rear have LEDs which seem to have come from the same hand that styled the rest of the car. There is a certain visual coherence to it that takes a while to understand. But when you do, you appreciate it all the more.

The interior is pretty much a straight lift from the GLA. Which, by no means, is a bad thing because it's a wonderful place to be. The electric sports seats are comfortable yet fitted with high bolstering. This is a clue into this car's character. Gizmos abound in the CLA as well. Electric seats, Harmon Kardon Stereo, brand new satnav from Garmin, a whole new media interface, panoramic sunroof that closes itself when it starts raining, 'Mercedes Benz' illuminated on the door sills and tonnes more.

The car that I tested was the CLA 200 petrol. That's 181bhp and 300Nm of muscle from a 1991cc turbocharged four-pot. If you throw in the same 7-speed double-clutch gearbox, it's the same drivetrain found in the GLA, New C and E Classes as well. Only the CLA is the least amount of car that it has to push around.

The result, as you'd expect is that it's smooth, unruffled, quiet and properly brisk. In the real world it means that you get to where you want a lot sooner than you thought you would. Despite that gearbox, it's supremely well behaved in the city. It seems to glide from place to place without really affecting its surroundings. All the controls you need to operate it almost feel subservient to your commands. This alone will remove most of the stress from city commuting.

As long as you drive it, of course. And drive it you will, because there is hardly any space at the back. I'm 6'3" and I just didn't fit. Not nearly enough headroom even for short journeys. It's the price to pay, I suppose, for the beautiful roofline and the structural beef necessary to accommodate the pillarless windows. But if you don't really need the back seats, or if you've got young kids, you won't mind it at all.

Because of the A Class underpinnings, you'd think that it was good to drive. Well, you're wrong. Good isn't a good enough word. It's fantastic. Genuine balance, fantastic steering, proper power and no body roll add up to a brilliant driver's car. And the ride's plush and forgiving as well.

And no. It won't graunch its belly on speed bumps. Merc's made sure of that.

Whichever way you look at it, the CLA is a great car for a few reasons. Whether you buy the petrol or diesel, you'll get a proper Mercedes with hundreds of features, looks that Ray Charles will still approve of and driving dynamics like an A Class. All this shouldn't cost more than 35 lakhs when it launches on the 22nd of January. We're happy. Very happy.

Il Tornado
Benelli TNT 600 GT

What we have here is one-chuffing-hundred-and-four years of motorcycles and guns. They still do both with equal gusto. That, children, is Benelli.

Stands to reason, doesn't it? That the modern-day interpretation of something that predates Ferrari and Lamborghini by decades ought to be, in the very least, exciting. Cracking motorcycling world championships in the 250cc class in 1950 and 1969 may seem easy. But try the Isle of Mann TT. They won the 250cc class in 1939, 1950 and 1969. Wrap you head around the fact that making fast Italian bikes is something they invented. But now they're owned by some Chinese buggers. Has that ruined everything that Benelli stood for? You bet your brown cheeks it hasn't.

The one we rode is called the 600GT. And it's as violent as a terrorist on cocaine. It's a raw, vicious, pure-play sports-touring motorcycle with a 600cc inline-four. If that seems a bit short on capacity, then Honk will there to laugh our heads off when you try it.

It's a super sport in disguise, I tell you; no two ways. There's nothing sane about 82bhp from an in-line four. 'Specially when it's genuinely (and perpetually) angry.

Honestly, it simply refuses to cruise. It knocks at anything below 3000rpm, and it pulls maniacally above 4000. So that's the agro explained.

But what about the fact that it has two hue-mung-gous panniers? And the straight-up riding position?

Most large-capacity motorcycles give you a thrill-a-minute experience. And the GT (GT=Gran Tourismo=Grand Tourer=Fast-as-bloody-hell-over-long-distances) is no different.

The windscreen (bikes have them too) is nothing short of brilliant. There was a point where I was doing 180kph, with one hand on the throttle and the other making waves in the invisible air and sitting upright. Yes, you do feel the wind, but only after it's been through a committee which has decided that the rider is not a kite.

It doesn't look particularly Italian. There's none of that knee-buckling beauty that we've come to expect from Italy. It looks big, badass and functional. If you throw in massive panniers, it's about as big as a Bombay flat. As a stroke of utter genius, Benelli's given it a 27-litre fuel tank. If you're riding like a complete loon, you'll get about 12kpl. With a full tank that's Bombay to Pune and back without breaking a sweat.

Mind you, the amount of fuel you have on board directly affects the handling. With a full tank of fuel, it brakes a lot better and the nose stays planted when you throttle out of a corner. If it's running low, it wheelies all the time. Yes, even amateur riders will be able to make this 233kg (without rider and luggage) wheelie until the cows come home.

The gearing is something else that stands out. While each gear goes comfortably from 4000 to 12000rpm, they're stacked really close together. There's barely any drop in revs from one gear to the next. The sweet spot is sixth gear; 50 to 210kph without having to shift. On the highway, I rode it like an automatic. While the torque spread isn't exactly even, it does kick in once you get past about 4000 revs.

But what I've failed hopelessly to describe until now it its personality. It loves to run. It loves to eat up tarmac and destroy long distances. It's one hell of a mental. But more than anything else, everything about it is endearing, including the size and weight. If you could ever conceive of owning a pet tiger, you'll like the 600GT. It's just as exciting.

Captain Sensible
Volkswagen Jetta 2.0 TDI

This isn't the kind of car we normally review. In fact, it's the kind of car that we don't really know what to do with because it has absolutely no appeal to the petrolhead. So what follows is a review of the Volkswagen Jetta which is as sober as the car.

The Skoda Octavia and Audi A3 are based on the VWs current MQB platform. This Jetta is based on the previous –gen (Mk VI) VW Golf. That means it's a generation older than its supposed siblings. Although, from where we're sitting, that's not necessarily a bad thing. This is the result of six generations of ruthless German engineering. And it certainly shows because as a car; a machine to get you and four others around, it is nigh-on perfect.

The looks won't offend anybody. It's simple, subtle and handsome. In fact, part of the deal is a touch of anonymity that comes as standard. The result of being completely inoffensive is that it just might be forgotten almost immediately; ideal for people who value discretion.

Inside, it feels like every component, every piece of plastic that's been fitted has been built to last a thousand years. Even the fabric seats in the lesser models feel perfect.

As far as drive goes, you can choose between a 1.4L turbo petrol with a six-speed manual or a 2.0 turbodiesel with either the manual or a six-speed DSG automatic. The diesel DSG is the one we'd recommend because it works best for this car.

Unless you drive a racing car every day, you'll find that with any of the drivetrain options the Jetta isn't bad to drive. It's not particularly sprightly and involving, but for a car of this nature, it's not bad at all.

My only complaint is about the petrol engine. The turbo lag is horrendous. The was a point where on a slight incline, in first gear with one foot off the clutch and the other flooring the throttle, it still took a good 4-5 seconds to get going. I really thought it was broken. And I stalled it a lot. But once you get it moving, there's a fair amount of power (120bhp) to make brisk progress.

As is the case with most cars today, it's the diesel engine that really shines. It's smooth, quiet and married to the DSG gearbox very well. The 140bhp 320 torques are always there. If I were running VW, this is the only drivetrain option I'd provide for the Jetta. Everything about it just feels coherent with the rest of the car.

In the corners, it's best to take a slightly less enthusiastic approach. While there are tonnes of safety features that prevent an accident – and many that mitigate its effect once it's happened – it doesn't particularly enjoy enthusiastic motoring. It's just not that sort of car. Treat it gently and it'll give you over 14kpl in the city.

What you get in return for 20-something of your hard-earned lakhs is a car that's been ruthlessly over-engineered for 35 years. You get a car that was conceived, designed and built to be as good as a car can be by people who are probably the best in the world at engineering fidelity.

If I may liken cars to people, the Jetta is a middle-aged IIT-IIM technology consultant who also happens to be a really good husband and a great father. Not someone you'd want to go to a nightclub with, but the perfect matrimonial advert. Just don't hold out for any sort of excitement whatsoever.

Yes and No
BMW X3 20d xDrive

It's actually quite a good car to drive, the BMW X3. But it's the worst driving BMW on sale in India. What did we expect? All the other BMWs are so damn good, that the poor X3 didn't stand a chance. It's nicely styled, too. But it's still clearly far from BMW's best efforts.

But at least it's comfortable. Except if you're in the city. Because in the city it's as bouncy as being on an elephant that's dodging machine gun fire from a helicopter gunship while running through a jungle.

As you can see, it's a big SUV. But it can't go off-road. AT BEST, it could drive you up a slightly rutted path to your farmhouse.

It has a 2.0 litre diesel engine that's good for 190bhp and 350Nm of torque. But because it's big and heavy, you only get about 11kpl, not 18 like BMW claim.

What we have here is the result of having to pack too many skills into a car. And the inconvenient truth is this; the X3 is really rather good.

First, the size. The new X5 has gone on to be a size bigger than the old one. A little too big, to be honest. The X3, on the hand, is bang on. You want a perfectly-sized SUV? This is it. This shows in its interior. There's just lots of space everywhere; for the driver, rear passengers and in the boot. I've got to hand it to BMW. Their best stylists may have been involved in other projects but the interior packaging engineers have done the job as well as I've seen.

Next up for praise is its ease of use. Like most BMWs it's unlock, get in, start, into D and you're off. From this point on in your daily commute, you are immune to the outside world. Sound deadening is absolutely brilliant. Through bumper-to-bumper traffic, it lulls you into a semi-coherent zen-like state where you are a little more than oblivious to the outside world. Imagine having this on a daily basis. Imagine also having a brilliant stereo which takes every sort of input short of a hamburger. And then what you have is probably one of the best of the urban SUV breed.

Petrolheads, please gather around because this last bit is for you. That annoying trait of bouncing around in the city means that it has stiff suspension. It also has buttons where you can set up the engine and throttle in EcoPro, Comfort, Sport and Sport +. Even the gearbox has a Sport mode for faster shifts and taking each gear to higher revs.

The result is that on the highway, it's as good at covering long distances as I am at being idiotic about a car. Not only that, but this is where you get to enjoy two very intrinsic aspects of this car – the steering and the brakes. The steering is point and squirt; not suggest and heave. Inputs have to be measured because it gives you precisely as much change of direction as you ask of it. Precisely.

The next great bits are the brakes. BMWs have always really good brakes. More than their actual stopping power (tremendous in their own right), it was always their feel that won us over. The X3's are no different. On my 350km highway thrash, I never got any fade. There were times when I panic-braked without any reason from 180kph just to see how good they were. And each time, the car neatly pulled up where I was expecting it to. It does a brilliant job of keeping the driver in control even when he feels he's lost it.

How do we sum this car up, I'm wondering. Tell you what, everything you actually need to know is there above. Tell us what you think. Would you buy one?

Did Someone Order a
Proper Luxury Car?
Mercedes Benz C220 CDI

Luxury means many things to many people. For some, it's simply time. For others, it's a sense that all is well because they have the best of something. Merc's been at the forefront of the latter for a while now. And they don't look like they're tending towards austerity anytime soon because in 2015, they're bringing in 15 (16 if you count the new A Class) of some of the finest luxury cars the world has ever known.

In all honesty, Honk and its keen posse should dislike the brand-new C Class. It isn't what you'd particularly call sporty. It doesn't look racy enough to set our trousers on fire. And it is as exciting as being asleep.

BUT - and this is one hell of a 'however' - It isn't meant to do any of those things. It's meant to be luxury saloon. And it does that way better than any of its competitors.

As a device to take you from A to B, it really doesn't need to feel as good as it does. I mean, just look at that interior. Our test car had electric everything and Merc's new Command system which is very user friendly once you learn it. But the gorgeous wood, brushed aluminium and leather are just elements. It feels as though they have been given to Bach or Chopin to be composed into a container for humans that feels much more opulent and tasteful than its 42-lakh price-tag suggests. Speaking of Bach and Chopin, our car also had a Burmester stereo. This is some serious top-of-the-line sound that's tuned for pure fidelity and reproduction of natural sound. Leave your Katy Perry and Justin Bieber at home and try Eric Clapton unplugged instead. You'll feel like he's sitting under the bonnet and crooning just you and your passengers.

But he isn't. We checked. What we found instead was Merc's superb 2.14L diesel engine that, in 220 CDI guise, puts out a smooooth 170bhp and an equally creamy and relaxed 400Nm of torque. Again, our only crib is the 7-speed double-clutch gearbox. It's sublime at low speeds and while cruising down a highway. But the minute you press it into action, it loses its wit. This, I don't think was ever meant for high performance. But, like in the S Class, it suits the nature of this car.

Driving the C Class respectfully in any environment is almost zen-like. It lulls you into a state of calmness where you find yourself pondering life's imponderables while you sashay from traffic light to speed bump. It's a proper Mercedes saloon in that respect.

I think we've said everything that needs to be about this car. Except that the diesel engine is so quiet, you'll need to come out and check the CDI badge on the boot to make sure. And this means 750-1000km on a tank of fuel while you'll easily get 15kpl in the city and well over 20 on the highway. We did.

This is one of the very few wilfully un-sporty cars that we truly love - simply because it feels so damn good. Only Mercedes Benz could have pulled this off. If this new C Class is anything to go by, we should all pay close attention to them this year.

Dynamic? Really?
Audi Q3 2.0 35 TDI Dynamic

When we brought you the road test of the Audi Q3 sometime in 2013, we got a lot of criticism for our criticisms. While it was a very good car in the technical sense of the term, it didn't really float our boat because there wasn't too much to get excited about. The biggest problem with that particular car was the lack of DriveSelect, without which, the steering was permanently stuck in comfort. This meant steering so light that going around corners at anything approaching 'quick' was as hazardous as getting a lap-dance from a slightly irate Cobra.

Thankfully, the Q3 Dynamic has DriveSelect. It also has the other two pillars of Audi's holy trinity – Quattro and S-Tronic. For Honk, these three aspects define a proper Audi. So let's start with the DriveSelect.

It gives you options between Comfort, Auto and Dynamic. In comfort mode, it's much the same as old one. That said, it is completely God-sent for city driving. The impossibly light steering takes what feels like half the effort out of your daily commute. It's just so easy and so forgiving. Auto sort of works too. It backs off the power assistance very slightly to give you a smidge more control when it feels you're being enthusiastic. But the Dynamic mode, the very thing the car was named after, is a bit confusing. On paper, it's supposed to give you more control during enthusiastic driving by backing off on the steering power assistance. And back off, it does. What it doesn't do is provide any sort of feel or feedback whatsoever. This means that you never have a clue how much grip you have or when the rear is going to let go around a corner. You just have to use your experience as a driver and… erm… guess. Quattro helps in this respect. When you feel it shuffling power around the four wheels (and you can feel this) it's time to back off.

Speaking of Quattro (possibly the best AWD system in the world), we tried going off-road a bit. Despite the road tyres – they don't work at all on loose surfaces – it wasn't half bad. Anything reasonable we threw at it was dealt with to satisfaction. No complaints for a car of this size.

But the best part of the Q3 has always been the drivetrain. The 2.0 TDI engine with the 7-speed S-Tronic gearbox is one of the best drive packages money can buy for daily use. Expect supreme fuel economy, linear power delivery and the smoothest quickest changes this side of a politician jumping loyalties. It's always been an absolute joy to use this gearbox on a daily basis, even if the engine is a bit rough at low speeds.

The end result of the *Dynamicisation* of the Q3 is a car that feels a lot more complete than its less equipped siblings. That it isn't a car for keen drivers is an unequivocal fact. But with lots of features, simple, handsome styling, a supremely competent drivetrain package, it's become the car it always should have been. Our only crib now is the name. They should have called it the Q3+ or the Q3 No-seriously-we've-got-it-right-this-time. Not Dynamic. Because it just isn't.

Style and Substance
Mercedes-Benz CLA200 CDI

This is my third review of the CLA. The AMG version is probably the most accessible performance car I've ever driven and the regular petrol version is just impossibly smooth. And now I've spent some quality time with the most sensible option – the diesel.

Now imagine it in the flesh. Times that by ten. That's how good it actually looks. It has the capacity to make people stop and stare. In red, it's one of the best-looking cars on sale today. No arguments, please.

The inside, though beige, it a beautiful place to be. There is much leather and brushed aluminium and superb plastics. To be beige and stylish at the same time in a car which is low and racy must not have been easy. Still, trust Mercedes to pull it off. Unlike some other manufacturers who make you pay for the key with which you start your car, Mercedes has filled the CLA up everything they could as standard. Here's a small list of the kit on offer – Body-hugging electric sports seats, Harman Kardon stereo, proper panoramic sunroof, satnav, dual zone climate control and a million other bits and bobs.

If you're daily driver is an SUV, or another luxury saloon, then be prepared to get used to a really low seat. And this does play tricks on your mind initially because you sit there thinking, 'hmmm, this is a low car. And if I'm sitting this low it must mean that every speed bump from here to my office is going to help itself to bits of the sump.' But don't worry, that paranoia soon dissipates after you've gone over a few man-made mountains that masquerade as speed-breakers and the only things that make contact with the road are the tyres. Mercedes was adamant about the ground clearance. They ensured that it'll be good enough for India without messing with the CLA's low profile.

The laziness of the power delivery and the gearbox may trick you into thinking that this is a slow car. And…it sort of is in some ways. 0-100kph in 10 seconds isn't quick by today's standards. But in the city, the laziness makes life so much easier. It doesn't dart forwards every time you go near the throttle. It's a lot more relaxed than that; progressive as well.

On the highway, the CLA is a different animal. If I were ever to rob a bank, this would be my only choice for a getaway car. Why? Because the CLA can do 1200km on a tank of diesel on the highway. At 200kph. This is down to the a nice lazy 2.14L diesel that's been tuned for economy, a nice lazy gearbox with widely spaced ratios and, most importantly, the CLA has the lowest Coefficient of Drag of any saloon car in the world. What that last bit means is that it has very little resistance to the air.

And it handles like an A Class. Which means it handles as good as a front-wheel drive car can. At high speeds you can feel a direct connection between the wheel in your hands and the two it turns. In terms of being one with the car, the CLA encroaches deep into BMW territory. You don't need to be Hamilton to push this thing either because it has an inherent sense of safety, of being planted and obedient to your inputs.

As you can probably work out, we really love the CLA. Even more than A Class. It pushes all our buttons; mental, beautiful and sensible. Apparently over a lakh people across the world agree with us because that's the number of cars they sold in 18 months from its launch. We don't generally do buying advice on Honk, but this is different. The CLA200 CDI in red costs 33.5 lakhs in Mumbai (Ex-showroom including octroi). Buy one. Now.

It Makes Perfect Sense
Mercedes–Benz B200CDI

Honestly, I'd hate the job of being a designer at Mercedes. They've got so many great looking cars that when the boss walked into the design studio and said 'bring that rather vegetarian B Class up to scratch, will you?', I can only imagine that Hans and Friedrich (made-up German car designer names) may have even allowed a tiny bead of sweat to dribble onto their impossibly thin spectacles. The old B really wasn't pretty. In fact, it sat in the Merc line-up like Justin Bieber would at Woodstock.

Anyway, after Hans wiped the sweat off Friedrich's forehead, they set about improving the B Class's visual appeal. And after considerable effort, we've got to say it's the best-looking box-shaped minivan-esque hatchback-type-thing we've seen in a while. Changes include new lights all around and Merc's now familiar styling. You can have it in racy red, if you like. And you probably would.

I bet you'd like the interior as well. It's jet black, with a strip of grey plastic running across the dash where you'd normally expect to find wood. It has the look and feel of pinstriped suit. Very elegant. Of course, this being Mercedes, they've loaded it to the overflowing with equipment. Great stereo, satnav, electric seats, panoramic sunroof, driving modes, gearshift paddles, but sadly, no Angelina Jolie. Jokes apart, this is a very good interior. In terms of space, you can fit anything this side of a giraffe in the back. And even with the spare wheel, the boot's not bad either.

Once you've got in, adjusted your electric seat just so, put some tunes on the stereo and settled down to drive the thing, the first thing you'll notice is how good the visibility all-round is. And when you've turned the key, you'll honestly believe you're driving a petrol-engined car. This has to be one of the most refined diesel engines in the world. In 200 CDI tune, you're looking at about 135bhp and 300Nm of torque from the 2.14L four-pot diesel. This is channelled to the front wheels - using the gentle power of suggestion – by the 7-speed double-clutch auto box.

What's it like to drive? In a word, relaxing. It's a quiet car to begin with, being a Mercedes. But this engine in this tune adds even more calm to the experience. You could easily forget on your daily commute, that you are in fact on your daily commute. Even that lazy gearbox is ideally suited to this. It blurs changes so perfectly that you often need to consult the rev counter to work out which gear you're in.

Out on the highway, it cashes it's 'Luxury Tourer' cheques quite nicely. Again, in complete silence. But this is where we find the apparent lack of power. You see, 200 CDI is the lowest state of this 2.14L diesel engine's tune. Which means that while this very engine is capable of producing 204bhp and 500Nm of torque, it's been tuned down for economy and probably because 500Nm in a front-wheel-driven car will cause many things to explode. Still, what it lacks in outright power, it makes up for in smooth and effortless delivery. There is a moment when you pull out to overtake someone where you think to yourself 'Will I make it? Is there enough power?' By the time you've had this thought, you'll be a few hundred metres ahead of whomever you were trying to overtake without realising it. See what I mean? There's no perceptible urgency, just smooth linear acceleration.

Of course you want to know what sort of fuel economy it can do. I got about 15kpl while pootling around gently in the city and WELL over 20 cruising on the highway. Here's something interesting. My test car came to Mumbai from the Merc factory in Pune where it was fuelled up. When it reached me, the fuel needle (which I checked and worked fine) still read a little more than full. It hadn't moved in 130km. I'll leave you with that thought.

BMW's Secret Weapon
BMW 328i

Honk has had the good fortune of having spent a lot of quality time with the diesel 3 Series BMW, both the normal one and the GT, and we liked them tremendously. The normal 3 especially won our hearts for being so good at so many things. And so we arrive at a point where we review a car that none of you will buy – a petrol 3-series.

We all know the 3 is very handsome car. Car designers do tend to balls up quite a lot these days, but on the day the 3 was bring scribbled, the sun was out, the birds were chirping, pencils were sharp, nobody was angry because they'd fought with their wives and there wasn't so much as the thought of a hangover in the room. As result, it'll have its place in the history books as one of the best saloon cars ever designed.

The 328i's got the edge over the diesel in terms of looks in two important aspects. First up the swish 18" wheels. Not only do they fill up the arches beautifully, they also complete the package of the sports saloon visually. The second and far more importance visual cue is the 'i' at the end of the '328' on the boot lid. It's a very satisfying sight to behold. 'There goes a proper petrolhead', you think to yourself.

The interior is very refreshing. After having driven so many cars with so much beige and so many hideous browns, this one's a simple black, with a thin red stripe running across the dashboard. It reminded me of my beloved M5. If I had my way all BMWs would have a simple black interior. It gets better because this sublime container for humans and their rubbish comes with superb sport seats which adjust every which way. The side bolstering can be adjusted so you aren't flung around in corners. Another brilliant thing about the seats is that for some reason, your shirt doesn't get as crumpled as it would otherwise. Even if you're daft like me and wear linen in Delhi when it's 40 degrees outside.

Certainly, some big-hearted person has worked out the equipment for the 328i. Short version? It has everything. Proper big screen, sunroof, iDrive, Navigation Pro, great audio system, head-up display, driving modes and plenty more to fiddle with when you're stuck in traffic.

Being stuck in traffic is no real hardship in the 328i. It's as docile as an ageing spaniel. It's extremely easy to potter around town all day. It doesn't have the low-end of a diesel engine but it's much more progressive. And more predictable as a result. I did a whole day's drive in Delhi and at no point did it even begin to ruffle my feathers.

But then I got bored and took it out to the Yamuna Expressway. Engine in Sport+, gearbox in Sport, time to find out what this mother can do.

Strangely, it sounds like a straight-six. But it isn't. It's a two-litre four cylinder with turbos. But there's nothing strange about the pace of thing. Smooth, firm acceleration is what this motor was meant for. The only bit of harshness comes from the differential when you shift up at full throttle on the 8-speed automatic sport gearbox. And the shifts are done in half a second (real-time) when you pull on the right paddle (Oh yes. It's got paddle shifters). In Sport+ mode, you can choose the way you want to corner; smoothly on the ragged edge, or if you turn off the DSC, well beyond it with smoke pouring off the rear tyres. Whichever you choose, you'll be a lot happier than you were before you set off.

This is one of the finest all-round cars we've ever driven. We still can't find a single thing we'd change about it. Until we do, it gets a 10/10 score and a proper standing ovation from us.

India's People's Car.
Or Rather it Should Be
Tata Genx Nano Twist EasyShift XTA

Keen readers have probably clocked me as being a little elitist. That's not entirely false because I've brought you more luxury and performance car reviews than anything else. And my rule has always been that a lesser car or bike will only be reviewed in these pages if it is unique and genuinely interesting.

With that, we arrive at the Tata GenX Nano Twist EasyShift XTA, the first car in the world (probably) whose name is longer than it is. Don't worry, though. I haven't gone off the boil. This little scamp is a very interesting car.

Let's start with the 'little' bit. If the Mercedes GL is the largest car you can buy in India in terms of sheer acreage, the Nano is by far the smallest. It is remarkably small like a Smart car. The weird part is you don't feel this sitting inside. Because it's tall and because the packaging is extremely well thought out, I could have the driver's seat in my preferred position – all the way back – and still be able to fit in the seat behind it. At the cost of being annoying I'm an ungainly 6'3".

It's the interior where this Tata really gets going. Aside from the aforementioned space, of which there is definitely more than you could expect, it gets cracking with power-assisted steering, powered windows for the front, central locking, a 12V charging point and a stereo which can take a USB and Bluetooth. Come on, you didn't get any of this on the original Nano. Throw in an aircon that works even in the oven that was Pune during her hottest day of the year and, even as a devout follower of and firm believer in luxury and high performance, I find myself thinking *hmmm. As an everyday runabout, this makes a lot of sense. If only it had an automatic gearbox.*

Tata Motors is ahead of me on this because they've given it a 5-speed automated manual. Think of this as a normal manual gearbox where computers and hydraulics are drafted in to do the work that your left hand and foot normally do while shifting gears. So, to the user, it works just like an automatic, because it reduces effort and stress. If you fancy getting a bit of a lick on, there's small button marked 'S' for sport. It doesn't turn the Nano into a snarling supercharged Jag, but it does hold revs until the redline. And there's manual override as well.

The engine's at the back like a Porsche 911's. Unlike the Porsche's it's a 660cc V twin that makes a proper racket if you're standing behind the car. While the inside's much better, I'd like to propose the Nano for the title of India's Noisiest Car.

Anyway, the drive. There's no other way to say this; with tiny 12-inch wheels at the furthest possible corners of the car, steering that actually has some weight, an automatic-ish gearbox that does the shifting this isn't a bad car by a country mile to drive. If you're even a little keen (or late for work), you'll be squeezing though the tiniest gaps and giggling to yourself because you've just realised that the Nano, with all these gizmos and that gearbox has suddenly become great fun to drive. It's a happy car, is the Nano. It's almost as if humour and joy are now part of its DNA.

So, what Tata Motors has done here is reinvent the people's car. Like the old Mini and Fiat 500, this is India's chance at making a people's car that is practical, clever and has tonnes of character. It also has endless scope for customisation. I'm getting one with a psychedelic paintjob, whitewall tyres and chromed wing mirrors from a '60s Vespa.

At the time of writing this, we don't know how much it'll cost, but we asked Tata if it would be 3 lakhs on-road and they didn't say no.

When Artistry Meets Ruthless Engineering
Feature – Moto Exotica

Seven and a half hours. That's how long it took us to do the measly 279-kilometre drive from Delhi to Dehradun. I tried to uphold my standards of blitzing long distances in record time and I'm deeply sorry to disappoint. Blame endless traffic virtually the whole way.

All my photographer and I wanted when I got there was a hot shower (separately, of course) and some nice cold beer. Thankfully, Arjun Raina is just that kind of guy. His workshop, if you can call it that, is exactly in the middle of absolutely nowhere. Getting there meant, going right through Dehradun and all the way out the other side, through the rural outskirts, through a jungle, then a few kilometres of dirt road into the valley and suddenly Moto Exotica appeared on a hillside surrounded by paddy fields.

Inside we found not a single chopper, which is rare for custom bike builder. The place itself is part studio part laboratory. And all their motorcycles are and have been engineered using the best available technology.

"Let me show you our latest toy", said Arjun as he took me to see his new 3D printer. "With just this, we can make prototypes of just about any component in plastic. It saves us a lot of time and money, not to mention trial and error", he explained as the printer furious darted about the place turning what appeared to be plastic thread into a gear shifter.

There's one thing you must know about Arjun and, by extension, Moto Exotica; he is an absolute pedant about lightweight and he loves his Yamaha RD350s. "There's something about that two-stroke twin. Once it gets under your skin, nothing else will do", he said, pointing to the scrambler that won the build-off at India Bike week 2014. "Take it for a thrash, you'll know what I mean."

See, I know how popular RD350s are. I know that people who love them are not too keen on anything else. I understand all that. I know and respect the RD350 in the same way that I know and respect Pink Floyd. I just don't dig it.

Or rather I didn't. This bike on loose gravel and broken, dusty tarmac is an absolute animal. The exhaust has been designed to have roughly the same effect as a turbocharger. Essentially that's nothing, nothing, nothing, BANG! A wall of noise, a streak of white two-stroke smoke, and enough power to rip your face off. When it's not in its power band, it feels clunky and unbalanced. But when the revs are high and the throttle is fully open, it comes alive and pulls violently like only a two stroke can.

But the bike we came to review, as promised when we did the IBW story, was the 92 kilo Neo Café Racer. Sadly, we couldn't ride it because it was missing some crucial part that was yet to arrive. Still, semi-slick tyres, partly-carbon bodywork, RD350 engine tuned to produce much power and the real-world performance of a Yamaha R6. Is that bonkers or what. This is a very hard motorcycle to take your eyes off of. It has a minimalist elegance. You can visibility tell that it is completely devoid of any sort of frivolity. What isn't needed isn't there.

This is the mantra of Moto Exotica. They use science and maths and engineering know-how to build lightweight performance machines. They have pretty much the same ideology as Lotus; fast, agile pared down, pleasurable but most importantly, light.

X5 vs. India's Worst Road Trip
BMW X5 3.0d xDrive

It couldn't have been easy making this car. Imagine the effort that went into studying the Porsche Cayenne and the Range Rover Sport, only to find that in many ways their qualities of being able to provide abject luxury, off road abilities and excellent driving dynamics can't be bettered.

That didn't stop BMW from trying. And the fruit of that labour is this smashing new X5. Before we get to what we did with it, you need to know something about BMW. No BMW we've ever driven has been bad to drive. Some have been better than others, but as driver's cars, almost all of them have stood head-and-shoulders above their competition. The problem the X5 has always had is that it had to be seen competing with the Range Rover Sport and Porsche's Cayenne while costing significantly less. This new one has the same mountain to climb. Having spent many days with the Range Rover Sport, I can tell you straightway that that's a really tall order.

To find out what it was capable of, we drove from Delhi to Dehradun and back. Like idiots, we were hoping for scant traffic, beautiful mountain roads and some nice local grub along the way. What we got instead was bonkers traffic for all but 50 kilometres in both directions, endless roadworks, some of the worst driving we've ever encountered and KF-bloody-C. Don't even get me started.

Through all this, I was endlessly thanking the powers that be for the X5. Here's why.

This is one of those cabins you just get comfortable in immediately. It takes no more than a few minutes to feel right at home. It could be the well-designed seats, or the superb visibility, or the big slab of warm wood running across the dash, or the full-length sunroof, or the superb aircon that kept Delhi's 42-degree temperature firmly out. Throw all that lot together with an endless array of gadgets and what you end up with is a wonderful place in which to commute.

The combination of this 3.0 straight-six diesel and the 8-speed auto box is one of the finest drive packages that money can buy. There is a certain smoothness and progression to it that most other carmakers simply cannot replicate. On paper there's 258bhp and 500 torques. But out in the real world, numbers count for as little as a politician's pre-election promises. No matter what speed you're doing, there's always power when you want it. It's not served up in one big lump either. It's a constant, even surge all the way to the redline. Overtaking in the X5 at virtually any speed is but a twitch of your right foot.

Driving modes work particularly well in this car. We used EcoPro in Delhi's rush hour(s) and it's great for city driving. It keeps the engine completely quiet, shifts up as early as 1500rpm, cuts the engine when you're stuck in traffic and generally does everything in its power to sooth your brow and conserve fuel at the same time. Once we hit what is laughably called a highway, we switched to Comfort mode. This lets you maintain good pace regardless of what your conditions are by kicking down the gearbox sooner and letting you have more power. Squeezing through traffic was no hassle. For the first 150 odd kilometres at any rate.

And then we hit highway roadworks. The indignation one feels when one is asked to pay toll for a road that is still under construction cannot be adequately described in 800 words or less. To have to do this several times not only cost us a lot of money, but a great deal of time as well. The only good news is that we were in a luxury SUV. I remember thinking that if I had to go through this, I can't think of a better car in which to do it. And I kept thinking that until the roadworks ended because the X5 dealt with the conditions beautifully. We could see cars bouncing around over bumps and ruts all around us, but we were alright.

In the mountains, we were in Sport+ all the way. This turns off the ESP and tightens everything up. This with paddle shifters was an absolute blast on the final climb up to Dehradun. For the first time since we set off, we felt like we in a proper BMW.

Crunch time. Is it better than the RRS and Cayenne. Honestly, it's up there, but feels very different. In spite of its size, weight and girth, it feels like a BMW should. And that's good enough for us.

Sensible Little Rascal
MINI CooperD 3 Dr

This is a big moment for me. I was unnaturally in love with the old MINI because it was just the ultimate city car. This new one is a bit bigger, a bit porkier but the one we had on test was very diesel. Does this kill the Joie de vivre of the MINI? Or does this make it more appealing?

If you park it next to the previous generation car, you can see that this one's bigger. I've heard many people go on and on about how it shouldn't be called a MINI anymore because it's grown too big. All balls. It's a beautiful size. It still fits in the tiniest of gaps despite being wide, and it still is the easiest car in the world to park. And most importantly, it's still cheeky.

Then there's the interior. Oh man. They've pulled out the stops. Satnav, head-up display, full glass roof, and that's only the beginning. Virtually everything in the cabin is operated by a selection of beautifully milled metal toggle switches. Jet fighter enthusiasts will go nuts with this. I certainly did. But then there's a little bit of a let-down because the seats are manually adjusted and for a fun and sprightly little car such as this, there are no paddle shifters for the 6-speed automatic gearbox. Not cool, BMW. Not cool. It gets a little worse because my test car didn't have leather seats. Come on. My 11 something lakh Fiat Linea had leather seats as standard.

And then we arrive at the heart of the matter. Literally. This MINI CooperD has a diesel engine. And it's a tiny 3 cylinder which have 1.5 litres in which to shuffle about. It's boosted by direct injection and a turbo, but that really isn't enough engine for a car with a Cooper badge on it, surely? Actually, it is.

This blend of small but torquey engine with a genius chassis setup means that the CooperD performs very differently to the petrol engine. Here you get up close and intimate with the little droplets of feedback, the crispness of the steering, the sheer balance of the whole setup, while getting over 20kpl. But is that what a near 40 lakh (On road) super-hatch is meant to be? Or is it critical that it have a petrol engine?

It's not that the diesel is underpowered or anything, it's just that it happens to be diesel. In most cars, I wouldn't bat an eyelid about it. Modern diesels are clean, torquey, efficient and very economical. But the MINI isn't most cars. It's special. It's one of the most recognisable shapes in the automotive universe because it is unlike anything else in the world. And it feels like it. The diesel's fine to pootle around in the city, but there are times when you'd like some proper grunt to go with the handling. And sadly, the diesel falls a bit short.

Of course it makes more sense than the petrol. But buying a MINI isn't a cold and calculated decision. You buy it because you must. Because your heart is set on it. And to complete that emotional connect with it, it needs a petrol.

The CooperD then will always be a gift-to-the-kid-when-he/she-turns-18 sort of car. And I've got no problem with that. But my MINI will always be a full-fat very petrol Cooper S.

Into the Night
Indian Chief Classic

It was a stormy, windswept night in the city. The sort of night in which you'd make sure your doors were locked. The sort of night when the wolf howls at the moon. As people drove a little faster than usual to get home sooner, their minds occupied with an irrational fear they couldn't quite understand, their dizzy white lights reflected off her naked curves. This was her element. And she owned it. I could feel the eyes on her as we rode through the city. I could feel them all saying the same thing – I want you.

I couldn't imagine myself getting so emotional about a motorcycle. I'm even referring to it as 'her'. That's a cardinal road testing rule I'm breaking that'll probably have me fired. And yet…

This is that kind of motorcycle, is the Indian Chief Classic. It is utterly bewitching when you see it for the first time. Or for the twenty thousandth time, for that matter. Just look at those valanced fenders. Just think about how painstakingly each one is made by hand. Look at the War Bonnet light with the chief himself. Just look. Tell me if you find a single detail on this motorcycle that isn't exquisite.

Being American, the Chief Vintage is rather large in every possible way. From the oversized body panels, engine, handle bar, seats, headlamp, wheels and tyres, this definitely Americana. But it's the most tasteful Americana I've ever seen.

Under the exquisite body, it's got Thunder Stroke 111 cubic inch v-twin. That's 1811 Metric CCs. This is then married to sublime 6 speed gearbox. The result is the delicate sound of thunder; remastered for the 21st century. It's loud, but doesn't shout. It can trouble seismographs on other continents without troubling the rider. It sounds like God whispering.

To ride it is no more difficult than riding any other bike. It's very forgiving. Of course, you need to understand that 370kgs (with fluids) is considerable weight. But it's beautifully balanced and the handlebars are low and wide, so you very quickly learn that provided you ride it with the utmost respect, it won't kill you.

The gearing is very tall, so you'll find that in traffic, you're still in first while other bikes have gone into third gear. Steering a motorcycle this heavy is bit different. Manhandling the handlebar is out of the question. It's just too heavy. A better option is to lean gently into corners and let the front gradually fall in that direction. Think of it like dancing. You lead, the bike follows.

But the first time you hit 6th gear and the Chief settles into a 130kph cruise is a bit of nirvana. It feels so good that you'll find the hair on your arms standing on end, and maybe even an erection. There's something so perfect about flying down the highway on this thing. And there's no effort because it has so much torque (139Nm) and such a supple ride. You'll wonder how you did without this your whole life.

I'm not the biggest fan of American engineering, truth be told. Yes, their muscle cars are iconic because they all have V8s and romantic names. But they all handle about as well as each other. Harleys are superb motorcycles and the torchbearers of American motorcycling. But they also make the Street 750 and 500.

The Indian Chief Classic is in another league. Not only is it pure Americana with generous helpings of chrome, it's as exquisite as a Rolls Royce. Yes, it costs 30 something lakhs, but as Pankaj Dubey, MD of Indian Motorcycles India said, "some dreams cannot be realised immediately. They must be big enough to keep you dreaming for a long time. It makes their realisation that much sweeter."

This is my new dream. Someday I will own this motorcycle.

Over Here, Cadbury! It's Your Lucky Day
BMW 730Ld Signature

This week, we discuss the 7-Series, which – in my opinion – is the only car in the world to possess supernatural powers.

First, it somehow has the ability to make an impression and be utterly discreet at the same time. You'll recognise it of course, but it just sort of slips out of sight just as you started to pay attention. The styling is so basic and rudimentary that visual appeal - in its entirety - is the responsibility of the basic shape itself. No worries there. BMW knew that they needed to be a little conservative with the 7, and they've done just that. The result is a master-class in limo design. The visual bulk is properly offset by the near-perfect proportions.

The interior is very generous in terms of space and creature comforts. As you'd expect, there's electric everything, but only for the back seats. There are two separate screens, reclining seats with air conditioning and massage functions. It fair to assume then, that in this Signature, the 730Ld, has been turned into a pure-play chauffeur-driven limo.

Think about that for a minute. The makers of The Ultimate Driving Machine are stating verbatim that this car is completely inclined toward its rear passengers. That it has no air-con or massage functions in the front seats, or even paddle shifters or head-up display for the driver communicates this unequivocally. This is the part that I don't understand.

How much do you need to love your chauffer to buy a 7 series for him to drive around in? I mean, if all you intend to do is sit in the back, the S Class is much more spacious and sensible.

And that little ejaculation brings me on to another one of its supernatural traits. After 10 minutes of driving, the whole car shrinks around you. That's a tall order when the car is just over 5.2 metres long. I found this out as I drove through typical bazaar streets in Jaipur with street vendors, cycle rickshaws, cattle and everything else you'd expect. Was I flustered? Yes. But as no point did I think that it was unmanageable.

Here's another bit of sorcery and witchcraft for people who think that BMW have gone soft with this back-seat-only limo – it covers ground like nothing I've ever driven before. You've probably worked out that, at Honk, we love cars that cover ground quickly, in great comfort and, if possible, economically as well. The BMW does all this better than any car we've ever driven. There. I said it.

A tank of fuel will get you from Delhi to Jaipur and back with over well over a quarter of it left. We did over 600km (most of it in Sport mode) and this was the result. That's complete madness. Especially when power is produced from a turbocharged straight-six diesel. The engine puts out 248bhp and 560Nm of torque and that's plenty considering that none of it is wasted thanks to the superb ZF 8-speed automatic gearbox. It may not have paddle-shifters but it is as smooth as an unobtrusive as they come.

Let's say for example that you've left Jaipur at 5:00pm and you have a dinner date in Delhi at 8:00pm (I did). It's only 275-odd-kilometres so the distance is manageable. But the traffic is insane. It's as though all of the world's lunatics turn up to practice their lunacy on this particular stretch of road. Of course, the 7 has the pace to deal with this but what you need here are proper brakes. On smooth tarmac the brakes are powerful, but even if the road is slightly undulating – as it is in India quite often – be prepared to find out exactly how Electronic Brake Force Distribution (EBD) works. You can just feel the electronics intervening sending different amounts of braking power to different wheels as the steering wheel bucks and kicks in your hands. This, sadly, I could never get used to.

All in all, it's a formidable piece of kit. Bear in mind that there's an all-new 7 series due next year and you'd be fooled into thinking that BMW have given up on this one. They haven't. They've tickled and fettled it until they've ended up with a creature that that belongs to the open road.

Small Ford = Big Fun, Right?
Ford Figo Aspire

Let's get your misconceptions out of the way first. No, it's not based on the old Figo. Neither is it based on the current Fiesta. It's based on an all-new platform that underpins the Ford Ka for global markets. Yes, the Aspire is a made-for-India product because no other country has this ridiculous four metre regulation which has given us some of the ugliest cars on sale. They all start beautifully at the front and literally hit a wall some way down.

The Figo Aspire has been much more successful in this respect. It's not ugly for a kickoff. In fact, it's got Ford's new signature front end which makes it sort of handsome and cheeky at the same time. On the road, it looks tiny. Really quite small. The little 14" castors that are meant to be wheels don't help. This car could do with proper 15" wheels.

There's more bad news, I'm afraid. Bucking the trend of the hour, Ford's gone and given the high-end Aspire an old-fashioned monochrome LCD screen as oppo-to a touch-screen that can tell you the humidity in Belize. They explain that functionally, it syncs up with your phone and does most things that the new touch-screen ones do using Microsoft's… erm… SYNC. That's all very well.

Respect where it's due, though. This little fellow is quiet, comfortable and peaceful. But it has a better power-to-weight ratio than the current Mercedes A Class diesel. That's only half the story because it's also supremely tractable. It does 45kph to 190 in one gear. This power delivery's been worked out very well. It's got plenty of torque at the bottom end and a sweet midrange. It gives the impression of being a satisfyingly large engine in a small car. It leads one to believe that no matter how much power you need or when, the answer is always 'sure, here you go'. Throw this in with superb real-time fuel economy (easily more than 20kpl) and a slick five speed gearbox, and you've got all the makings of a proper European-standard city slicker. If only that chassis were up to scratch.

Are you kidding? This is a small Ford we're talking about. Of course the chassis is good. In fact, it's a hell of a lot better than good. This car handles well enough to justify the Blue Oval badge, and that's a very big ask of any car. The way it works is that for a small car to carry a Ford badge, it has to out-handle everything that it competes with. And this little Figo does. There is a particularly fundamental joy to driving it. It's as though the car's smiling; it's happy.

Yes, the wheels are small for such a high power-to-weight ratio and the multimedia system is seems a bit last year. But one could quite simply buy one of the lesser models which gives you a phone holder where the screen used to be and – hey presto – you have the all the functions from your phone with Bluetooth audio. And if you too think that the wheels are too small, simply ask your dealer to fit a set from the Fiesta.

This is one car we'd happily recommend because not only is it brilliant as just a car, it's the only car for its money that's made to be driven.

Cross Referenced
Maruti Suzuki S Cross 1.6 Diesel

I'm confused by the new breed of crossovers. They all appear to be utterly shameless visually beefed-up versions of hatchbacks that sell for a lot more than the cars they're based on. We're referring, of course, to the VW Cross Polo, Etios Cross and the Fiat Avventura. Mercifully, these particular cars have sold bugger-all in India. We're really proud to see that India's growing up as a market and can't be conned with some extra ground clearance and plastic body cladding.

On the correct side of this crossover conundrum, you've got cars like the Renault Duster, Ford EcoSport, Skoda Yeti and the forthcoming Hyundai Creta. The primary difference between these and the pretenders is that these are all-new cars and not jacked-up hatchbacks. They might be based on normal cars but they've been completely redesigned and rebuilt with a separate identity. And most importantly, they all look like SUVs and a few (Duster AWD and Yeti 4x4) even perform like them.

And then comes this Suzuki which looks decidedly like a hatchback-on-stilts crossover. It doesn't look at all bad from any angle but anyone who looks at this and gets excited has either been living under a rock their whole lives of they are well overdue to get their eyes checked. It's neither particularly beautiful nor particularly attractive.

But they wouldn't have lived under a rock all their lives because Maruti Suzuki has aimed this car squarely at what it calls an 'evolved customer'. Maruti says that this is someone who is well-travelled and well versed with international standards of car-buying. To this end, they're even rolling out an entirely new range of premium showrooms called NEXA, which will be all black leather and bright lights, just like ZARA - which they openly admit it was styled after.

Here you'll be treated to some posh coffee, while a salesman with an iPad (they're very particular about this) gives you a 'buying experience'. This person will also manage your relationship with the brand. We could write this off as blarney but Maruti still pretty-much OWNS the Indian car market. They must know what they are doing.

Or should they? Because every question that was asked about the car or NEXA was answered beginning 'Our survey showed that…' So the S Cross doesn't have an automatic gearbox or AWD because their survey of 'evolved customers' said they weren't important. Suffice to say this car is basically the result of survey results. Begs the question, since when did people know what they wanted until it was shown to them?

Anyway, the car. The interior is, mercifully, black. It's very tastefully done. The steering wheel is packed full of buttons. Don't worry, they work quite well and fall easily to hand. Except the ones that operate the phone which are hidden inside the wheel like a Range Rover Evoque's. The centre console is squeaky clean, with the touch-screen interface dominating your vision. It's a simple device cooked up by Maruti and Bosch. And let's be honest, it feels more tactile and better to use than the Range Rover Evoque's.

The S Cross has a very strong party trick – the sheer acreage at the back and supernatural ride quality. Turns out that Mr Evolved Customer was good for something after all because along with being packed to the rafters with features, fantastic NVH management, an incredibly spacious back seat and a ride worthy of a European badge, it also has a beautifully long-legged drivetrain which makes it a great highway car. The 1.6 diesel engine feels grunty and robust and the 6-speed manual works well in the last 3 gears.

We're still slightly confused about this car, if we're honest. It's not particularly fun to drive. It's let down by a notchy gearshift and over-assisted steering. It's forgettable to behold offering nothing India hasn't seen before. But its strengths are rock-solid because as a place to be in and a device to get about in, it can still kick many a 20+ lakh car in the nuts. If ALL you want is a great ride and lots of space for anything this side of a Yeti, the S Cross is your new default choice.

Less A Class, More Mercedes
Mercedes-Benz A200 CDI

I'll never forget the sight of the A Class flying up the beautiful drive at Ratan Tata's Officer's Holiday Home in Ooty. It was my first ever Mercedes road test – the first time someone had said 'here's a Mercedes, go play with it.' Of course, it helped that the A Class was a cracking car. It took Mercedes deep into BMW territory with its crispness, precision and poise. It felt - what's the word - alive.

This new diesel A200 CDI has the exact same engine as the old A180 CDI, only in a different state of tune. In fact, this same motor stretches all the way to the 204bhp and 500Nm 250 CDI. Flexible, eh?

In 200 CDI tune, it's 136bhp and 300 torques. And it's lazy. It's as easy going as a Goan at 3:00pm on a Sunday afternoon. You put your foot down and nothing actually happens. You can feel a downshift. Eventually. And a few seconds later you find yourself doing 150kph without really knowing how you got there. You can't really feel it accelerating, and yet it does, smoothly, silently and without making a fuss about it. The tyres have had a big lunch as well. They're fatter for a better ride and the wheels have gone down from 17" to 16". They're now the same Eco-Comfy size as the B Class's.

Mercedes has taken the A Class out of the rock band, cleaned it up and sent it off to college, which should upset us. But it doesn't.

The result of this *lazification* is actually quite a lot more real-world pace. But more than that, it feels more like a Mercedes than it ever did. It's developed an ease of operation it never had. This is most apparent in the city. In the earlier car, you had to forgive the slightly firm ride because you knew that it handled well. With this one, there's nothing to forgive. It's a lot plusher than it used to be. It's slighter higher as well which means it can easily deal with speed bumps and big potholes. As an automobile, a car, a device meant to take you, your passengers and luggage from A to B, Mercedes has improved it in every way. It's even got a panoramic sunroof now.

On the highway it feels like a proper Mercedes. It's silent, efficient, predictable, un-dramatic and fast. If you're reasonable with how much speed you carry into corners – most people are – then you'll really enjoy that reassuring feel that Mercs do so well. It will easily do 900km on a 50-litre tank of diesel without batting an eyelid if you just drive normally on the highway. A word of caution, though. As with all Mercs, the 7-speed double-clutch auto box is geriatric. Lightning fast, it ain't. In fact, we'd advise manual control on a mountain road or if you're on a road where you need to make quick overtakes. Treat it like a proper manual. Get into gear before you make your move.

It pains me to say that that the crispness is almost gone. That magic, that almost organic connection it had with the driver has all but withered away. It's still there, but it's been watered down. But it's alright because it's much better at being a Mercedes. If that doesn't fly, there's a new one coming soon. It'll be better to drive. And even more beautiful.

Breaking Balls
Scott Scale 770

I wonder what it's like to be normal. I mean really average. I'm sure it must have its advantages. Anonymity, inherent discretion, the ability to keep a straight face when a Lamborghini passes by. All this seems – on paper – invaluable.

I have no such luck, sadly. Aside from being ungainly tall, I have a receding hairline, a face like a fish that died last month, two huge ears that can pick up local radio stations from Uzbekistan, a crooked nose, teeth that look like they were discovered (and immediately abandoned) by pre-Nazi archaeologists and an entirely illegal amount of enthusiasm for most things automotive. To top it off, in the last eight years, I've become probably the only person outside rural Africa who is thin and fat at the same time; like a pumpkin propped up by two chopsticks.

Just for good measure, throw in chain smoking, the occasional booze binge, a diet consisting mainly of dead animals and zero exercise and you see why it's not hard to convince people that men can indeed get pregnant.

If I'd gone on living like that, I wouldn't have seen my thirty-fifth birthday. Something had to be done.

Fortunately, Scott Cycles called just as I was staring at myself in the mirror wondering how a proper six-pack turned into a bloody football. This was it. Cycling would get me back in shape.

The bike they sent round for me to 'test' was called the Scale 770. It was essentially a mountain bike with knobbly tyres and more than three times the number of gears of any car I've ever driven.

Apparently, bicycles such as this are made using the same cutting-edge tech you see in posh cars, fast motorbikes and even aeroplanes. And so it went with the 770. This thing rocked up with a 30-speed gearbox, disc brakes fore and aft, lockable front suspension for tricky uphill bits, easily detachable wheels and proper MAXXIS off-road tyres. All this came in at about 80 thousand INR. Spanking value. Apparently.

Inevitably, there are one or two issues. As with most fancy bicycles, you sit on the most delicate part of the male anatomy. It's that bit just between… ahem… your two organs of excretion. In the first week, things get frightfully sore. And the chaffing is actually bad enough to make you think twice about the whole business.

There's more. A bicyclist's fuel is pretty much what's in his belly and the air in his lungs. In a city like Amsterdam or Copenhagen where there's virtually no pollution your lungs are full to the overflowing with the respiratory equivalent of Shell V-Power. In Bangalore however, you can actually see the air. It's mostly grey or brown. Or a worrying mix of both.

In the first week, I started out doing between 10 and 15 kilometres a day. All the things you take for granted in a car or a motorbike cause such strong emotional reactions when you're on a bicycle. The hammer-blow when you see an up-hill incline. The sheer elation when you see a decline. The vivid rage you feel when someone carves you up and you have to accelerate all over again. That excruciating burn in your legs. The cotton-mouth. Dry throat. Empty, overworked lungs. Your heart pounding so hard that the only thing it purports to do next is stop altogether. So you do before it does.

Here's the funny part, after precisely a minute (and 100ml of water), you feel absolutely normal again. I'd stop whenever I was completely shattered, take a minute's break and a sip of water, and get going again.

The second week was worse. Because I'd built up a bit of a tolerance, I started doing 25-30 kilometres each day. And that's when I started to understand this bicycle. It may be billed as a mountain bike, but what it likes best is to be ridden viciously across all surfaces.

With a normal bicycle, you turn the handlebar or lean into a corner to change direction. On the Scale 770, you tap the back brake, lock the rear and slide. This is a very effective way of changing direction provided you use it correctly. If that doesn't work, flicking a switch locks the front suspension and a careful index finger brakes the front wheel just hard enough to lift the rear into the air. This can then be placed anywhere you want by shifting weight. This is particularly useful in tight spaces. Traffic jams particularly.

I can't say I've got any fitter or healthier as a result of cycling, sadly, because I only rode it maybe 20 times in the month that I had it. But as bicycles go, the Scott Scale 770 presents that perfect all-round package of practicality, kicks and cracking value brought to you by one of the best brands in the business.

But cycling isn't for me. Mainly because it's done what feels like irreparable damage to my scrotum. And since I really haven't been able to find a replacement within budget, I think I'll just give up smoking and eat healthier. And go to the bloody gym like normal people.

Super Cat
Jaguar F Type R Coupe

The Jaguar F Type R Coupe is not the best-looking car in the world. That said, it is an agonisingly close second only to its convertible sibling. It is Greek-Goddess beautiful. It's as classically correct as Sophia Loren's sunglasses. It's the kind of beauty – I'm ashamed to say – that even I can't aptly describe.

You'd expect this, of course, because a) it's a Jaguar and b) it was designed by Ian Callum. He's given us extraordinary cars like the Aston Martin DB7 and DB9 and all the Jaguars currently on sale. Suffice to say that we think he's the best car designer alive today. Either way, I can guarantee you'd whip your phone out and take pictures if you saw one; as did about 500 people during my two-day test.

The cabin is pretty much the same as the convertible. Which is to say immaculate quality and functionality, beautiful ergonomics and more than enough space for yours truly, who's 6'3". The car itself is only slightly taller than my waist-line. And this is all the more astonishing because not only did I fit in it, but it also had enough ground-clearance to deal with just anything that a luxury saloon could.

But you don't want to know about the ground clearance, do you? You want to know what 542bhp and 680Nm of torque feel like from the 5.0 supercharged V8. Imagine the sound a sleeping tiger would make if you were to suddenly and without warning, stick your finger into its bottom. That's what it sounds like. Loud, angry, vicious and very scary.

It is, without a doubt, the best automotive soundtrack in current times. And it gets even better because Jaguar has fitted a little button on the centre console that opens valves in the exhaust and makes it even louder. I'm going to stop short of saying that it's better than Merc's erstwhile 6.3 AMGs. But it's as good as. Which makes it as good as the best engine sound I've ever heard. This is sonic euphoria.

It's Felix the house cat in the city – gliding gracefully from one traffic light to the next without so much as a murmur of complaint. I drove it in peak hour traffic for four hours non-stop and it didn't bite once. What was apparent was the very firm ride. At low speeds, there is very little give in the suspension. The fact that the tyres are skinny doesn't help its case. It's very well damped so it never crashes over bumps, but it does transmit every single surface imperfection to the seat of your pants. Don't worry though, because there is a way to get past this.

Take it out onto the open road, lower the windows, push the exhaust button on the dash, select Dynamic Mode and hit the loud pedal as hard as you can. Don't panic if you see a corner coming. The brakes are superb. And you'll know just how great the chassis, steering and suspension are when you corner at the limit or beyond.

As you watch yourself smiling the smile of someone about to 'arrive', the G-forces attacking your vital organs, the wall of noise, and the buzz you get from being so comprehensively in control of this beast, you'll realise that you're driving one of the all-time greats.

With the F Type, Jaguar has proved one very important point that all sporstcar and supercar makers have ignored in recent times. It has proved that performance figures are just numbers. What actually matters is feel. And that's where the F Type stands above just about anything else. This is a true sportscar because it looks superb and feels fantastic to drive.

Smooth Operator
Mercedes-Benz GLA 200

A few weeks ago, we brought you the review of Mercedes' answer to the clinical Audi Q3 and BMW's apocalyptically hideous X1. It was called the GLA and one thing was readily apparent; it had all the right SUV vibes even without having four-wheel drive. But that was the diesel. And even if I told you that it sounds like a road drill and rides like a medieval wheelbarrow (it doesn't, by the way), that's the one you'd buy.

So what's the point of a petrol version? In this day and age when petrol costs more than both your children's kidneys and then gets consumed before you've ever got to pump to get some more, why did Mercedes bother with a petrol version? Is it some sort of 'look, we're still selling petrol cars even when BMW and Audi and phasing them out'? Or does it have to do with the fact that it's cheaper to build petrol cars and therefore more profitable?

The answer to both those questions is a definite maybe. But you should be glad they're making the GLA 200.

I'll be the first to admit the fact that it might not be the prettiest car an obvious way. It's the opposite of cutesy. It's chunky, massively detailed and sits on thick, muscular haunches at the C-Pillar. Altogether, it is a properly aggressive small SUV; like a Lladro British Bulldog. I saw one of these at night outside Bangalore's UB city and it looked right among the endless Range Rovers and posh shops. Staunch aficionados of showing off will like the attention it gets.

The interior is different from the diesel version we drove earlier. It's predominantly beige. I don't understand our fixation with beige. I mean, yes, it makes a cabin feel a bit bigger, but black is infinitely sexier and more timeless. Still, as it turns out, it feels like a proper Mercedes so that's good.

And now we get to why this is one of the best cars we've driven this year; that engine. It is smoother than the love child of Frank Sinatra and Monica Bellucci smeared in honey. It's been ages since I've driven anything that is just so creamy. It means you'll never hear it in the city. Ever. And unless it's in Sport mode, you'll never hear it on the highway, either. And even the less-than-perfect 7-speed double-clutch gearbox seems to be more in tune with the progressive nature of this motor.

It flies down the highway with a composure that I've never experienced in a front-wheel-drive. Along with being massively planted, it feels progressive and does a wonderful job of isolating you and involving you in the drive in equal measures. That last bit was normally the core of BMW saloons exclusively. It's A Class genes are more than prevalent.

In most cars, when you arrive at a corner, the instinct is (and racing rule, for that matter) to brake on the way in and throttle on the way out. In the GLA, I found myself braking well before the corners only so I could throttle my way right through them. This is where the chassis, the suspension and the steering start to play their little number. Even if the front starts to drift wide half-way through the corner, backing off the throttle brings it smoothly back into line. To be honest, this is how a proper road-tester describes the handling of a hot-hatchback. But that's what was going on here.

None of this matters, I suppose. I could tell you if costs fifty rupees and it comes with ten free Megan Foxes. But you'd still buy the diesel, which is a great luxury car by any measure. But the GLA 200? This is the very essence of how a modern luxury car should feel.

Dad's Army
BMW 320d Gran Tourismo

In thirty odd years of me having known my father, it has so transpired that he is a responsible ex-army officer with a penchant for discipline and life's finer offerings in equal measures. All very normal. But last year, we discovered that he could play the flute. Quite well, in fact. Even my mother didn't know this. He'd never thought to play it or even divulge the fact he could for all these years. This is something I respect but don't fully understand because here we are in 2015 where people publicise even their wind-breaking and nose-picking abilities in an effort to get famous on YouTube.

And that brings us neatly onto the BMW 320d Gran Tourismo. With the GT, BMW has targeted the more mature buyer. It's softer, more spacious and generally more relaxed than the normal 3 Series. To be fair, we really like the normal 3 Series at Honk. It's probably the most balanced saloon car in the world. There's a real sense when you drive one that all the intrinsic engineering that could possibly go into making a keen driver's car has gone into it. With the GT version, it feels like all the intrinsic engineering has been watered down to make it more forgiving; easier to live with.

It's got a lot heavier as well. The rear end has been redesigned to be larger, more commodious and crucially, uglier. On the plus side, there's a vast amount of space in the back seat, the boot's big enough for about four medium-sized corpses and the lid can be opened and closed electrically. Not to mention the retractable spoiler that sits on top of it. A spoiler on a 2.0L diesel saloon which weighs two tonnes. Right.

Put a GT badge on any car and you'd presume it's meant for long distances. And the GT isn't too bad at that. But it doesn't come close to being as much fun as the regular 3. Let me put it this way, in a regular 3 series, you'll arrive at your destination happy and excited. In the GT, you'll arrive relaxed.

So we can safely assume that BMW has gone after a piece of Mercedes' pie with this. And, to be honest, I wouldn't have it over a C Class. Because while it is supremely comfortable, as easy to drive as a shopping trolley and as relaxing as being in bed, the C Class is better at all of these things.

But I haven't got to the best part yet. Just like discovering my father's hidden musical inclinations, we had a revelation with the GT – it's a proper leathery drift machine. Say what you want about the laziness, the looks, the market positioning and whatever else, but this is still a BMW. Turn the ESP and DSC off and it'll spin it rear tyres until they burst. Yes, it's only got 184 odd horsepowers and 380 torques from a modest 2.0 diesel, but with electronics off, the 8-speed auto box gives you everything every time you put your foot down. It is honestly like your dad joining your jam session and playing brilliantly with your band.

Add that to properly good manners in the city, a brown leather interior in a black car (perfect combination, by the way), cabin space better than a 5 series', lots of electronics and gadgets, very strong fuel economy and all you really need to get past are the looks. Sorry dad, but I'll stick with the regular 3 series. It's just more BMW. Still, it was great fun jamming with you.

Renaissance Man
Fiat Punto Evo 90hp

Good news! Fiat's finally got its act together. After years in the sales doldrums, they've finally worked out that sharing showroom space with Tata motors wasn't the best idea. I found this out first hand when I went to buy my Linea T Jet Plus in back in 2011. The salesman tried his hardest to convince me that the Tata Manza was better in every way. I punched him and bought the Fiat, of course, but I can imagine the hundreds that were actually swayed by the pitch and bought the taxi instead. They've got their own dealer and service network now and, all things considered, Fiat is now a brand that even evangelical enthusiasts of boredom and bean-counting can buy into.

The cars were never bad. Far from it, in fact. Fiat provided the only options for the petrolhead on a budget. And three years later, they still make the best driver's cars in their respective segments.

This, by no stretch of the imagination, means that they were perfect. In my car alone, the window lining fell off, the ABS warning light came on and stayed on for weeks after it had been fixed. The handbrake button fell off, the Bluetooth Blue & Me system is the hardest in the world to connect a phone to, and the list goes on. But I would take all that and more all over again because as a device to comfort you on your daily commute, it's up there with a bed. And as a source of entertainment, it's like being on stage with Aerosmith.

So when the Punto Evo came out, I was priapic with anticipation. You see, the Punto is the very essence of budget Italian city car. And the new Evo seems to have slightly lost the plot with its styling. It looks good, no doubt. But the Evo's fussy styling is not something that Giorgietto Giugiaro, its original designer, would approve of. The subtlety has given way to aggressive detailing that we associate more with Hyundai than Fiat. But the flipside is that it does look more modern. In a country like India where 'new is always better', this matters a lot.

The Evo's interior is vastly improved over the old Punto's. Great design, many buttons and corresponding features and great use of black round off a very cool place to be. It comes alive at night with soft but prominent amber illumination in the cabin. Feels a lot more expensive than it is, to be honest.

Then it goes a bit downhill, I'm afraid. Turning the key seems to wake up what sounds like a building site. That little 1.3 litre diesel sounds positively agricultural. This is where the Evo starts to reveal its bipolarity. The clutch pedal appears to travel to the moon (plus 18 inches) each time you shift gear. I ended up riding it – something I never do otherwise – to keep it going smoothly in city traffic. The throttle pedal is more suggestive than precise because it gives you the kind of power it thinks you want. Vague, I think would be the kindest way to describe it. And the turning radius makes every three-point-turn into a four or five.

But find a twisting road and the Evo comes over all Italian. All the looseness and fluidity of the old Punto feel enhanced. Almost like the Evo's taken a 'blue pill'. It flows from corner to corner like nothing else you can buy for this money. And that building site of an engine has so much torque that you can choose either third or fourth gear and leave it there. From there on, it's pretty much untouchable for the way it feels. It doesn't matter how fat you are, your bum will experience feedback like never before. And that steering. Oh, the steering. Feel, feedback, predictability are what it does best.

The only dynamic niggle I found was from the tyres. The Apollos that my test car had were a bit kak. Insist on the Goodyears at your dealer. They're a hundred times better and complete the experience.

Please make your own decision about whether or not you can live with its foibles. And if all you want from a car is engineering fidelity and reliability, there are plenty of other options. But if you have about 7.33 (Ex-Bangalore) lakhs and you love driving, there is still only one way to scratch your itch – the Italian way.

Badassery is Alive and Well and Lives in Jaipur

Two Years Later – Rajputana Customs

Keen readers will remember that Honk featured Rajputana Customs two years ago. We knew very little about them back then. But going there, meeting Vijay Singh and getting a first-hand feel of their work was a bit of a revelation. We'd never thought that India would produce a bike builder of this calibre.

But here we are in 2015, and all that changed about Vijay is that he's lost a lot of weight; all of which seems to have made its way onto his upper lip to form a mammoth moustache.

It's refreshing to see that he's the same laid-back humble guy he was two years ago. We've all seen success change people. We've seen their horns grow and their egos explode. I'm really glad this BS hasn't got to him. And I'm glad because this 29-year-old has a social responsibility – to continue making India's finest custom motorcycles.

Apparently, we're not the only people who think he's at the top of India's bike-building food chain. While we were busy taming dunes and racing Range Rover Sports against paragliders, Rajputana Customs popped up on the radars of no less than Harley Davidson and Triumph Motorcycles. This tiny motorcycle coach-building outfit from Jaipur was commissioned to build for two of the biggest bike brands in the world. Whichever way you look at it, that's a bloody big deal.

Let's start with the Harley. It started life a bog-standard Street 750, complete with MRF tyres. But Vijay and his team have taken it somewhere else. The finished article appears to be the love child of a café racer and an angry special-forces soldier. It has an intrinsic brutality to it that we haven't seen since Jens Von Brauck made the InfraRed V Max for Yamaha (Just Google it, please). We just took to calling it a Brawler because it reminded us of someone who's always looking for a fight. And it's loud. Really, spleen shatteringly, thunderously loud. Even here, there's a visual elegance that's come to be the signature of Rajputana Customs.

Next up was the Triumph Scrambler, aka No.1. This started out as a stock Bonneville. Triumph was nice enough so give them all the parts they needed. But I doubt if they could've known it would be so different in character to their own Scrambler. The No.1 is civilized in the same way as Bappi Lahri is handsome, I.e., not at all. The noise coming out of those exhausts is violent. The sound reminds me of the Jaguar F-Type R. Proper Braaap Braaap, this one. Surprisingly, it had knobby tyres, which of course meant that our boy (with the biggest smile on his moustache) threw it around in the dirt for our cameras.

I rode the No. 1 for a little bit as well, and here's my report. First, I made the mistake of wearing shorts. Bad idea. The exhausts are about 2.734 inches from your right butt-cheek, so it gets pretty hot. But it doesn't matter. From the first time you give it full throttle, you're hooked. If there's one thing I love about Rajputana is that they distil pure single-malt riding pleasure into their bikes. The noise and the sensations were quite the sensory overload. Going through the gears on a short stretch of open road is like pulling the trigger on a machine gun. The primeval part of your brain just doesn't want it to stop. I must mention at this point that, mechanically, it felt like a production bike. Which is to say that it felt beautifully made.

The time has come now to put all this in perspective. There will always be posers who turn up at bike shows and win build-offs because they've got access to big tyres and the continent's supply of chrome; and who cares if their bikes are damn-near unrideable. And then there's the Rajputana Customs, who just quietly go about their business of making fantastic motorcycles.

Japanese Gem
Honda Mobilio 1.5 i-DTEC V

To curb my gigantic ego – which I've got from reviewing virtually every posh car on sale – I've stepped into the world of the van driver with the Honda Mobilio. Make no mistake about it. This is a diesel van. This endless need to fill niches means that this seven seater is based on the Brio, and I know what you're thinking. The Brio is tiny, isn't it? So how in whatever's name has it been suitably adapted to seat seven? Very intelligently; that's how.

Call me mental but I like the way it looks. It's sort of round and edgy at the same time. It's got little kinks here and there to make it look fresh and interesting. It's no Lamborghini, but it's alright for a van.

The inside is typically Japanese. It feels very logical and functional. The car we tested was the V spec and, sadly, it had what Honda calls a 'Woody finish' on the dashboard. That's Honda-speak for fake wood. At least Honda is man enough to say it is. It's still a quite ghastly but some people like that sort of thing, apparently. It matches perfectly with their orange nylon shirts and fake gold watches.

As is the norm these days it has a touch screen infotainment system. You get satnav, Bluetooth, literally endless ways to play music, a DVD player for the full taxicab experience, Dolby surround sound that's hooked up to many speakers and lots of thoughtful little bits and bobs. There are a few oddities as well. For example, the bottle holders in the door pockets can't fit a one litre water bottle. The ceiling mounted air vents for the second row of seats also face the front seats. There must've been some logic behind it or Honda wouldn't have done it.

But what they've done really quite well is the packaging. You can choose between the third row of seats or a massive boot. As a five-seater, it's about as practical as a car can be. And it can actually seat seven adults. Even better is the flexibility of the seating. The second and third rows can be moved about and folded flat in different sections. This means you could be in the third row and stretch your legs out over the second row of seats. Or some such.

The engine and gearbox are ideally suited to chilled out driving. It has a hundred horsepower, but it only revs to 4000rpm. And because it has no turbo you've got to do quite a lot of work. And the gearbox doesn't like slick shifts. But there is a sweet spot. If you just drive it peacefully, it chugs along quite nicely and you and your six passengers can enjoy the very well set up ride. It feels like Honda has spent a lot of time tuning the suspension. And it doesn't roll in the corners either. This is proper engineering done by proper engineers. This means that it isn't all that bad to drive. It's not fun, but it's restful and predictable.

The result of all this is a car that feels complete. It is, sadly, still a diesel van. But it's a very strongly engineered and well thought out car with more toys than you'd expect.

Centre of Attraction
Range Rover Evoque

When Land Rover announced that Victoria Beckham was on its design panel, I must confess I felt a little knot in my stomach. What's a glorified former Spice Girl-turned-socialite-tuned-fashionista got to do with car design when Gerry McGovern was charged with designing it? McGovern knows how to design beautiful SUVs all on his own. Take a look at all the Land Rovers and Range Rovers on sale today. He designed all of them.

Mrs Beckham was brought in for two reasons; her exquisite taste, and to be used as a muse. She was the ideal customer for the Evoque. This meant that, above all else, it had to be supremely stylish. And it is. Since its launch in 2011, there has never been a better-looking SUV. Many have tried. All have failed.

The size is symptomatic of its known usage. Even LR knows that Evoques will spend their entire lives in crowded city centres with the occasional road trip. As a result, it has a tiny footprint; about the same as an Audi Q3. But that hasn't really affected the interior. It does feel a bit cosy, even in beige, but when you actually stop and look around, it's big. Simply put, I can roll the driver's seat all the way back and still fit comfortably behind it. The boot's pretty big as well. Honestly, you could have four proper fatties on board and it still won't feel cramped.

There's something about any Range Rover's interior. Something you can't really put your finger on. They just have great taste. Exquisite materials abound. Everything you can see and touch feels expensive; special. Everything falls nicely to hand. As places to be when one travels, Range Rovers are something else.

If there's one ergonomic glitch in the cabin, it's the steering wheel. It's huge. And it needs to be because it contains an entire computer keyboard. I counted 22 buttons. But I could be wrong. It could be 50. Honestly, there are buttons hidden behind buttons. How on earth is some posh actress-type-thing that this car is aimed at meant to make any sense of it all? The next day's headline should read 'Celeb undergoes counselling after accidently activating cruise control in traffic'.

It's really strange about the steering wheel because a) the other Range Rovers don't have nearly as many buttons and b) the dashboard has very few.

I loved driving the Evoque in the city. You get the sense that no matter what car anyone else has, yours is more beautiful. But then I arrived at a slightly bumpy stretch and the love was diluted to like. The suspension is stiff. MINI Cooper stiff. The kind of surfaces the larger Range Rovers would glide over are quite a jarring experience in the Evoque. I really didn't see that coming. And neither did my posh lady-friend whom I'd taken along for the drive. After her third angry and perplexed stare, I pulled over to check if the suspension was in some sport setting. It wasn't. So we went off-roading.

Those two words, Range and Rover, mean 'going places where no other car can go in complete comfort and supreme luxury'. And the Evoque didn't disappoint. It can climb, crawl on rocks, find traction where others simply spin their wheels and keep right on going. It is a proper Range Rover. Unlike its more expensive brothers, it has the old Terrain Response. You've to tell it if you're on tarmac, sand, rocks, grass or snow and it'll set up the ride height, suspension travel, throttle response, AWD system and traction control accordingly. And it really works quite well.

Long story short, it's a very pretty car, pretty enough to forgive the steering wheel, the stiff ride and a slightly agricultural-sounding diesel engine from Ford. But it has a party piece. If you see one driving out of a posh nightclub at 3am, you just know the party's left with it.

Thunder Nearing
Royal Enfield Thunderbird 500

Confession time – I, Sidharth Sharotri, am a Bullet-head – always have been and always will be. So, while you may lust for a Duke 390 or even a Ducati Panigale, all I want is a nice satisfying single-cylinder dug-dug-dug-dug at 60-80kph.

It helps that I've owned a few bullets over the years along with the old first-generation Thunderbird 350. Granted, it had its gear shifter on the left (which is like finding out that Axl Rose secretly listens to Britney Spears), but it was a great touring bike. I rode it to college, work, the hills the beach and everywhere else. All it asked of me was fuel. And the occasional clutch cable.

A few weeks ago, Royal Enfield sent the new Thunderbird 500 round for test. And if I'm honest, I was in a fix over my first impression. More capacity, more power, more torque, more refinement; but electronic fuel injection and, wait for it, LED lighting. To an old-school Bullet-head, that last bit's perfectly revolting. I didn't even like the idea of electric start.

But here's the thing, under the leadership of Siddhartha Lal, Royal Enfield is targeting a whole new market – people who want to ride for pleasure without the histrionics associated with Royal Enfields of yore. And the Thunderbird 500 is just that. It's just about everything the old one was without any of the fuss.

What's it like to ride? Let's pick it apart. The clutch is nice and meaty and it feels like shaking hands with an old friend. The 5-speed gearbox has very satisfying mechanical feel to it, like the bolt action of a rifle. Beware, though, because it has a couple of false neutrals. The new 500cc single-cylinder fuel injected motor puts out 27bhp, 41Nm of torque is an absolute peach. It's nice and quiet when you use less than 20% throttle and bellows like two angry Pavarottis to announce its awakening when you give it more.

At crawling speeds, the weight of the bike and the weight of the controls do demand more of you than you're initially prepared to give; almost as if it's trying to make a man out of you. So if you're used to riding one of those little commuter bikes whose names I can never remember, you might find your daily commute a little challenging to begin with. But once you realise that it demands and deserves a certain level of respect, you will wonder how you did without it all your life.

It must also be said this was the only time that I've asked for a vehicle for a second test because I didn't get to go touring the first time around. On the 400km it covered in two days of riding, it saw, chewed up and spat out everything that Indian roads threw at it. At 60-90kph, it did absolutely nothing wrong. I didn't bother maxing it out because it's a bullet, not a point and squirt racer.

As a touring companion, it's right up there with Harley Davidson. Except that it has its own identity and the sensations that it's capable of delivering are so unique and pleasurable that you won't get them from any other machine.

Here's my verdict, then. It costs about two lakhs on-road. Buy one, fill it up with petrol and write to us about your adventures. Have a good one.

Made for India
Hyosung Aquila 250

Just as there are different kinds of Petrolheads, there are different kinds of motorcycle enthusiasts. We all know about Bulletheads. We're also acutely aware of Harley's HOGs. There are many people who fancy wearing leather and rubber clothing for their sojourns on the superbikes. I've also just come across people who love doing gruelling, long-distance rides on their Pulsars, which, let's face it, were made to tear up city streets. But what if you don't belong to any of these factions? What if, for you, a bike is only meant to draw attention to yourself?

Fear not, because as usual, it's Honk to the rescue. Meet the new king of budget bling – the Hyosung Aquila 250 whose *raison d'être* is to turn eyeballs. The motorcycling equivalent of Soulja Boy's gold clock hung around his neck. Everything is shiny, including the candy white paintwork.

Let's see what this two-wheeled Liberace is all about. To begin with, it looks like a cruiser should. It's low, wide and long with very good quality visibly. There are no panel gaps or bits of exposed welding. The whole thing looks and feels very well put together. Seriously good quality levels here.

The riding position is bang on as well. It's been engineered in such a way that people of just about any reasonable size can get comfortable. And the slightly-lower-than-shoulder-height handlebars mean that it's easy to steer in the city and quite comfortable on the highway. The seat's pretty good too.

Everything works well in the city. The weight is easily managed and though it's not exactly nippy, it deals with traffic pretty well for something of its girth. The gearing really helps here because it's always well behaved. At idling, it's got a typical V-Twin sound – burble burble burble. Although this changes when you start moving. At low revs it sounds like a single.

Where it could use a little bit of work is when a little performance is asked of it. Let me tell you what I'm on about. It has five gears and you can get into fifth as early as 50kph. You can then hold this all the way until 150kph. This sounds great, right? All that flexibility. Well, it's not. Because at 80kph, it's in fifth at 5000 revs. This makes it feel stressed. And that makes cruising more stressful than it should be. The quarter litre V Twin makes its peak power, 26bhp, at 9000rpm and its peak torque of 23Nm at 7000 revs. Let me tell you the problem with that. A cruiser (with the exception of the Harley Night Rod Special which you read about here) is supposed to have long legs, ie., tall gearing, especially the last two. It's supposed feel effortless. This doesn't.

But that could be an easy fix – a sixth gear. DSK Hyosung hinted that there could be something to that effect rolling out of their plant in India when they start local production. That would take a product which is sort of interesting to a level it deserves. And take the price down from its current 2.8 lakh ex-showroom ticket.

There's some sound thinking behind DSK Hyosung, from bullet-proof products to owners' clubs and first-in-the-industry service packages. Yes, the bikes lack a bit of soul and the brand lacks petrolhead credibility. But give them time. They just might surprise you.

Perfection Reinvented
Mercedes Benz CLS250 CDI

Meetings generally don't work. I've had tonnes of them and hardly any of them resulted in something important. Even with Mercedes, I throw random ideas and elaborately constructed schemes in their faces every time I meet them, but the actual work gets done in about three minutes on the phone.

That said, I would've loved to be there for the meeting that conceived the CLS. At the time, Mercedes had had it up to here with Maserati's Quattraporte which was the only saloon car on the market with any real style. The result was a four-door car that had the low profile of a coupe and the styling to turn men into tripods. It was an achingly beautiful car. It was almost as if Mercedes had out-done Maserati at being Maserati.

Jump to 2015 and we've got the face-lifted version of the second generation CLS on test. And don't tell anyone, but I'm still massively priapic. Even if you drive a Lamborghini every day, you'll still look at the CLS and think 'yeah, that is beautiful'. It's long, low and wide, with a tapering tail. Like the Jag XJ, the CLS's proportions appear to be slightly off, but they work beautifully.

The interior, one gets the impression, was designed to induce as much emotion as the exterior. The big slab of wood that dominates the interior is now unpolished. It's got a dull, warm feeling that actually encourages you to touch it. The rest of it is a mix of leather, brushed aluminium and Mercedes level plastics. Being a Mercedes, there are hundreds of thoughtful features but there are one of two that we think have been left out. The first is a panoramic sunroof. If the A Class has one, there's no reason why the Agent Provocateur that is the CLS, shouldn't. Next are temperature-controlled seats, or the lack of them. At this price point, one does look for a real kicker on the features list, which for the CLS, seems to be headlamps (more on them later).

But the real heartbreaker isn't any of that. It isn't even the 17" wheels. The real knee to the gut is the engine. It's a 250 CDI diesel. In a car as extroverted and extravagant as the CLS, it is as appropriate as the Queen in shorts and a t-shirt. Merc's V6 diesel would be perfect for this car. It's smooth, silent and effortless at any speed.

But this is also where my case falls flat on its face. The CLS isn't particularly expensive. It's well under 80 lakhs (Ex-Delhi) and for that you get an extremely beautiful, superbly well thought out car with no rivals remotely near its price point.

Even that engine starts to make sense when you feel it do 0-100kph in 7.5 seconds. It can also do a 160-200kph cruise all day long while giving you mental economy figures. And come on, that's what you really want.

I'm not the biggest fan of air suspension. But it does have its benefits. While the ground clearance is enough to deal with most speed bumps, there's a button on the dash that raises the car even higher. In India, in the monsoons, you'll be glad it's there. There is another button which changes the suspension between Sport and Comfort. I wouldn't bother with Sport really, because it's just like Comfort, only bumpier and much less pleasant.

The fact is this. While the V6 diesel may seem more appropriate for a car such as this, I'd like to ask anyone to use the CLS for a few days; to do whatever they do normally with a car and then ask themselves if they thought it was underpowered. Unless they're Lewis Hamilton, or that German bugger that nobody really likes, they'll love the CLS as it is.

do whatever they do normally with a car and then ask themselves if they thought it was underpowered. Unless they're Lewis Hamilton, or that German bugger that nobody really likes, they'll love the CLS as it is.

The Teenage Dream Has Come of Age
MINI Cooper S Convertible

I needed to be sure so I went on the internet and checked. After two hours and a not inconsiderable amount of instant coffee, I discovered that, at 34 and bit lakhs, this is the cheapest convertible you can buy in India.

Just think about that for a second. The fully vegetarian Audi A3 cabrio, which has about as much personality as a Swedish accountant, costs 46 lakhs. But you get a proper full-fat fire-breathing Cooper S drop-top for 34.

As you'd expect, though, there are one or two little niggles worth mentioning. First, although it's six inches longer than the old one, the back seats are still only good for small children. Or that really bendy yoga dude from television. Second, even in what MINI calls GREEN mode, you're looking at 7kpl in the city. Third, the boot, while bigger than the old one, is still only the size of a hotel-room mini bar. And finally, the image. The regular MINI is quite cheeky, but this is on another level. Whether by some misguided need to sell single-malt attraction or because the styling team was made up exclusively of posh sixteen-year-old girls, the MINI cabrio is as look-at-me as they come. Can you imagine the amount of time you'd have to spend in front of the mirror before you could go for a drive?

And that's not even the whole story. Try to imagine someone in a business suit stepping out of one. In fact, try to imagine anyone you'd readily recognise as a heterosexual gentleman stepping out of one. See what I mean?

But get past the image and you immediately begin to realise that it is a deeply satisfying car. Every inch of it feels expensive and exquisitely detailed. Somebody's decided that the best way to keep people staring at a simple shape is to give them a lot to look at. And the head lamps and tail lamps have LED detailing. The 18" rims on my test car looked beautifully sculpted. At a glance, all this detailing appears very well integrated. But when you walk around the car, you realise just how much thought has gone into holding your attention.

The interior is much the same. Like the previous gen MINI, this one has toggle switches for various functions. It also has BMW's iDrive which is still the best infotainment system in the business. My test car had the optional Harman Kardon sound system which costs a cool 1.2 lakh. It also had something called 'Yours' which meant it wasn't 'Somebody Else's'. Anyway, that was about ninety thousand. Altogether, my test car cost just under 40 lakhs ex-showroom.

You can give me just about any car in Goa and I'll have something nice to say about it. Give me a MINI Cooper S Convertible and I'll be completely lost in a world of motoring nirvana. No car I've ever driven has felt more at home in its environment. It was as happy as I was, buzzing along on narrow country roads, freely distributing peace, love and positive vibes to all and sundry.

It's a happy car, and it's happiest when it's being belted along a twisting road. In spite of the image and all it implies, this is a Cooper S. That means that it was keenly crafted for the keen driver. It's got a lovely 2 litre turbo four which is very torquey and boomy at the bottom and middle of the rev range and nice and raspy at the top where it makes 192bhp. The oomph is transmitted courtesy a very well-tuned 6-speed automatic gearbox which somehow always knows if you want violence or peace and provides it instanter without so much as a murmur of complaint.

The result of all this, along with the superb steering, brakes and chassis is that this is by far the best driving hatch there is. There's a neutrality to it, an inherent poise that other manufacturers try to replicate using complex electronics because they simply cannot engineer a mechanical package anywhere near this competent. Even without adaptive dampers the ride is supple. And it clings on hard in the corners. It's just impossible to fault. It doesn't have a limited slip differential, but it doesn't understeer or torque steer, for that matter. You get the sense that it was conceived from the get go to be competent, brisk but not particularly fast. And most importantly, it was made to make you happy.

As a straight man chugging along on a twisting country road, the steering putting the car where I want it with microscopic precision, the engine making various melodic angry noises, the gearbox dispatching my whims through the paddle shifters with unerring consistency and 500 billion miles of blue sky for company, I caught myself thinking that maybe, just maybe, the16-year-olds might actually have a point.

Part 3

India Bike Week 2015

Honestly, they came in every shape and size you can imagine. Long, short, fat, thin, round, squared and so many other weird shapes. Oh, and there were some bikes too. Thousands and thousands of them, actually.

Roll your eyes up and try to think of a bike; any bike. There were probably five of them there. Our standouts of the show were the Indian Chief, Aprilia Caponord, Moto Guzzi V7 Racer, Triumph Tigers MotoExotica's 92kg RD350 mod (more on that later), Rajputana Customs' Harley Street 750 mod (and their superb Triumph Scrambler mod) and the heart-melting Vespa Super.

The concept of India Bike Week in itself has expanded to include many more things than it did. Last year it was very much a show of power for Harley Davidson. This time things were very different. While Harley stamped its authority on the show by being chief sponsor, Triumph, Benelli, Aprilia, Moto Guzzi, Indian and Vespa had their presence as well. Yuvraj Singh turned up to launch a modified KTM Duke which honestly wasn't that special.

But bike week isn't actually just about bikes. It's about the vibe you get from so many different kinds of people whom you meet. There were people who've ridden around the world a few times over, casual riders, racers and a Valentino Rossi look-alike. And then there was the generic festival crowd. With good reason, as it turned out because there were five stages with some great entertainment. Our pics were ViceVersa, Babyhead and the ever-present Nucleya.

But we can't go on without telling you about the biker build-off. Again, there was a modified KTM Duke, which didn't really float our boat. There was a modded Royal Enfield which was so ostentatious that it could only have been commissioned by Bappi Lahiri. Last year's build-off winner, Reza Hussain brought another crowd-pleaser in the form Da Bang. This is a completely custom Harley which has a front tyre as wide as Lamborghini Gallardo's rear tyre. I can't imagine for a second that it's anything less than tedious do ride, but the people loved it and he won the bike build-off again.

Our winner though, was a neo café racer from Arjun Raina's Moto Exotica. The headlines are as follows; 92kgs dry weight (lighter than a Honda Activa), tuned RD 350 engine, carbon-friggin-fibre used in the bodywork, Motogadget instrument console, the real-world performance of a Yamaha R6 and lightweight engineering that would've made Lotus proud. This was a fabulous bike. And we will bring you a review of it soon.

Funnily enough, IBW is about so much more than just bikes. It's a place where proper mentals come to be even more mental, and normal people go to be a part of a truly extraordinary event. What makes it even better is that it happens in Goa. Martin D'Costa and his crew at 70EMG have done a fantastic job of creating an event where people enjoy themselves more than they ever reasonably should.

If you were there, we were the pinball bouncing from one photo-shoot to the next. If you weren't, you should be there next year. They've got half-naked women washing bikes after all.

Inside Nissan

To the petrolhead, the Sunny and Micra offer no reason get out of bed. We also know that the Terrano, while still a great car, is a rebadged Renault Duster; which itself is a rebadged Dacia. That's their current line-up. So they dreamed up the Nissan Carnival at the Buddh International Circuit ('s parking lot), where unsuspecting jurnos and hacks such as self were invited to do some hooning in a selection of cars that they were considering for the Indian market.

First up was the all-electric Leaf. Honestly - pretty, it ain't. But it's very striking and looks like nothing else on the road. In lime green, it'll turn more heads than any sportscar you can think of. The interior is straight-up 22nd century Japanese. It's a blend of perfect ergonomics and beautiful digital instruments. And our test car was Dubai-reg; ergo, left-hand-drive. Ahead of me was a simple slalom course where we were meant to fling it from side to side, in the hope that it will reveal its handling characteristics in the process. It did. And for what is essentially an electric city runabout, it was rather good.

Next to face Honk's lead feet were the Sunny and Micra. I'm going to make it plain; I never liked them. They wantonly offer no excitement whatsoever. But on the handling track (complete with tight handbrake turns) they were a hoot. Nobody that ever buys one of these will ever drive them like I did on the track, but we tip our hats to Nissan for making even these cars great fun.

Finally, the reason we'd gone down there - the Nissan Patrol. This is a full-size SUV even by American standards. Use the Mercedes GL or Toyota's Land Cruiser for reference and you know what we're talking about. Being Honk, we had to take it off-roading. Like all big Japanese SUVs, it's designed to be utterly infallible when the going gets rough. And it was, until some journalist got it beached on a mound of sand. Then another one ran out of talent while tackling an incline of about 25 degrees. When Honk's turn finally came, we actually had no trouble at all. I mean, when you've got a 5.6L petrol V8 putting out 400bhp, enough torque to rearrange God's green earth, all the four-wheel-drive tech in the world in a machine that is specifically designed to do exactly what we were doing, it is absolutely no hardship. Yes, we go off-roading more often than most, so it must mean that it's only brilliant in the right hands. Good. We want one.

No sportscars were on offer, sadly. But Nissan is not averse to bringing the 370Z and GT-R to India. However, for fairly obvious reasons, they're very keen on bringing in their SUV line-up – Patrol, Pathfinder and X-Trail.

Goliath vs. Golaiths
T1 Truck Racing

Nobody. Not you, me, nor the so-called analysts and pundits could have predicted that the saviours of motor-racing as a spectator sport would be Tata Motors.

Let's face it. While many people like to believe that they're Formula 1 'fans', the sport has deteriorated into a sleep-inducing spectacle involving men in half-sleeved corporate shirts, laptops and cars that produce as much sound as the tree that fell to ground. When no one was around.

They go to great lengths to tell us that every unnecessary milligram is shaved of the cars to save weight. And then Lewis Hamilton turns up with an earring. And Fernando Alonso with his beard.

In motor-racing, it's the racing that's meant to be fun, not controversies and feuds between the drivers. We've got Hindi sitcoms and politicians who give us plenty of that.

This is why truck racing is my new favourite motorsport. First, the trucks. They're full-size Tata Prima lorries. Modifications for racing have been made in the form of stripped-out interiors with roll cages, racing bucket seats, all-weather racing tyres developed especially for truck racing by JK Tyre, smaller fuel tanks and some drastic weight-shedding to go faster that I'll explain in a minute. The result is that these identical 370bhp diesel monsters top out at 130kph. Not fast enough for you, eh?

The ground beneath your feet vibrates when these 6.6 tonne monsters rumble past you.

Aside from taking out all the creature comforts and other non-essentials, the rear trailer coupling has been removed to reduce 350kgs over the rear end. Couple this with stiffened racing suspension and you have trucks – proper lorries – that go sideways. A lot.

Before we get to racing, a quick word on the drivers. They were all professional truck racing drivers and champions from the UK. The difference between them and F1 wheelsmiths was that they were mostly middle-aged, a bit portly and looked genuinely happy. They were smiling to the crowds, laughing, playing the fool with one another and their pit crews and so on. The kind of people you'd love to go to the pub with.

Day one was the practice and the first qualifying. I'll tell you this - walking down the pit lane at the Buddh International Circuit is special enough. Standing at the pit wall, with your head poking over it when Lucifer, Leviathan and ten of their buddies are screaming down the main straight is enough to warrant a fresh pair of trousers. It is a glorious feeling being trackside; especially when these huge racing machines are banging wheels. In Practice. God alone knows how physical the race is meant to be.

Day two began with a mad rush to get to the track. And… what's this? Traffic? This one-make race series managed to fill up the main grandstand and the one beside it. That's a scarcely believable 48000 people. Along with the massive crowds came rain. This is something nobody saw coming. Thankfully the trucks ran on all-weather racing tyres. The qualifying race began in the rain with banging wheels, puffs of blue smoke from everyone's brakes and a general sense that all hell had broken loose.

The main race saw a rolling start with a crash on the first lap which immediately brought out the safety truck. The race itself was an extremely close contest between last year's champion, Stuart Oliver (Rig Stig from Top Gear) of the Castrol Vectron team and Steve Thomas of Allied Partners. In the entire 16 lap race, you could have measured the distance between them in inches. Flat out, no holds barred racing.

A few places behind, I saw my first motorsport accident happen in front of my eyes; literally 20 feet in front of me. Two trucks were jostling for position with the one in front being increasingly defensive. So, the guy behind pulled up alongside him and simply punted him out. That's it. A spinning truck coming right towards you is about as scary an experience as you're likely to have. Thankfully, he smashed into the barrier. The driver got out, examined his damage, shrugged his shoulders and walked away without so much as a hint of a tantrum.

Up ahead, Oliver and Thomas were still scrapping it out with Oliver finally taking the lead and holding on to it by the skin of his teeth to the chequered flag. As they came around for the victory lap doing donuts along the way, 48000 voices could be heard screaming in unison for someone they'd never heard of. Why? Because the racing was bloody excellent.

Of course, this being India, there was typical, crowd-pleasing entertainment in between the racing. Along with people we'd never heard of, there was Benny Dayal crooning, Shankar, Ehsan and Loy also tried to get the crowds going from under their umbrellas (owning to intermittent rain) and there were people dancing in shiny clothes. What was really impressive was Tata Motors' entire line-up of commercial vehicles. As a show of power, it was… erm… pretty powerful. But the variety is mind-boggling. If you've anything of any size that needs to be transported over land, they'll fix you up with the appropriate device.

But more than anything else, I'm going broke buying them drinks because they're doing so much to make the Indian petrolhoead proud and patriotic again. Big hand.